EXCAVATING JOHN'S GOSPEL

EXCAVATING JOHN'S GOSPEL

A Commentary for Today

Cornelis Bennema

WIPF & STOCK · Eugene, Oregon

Wipf and Stock Publishers
199 W 8th Ave, Suite 3
Eugene, OR 97401

Excavating John's Gospel
A Commentary for Today
By Bennema, Cornelis
Copyright©2005 Indian Society for Promoting Christian Knowledge
ISBN 13: 978-1-55635-799-2
ISBN 10: 1-55635-799-0
Publication date 12/14/2007
Previously published by Indian Society for Promoting Christian Knowledge, 2005

This edition reprinted 2008 by Wipf and Stock through special arrangement
with Indian Society for Promoting Christian Knowlege.

To my parents

Contents

Foreword xi
Preface xii
Introduction 1
  Reading for Meaning 1
  Setting the Stage 4
    Date and Place 4
    Author 5
    Audience 5
    Genre 7
    Purpose 9
    Characteristics 10
    Outline of John's Gospel 18
  Let the Play Begin 19

Commentary 21
  Prologue (1:1-18) 22
    The Introduction to the Word (1:1-5) 23
    John the Baptist as a Witness to the Word (1:6-8) 24
    The Reactions to the Word (1:9-13) 24
    The Incarnation of the Word (1:14-18) 25
    Reflection 27
  Jesus' Public Ministry (1:19-12:50) 28
    Setting the Stage (1:19-51) 28
      John's Testimony (1:19-34) 28
        John's Testimony before the Jewish Leaders (1:19-28) 29
        John's Testimony before Israel (1:29-34) 31
        Reflection 32
      The Call to Discipleship (1:35-51) 33
      Reflection 35
    From Cana to Cana (2:1-4:54) 36
      Jesus Supersedes Judaism (2:1-22) 37
        The Wedding at Cana (2:1-12) 37
        Jesus' Action in the Temple (2:13-22) 40

Reflection 42
Jesus and Nicodemus (2:23-3:21) 43
   Setting the Stage (2:23-3:1) 43
   The Birth of the Spirit (3:2-15) 44
   John's Commentary (3:16-21) 48
   Reflection 49
Jesus' Supremacy (3:22-36) 50
   Jesus' Supremacy over John (3:22-30) 50
   Jesus' Supremacy over All (3:31-36) 51
   Reflection 52
Jesus and the Samaritan Woman (4:1-42) 53
   Setting the Stage (4:1-7a) 54
   The Gift of Living Water (4:7b-15) 54
   The Giver of Living Water (4:16-26) 56
   The Responses of the Woman, the Disciples and the
      Samaritans (4:27-42) 58
   Reflection 59
Jesus and the Royal Official (4:43-54) 61
Reflection 63
The Opposition to Jesus (5:1-12:50) 64
   Emerging Opposition to Jesus (5:1-47) 65
      Jesus and the Lame Man at the Pool (5:1-9a) 66
      'The Jews' Accuse Jesus (5:9b-18) 67
      Jesus' First Argument – His Work (5:19-30) 69
      Jesus' Second Argument – His Witnesses (5:31-40) 70
      'The Jews' Accused Instead (5:41-47) 71
      Reflection 72
   The Bread of Life (6:1-71) 75
      The Feeding of the Five Thousand (6:1-15) 75
      An Interlude (6:16-21) 76
      The Bread-of-Life Discourse (6:22-59) 77
         The True Bread (6:22-33) 77
         The Bread of Life (6:34-40) 78
         The Giving of the Bread (6:41-51) 80
         The Consumption of the Bread (6:52-59) 81
      People's Responses (6:60-71) 82
      Reflection 84
   Family Debates (7:1-10:42) 86
      Jesus at the Feast of Tabernacles (7:1-52) 87

- Jesus Goes to the Feast (7:1-13) ... 88
- Jesus' First Discourse at the Feast (7:14-24) ... 89
- Jesus' Second Discourse at the Feast (7:25-36) ... 91
- Jesus' Invitation (7:37-39) ... 92
- People's Responses (7:40-52) ... 94
- *Reflection* ... 95
- Jesus and the Adulteress (7:53-8:11) ... 96
- *Reflection* ... 98
- Jesus and 'the Jews' (8:12-59) ... 99
  - Jesus the Light of the World (8:12-20) ... 100
  - Jesus Announces His Departure (8:21-30) ... 101
  - Liberating Truth (8:31-38) ... 102
  - Fathers and Families (8:39-47) ... 103
  - Jesus' Supremacy over Abraham (8:48-59) ... 105
  - *Reflection* ... 105
- Jesus and the Man Born Blind (9:1-41) ... 107
  - Light for the Blind (9:1-12) ... 107
  - The First Interrogation (9:13-23) ... 108
  - The Second Interrogation (9:24-34) ... 110
  - People's Responses (9:35-41) ... 111
  - *Reflection* ... 112
- Jesus the Good Shepherd (10:1-21) ... 114
  - Good and False Shepherds (10:1-10) ... 115
  - Jesus the Good Shepherd (10:11-18) ... 116
  - The Response of 'the Jews' (10:19-21) ... 117
  - *Reflection* ... 118
- The Rejection of Jesus (10:22-42) ... 119
  - The Unity of the Father and Son (10:22-30) ... 120
  - The Response of 'the Jews' (10:31-42) ... 120
  - *Reflection* ... 121
- The Resurrection of Lazarus (11:1-54) ... 122
  - The News of Lazarus' Death (11:1-16) ... 122
  - Jesus the Resurrection and the Life, and the Responses of Martha, Mary and 'the Jews' (11:17-37) ... 123
  - The Resurrection of Lazarus (11:38-44) ... 125
  - The Final Response of 'the Jews' (11:45-54) ... 126
  - *Reflection* ... 127
- The Last Phase of Jesus' Public Ministry (11:55-12:50) ... 128
  - The Approach of the Last Passover (11:55-57) ... 129

      Mary's Devotion and Judas' Defection (12:1-8) 129
      The 'Devotion' of the Crowd (12:9-19) 130
      Life through Death (12:20-26) 132
      Cosmic Judgement and Reconciliation (12:27-36a) 133
      The Closed Minds and Fearful Hearts of the
          Crowd (12:36b-43) 135
      Jesus' Public Farewell (12:44-50) 136
      Reflection 137
Jesus' Private Ministry (13:1-17:26) 139
    The Final Meal (13:1-30) 140
      The Footwashing (13:1-11) 141
      The Footwashing Explained (13:12-20) 143
      Jesus Foretells His Betrayal (13:21-30) 144
      Reflection 146
    Jesus' Farewell Discourses (13:31-17:26) 148
      Interactive Teaching (13:31-14:31) 148
        The New Commandment (13:31-38) 148
        Reflection 150
        Jesus the Way to the Father (14:1-14) 151
        Reflection 154
        The Promise of the Paraclete (14:15-24) 156
        Jesus Concludes the Session (14:25-31) 159
        Reflection 162
      Teaching on Discipleship – Privileges, Obligations and
          Consequences (15:1-16:4a) 163
        Obedience, Abiding and Bearing Fruit (15:1-17) 163
        Reflection 168
        Witness and Persecution (15:18-16:4a) 169
        Reflection 173
      Final Teaching (16:4b-33) 175
        The Work of the Paraclete (16:4b-15) 175
        Reflection 177
        Sorrow Turned into Joy (16:16-24) 178
        Reflection 179
        Parables and Plain Speech (16:25-33) 180
        Reflection 183
      Jesus' Prayer (17:1-26) 184
        Jesus' Prayer for Glorification (17:1-5) 184
        Jesus' Prayer for His Disciples (17:6-19) 185

Jesus' Prayer for Future Believers (17:20-26)	187
Reflection	189
Jesus' Passion and Resurrection (18:1-20:31)	191
Jesus' Betrayal and Arrest (18:1-11)	191
Reflection	192
Jesus' Trial (18:12-19:16a)	193
Jesus before the High Priest and Peter's Denial of Jesus (18:12-27)	193
Reflection	196
Jesus before Pilate (18:28-19:16a)	197
Round One (18:28-32)	197
Round Two (18:33-38a)	198
Round Three (18:38b-40)	200
Round Four (19:1-3)	200
Round Five (19:4-7)	201
Round Six (19:8-12)	201
Round Seven (19:13-16a)	202
Reflection	203
Jesus' Death (19:16b-42)	205
Jesus' Crucifixion (19:16b-27)	205
Jesus' Death (19:28-30)	207
Jesus' Piercing (19:31-37)	208
Jesus' Burial (19:38-42)	210
Reflection	212
Jesus' Resurrection (20:1-31)	213
The Resurrection (20:1-10)	213
The Appearance to Mary Magdalene (20:11-18)	213
The Appearance to the Disciples (20:19-23)	215
The Appearance to Thomas (20:24-29)	219
The Purpose of the Gospel (20:30-31)	221
Reflection	222
Epilogue (21:1-25)	223
The Miraculous Catch of Fish (21:1-14)	223
The Restoration and Commissioning of Peter (21:15-19)	225
Peter and the Beloved Disciple (21:20-23)	227
The Closure of the Gospel (21:24-25)	228
Reflection	229
Index of Subjects	231

Foreword

John's gospel is a wonderful book. Two things at least stand out: the first is the gospel's clear witness to Jesus, with its magnificent poetic opening on Jesus as God's word and with the climactic confession of Thomas 'my Lord and my God' in chapter 20. The second is its emphasis on God's love, the love that took Jesus to the cross and in which we can come to share through believing in Jesus. The gospel is thus a book that speaks to our hearts and our heads.

Such a wonderful book deserves careful study, and I warmly welcome Cornelis Bennema's commentary. The gospel is not always easy to understand, and it is helpful to have a reliable and well-informed guide. Dr Bennema is someone who has drunk deeply from the gospel, working on it for his doctorate (a very worthwhile work). Now in this commentary he takes us through the gospel in a way that is scholarly but not technical, bringing out the original author's meaning, but also reflecting on its relevance. The gospel is simple, but profound, and the commentary is similar – easy to follow, but full of insight.

Tradition has it that the apostle Thomas was the founder of the church in India. It is understandable that after his meeting with the risen Christ he will have wanted to share his experience of Jesus as his Lord and his God. Dr Bennema could be said to have followed in Thomas's footsteps – to India, which is where I had the pleasure of meeting him. I hope that his commentary will be instrumental in strengthening people's faith and in building up God's church in India and more widely.

David Wenham
Wycliffe Hall
Oxford, UK

Preface

My fascination with John's Gospel began in 1996 with what was to be a research topic for my Master of Theology degree but eventually led to a doctoral thesis on the role of the Spirit in salvation in John's Gospel. It was published under the title *The Power of Saving Wisdom: An Investigation of Spirit and Wisdom in Relation to the Soteriology of the Fourth Gospel* (WUNT II/148; Tübingen: Mohr Siebeck, 2002). Since 2002, I have been teaching John's Gospel at the South Asia Institute of Advanced Christian Studies (SAIACS), a postgraduate seminary in Bangalore, India, and keep discovering new things.

In my experience, the theological academy, to which I belong I suppose, too often does not (sufficiently) communicate its findings at a level that is accessible for the layperson. This book is aimed at (under)graduate theological students, pastors and lay people with an interest in theology. The purpose of the book is to give a well-informed exposition of the meaning of John's Gospel in everyday language. Although I have not explicitly used other sources, I must acknowledge that this commentary is the accumulative result of many years of reading, reflecting on, and interacting with the work of prominent Johannine scholars. The sections that I have titled 'Reflections', contain conclusions, further implications and possible application of the text for today. Although I have tried to maintain a global outlook, one will find more emphasis on the western and Indian contexts, since these environments have predominantly shaped my thinking and experiences. My desire is that as we go through John's Gospel you may acquire a deeper understanding of, and love for, God's message to us.

I take the opportunity to express my gratitude to those who have been influential in or have contributed to the completion of this book: To Professor Max Turner, my former supervisor at the London School of Theology (London, UK), for having 'fed' this sheep in a truly Johannine fashion and for his continuing friendship. Dr David Wenham at Wycliffe Hall in Oxford (UK) for recommending me for a project on John's Gospel with the Bible Reading Fellowship (Oxford, UK), which triggered off the idea for this book. SAIACS for the stimulating and challenging environment it provides in a non-western context so different from my native Dutch one. My parents who have brought me up in a Christian home and who have faithfully supported me throughout my life. To them I have dedicated this book. Rev. Ashish Amos (General Secretary/Director of ISPCK) for kindly having accepted this work for publication. George Korah, the manager of SAIACS Press, for his help with the layout, cover design and printing. Thanks are also due to my wonderful wife Susan for her love and support, and for copyediting this work. Above all, I am deeply grateful to God for inspiring, guiding and sustaining me through his Spirit. May this book please him and be of use in what he is doing in this world.

Cornelis Bennema (cor.bennema@saiacs.org)
SAIACS (http://www.saiacs.org)
Bangalore, India

Introduction

John's Gospel has been famously described as a pool in which a child can wade and an elephant can swim. Its basic message about Jesus is simple to understand, and yet the Gospel is deep and rich enough for life-long study by the layperson and 'professional' alike. A complementary image, which the title and cover of this book alludes to, is that of John's Gospel as an excavation site, and its study as an archeological investigation, in which we need to 'dig up' the underlying meaning from John's Gospel in order to understand it more fully. Before we step, plunge or dig into this wonderful Gospel, however, we need to deal with some preliminary issues.

Reading for Meaning

When you looked at the title of this book, you may have wondered why we need commentaries on the bible at various levels. People sometimes ask, 'Why can we not read the Gospel of John (or any piece of literature for that matter) as we want?' These questions have to do with the related issues of ownership and meaning: Who 'owns' a particular text and who attributes meaning to a text?

While reading, the reader will necessarily interpret the text in order to make sense of it; in this process, meaning is created. But the question arises, *whose* meaning is created? There are people who say, 'A text was written by a particular person – the author – who has determined the meaning of that text.' Others say, 'No, as a reader, I own the text and therefore I will determine what the text means.'

For the first type of reader, the focus is on the author and meaning is 'in' the text, that is, the text is the vehicle of the author's intended meaning and the task of the reader is to reconstruct that meaning. The second type of reader will assign meaning to the text without considering the author. For this reader, the meaning is 'in front of' the text; the focus is on the effect that the text has on him; the meaning is determined by the reader in the act of reading. This type of reader may have little or no concern for the original, authorial meaning of the text and the historical socio-cultural setting in which the text was produced. The chief concern is with what this text means for him now.

The danger is that with many such readers an array of meanings is created where each is entitled to their own personal meaning. This kind of reading seems unnatural. When we hear someone speak, we cannot interpret the words as we like. If we do, the speaker may say, 'But that is not what I meant.' Similarly, while writing, besides having a particular style and a particular audience in mind, an author also has a particular purpose: the intended meaning or message of the communication that is embedded in, or injected into, the text through the choice of words, sentences and structures. This creates the natural question and purpose for reading a particular text, namely, 'What did the author mean?'

This task of establishing the original meaning of a biblical text is no small one and comes with its own problems. John's Gospel was written in a different time (almost two thousand years ago), a different language (Greek), and reflects a different culture (Jewish) from ours. We must bridge as many of these barriers as possible to approach the original meaning of the text. This forces us to think about issues such as authorship (who wrote the Gospel of John?); audience (who were John's first readers?); genre (what kind of writing is this?); and purpose (why did John write this Gospel?). We will deal with these issues later in this chapter.

Although the text and the narrative world it creates remain the focus of our study, we also need, at times, to look at aspects of the world *outside* or 'behind' the text if the text invites us to do so. The reason for this is that we are often unfamiliar with the common knowledge that the author shared with his original audience. Therefore, we sometimes need information about the historical socio-cultural context in which a particular text was written in order to understand it properly. For example, the setting of John 7-8 is the Jewish Feast of Tabernacles, which is associated with the symbols of water and light. Knowing this helps us in understanding why Jesus applies this symbolism to himself in 7:37-39 and 8:12.

Unfortunately, the author of the Gospel of John is not around any more to assist us in understanding the text; the best we can arrive at is an *approximate* understanding of the author's meaning. However, this should not stop us from trying to approach the ideal as closely as we can. Also, as part of the bible, I presuppose that John's Gospel is co-authored by the Holy Spirit who *is* still present to guide us in our understanding. In fact, even if we do not share this assumption, John's Gospel itself attributes these interpretative functions to the Holy Spirit (15:26; 16:12-15).

It must be noted in light of the above discussion that views such as, 'I do not need a commentary because the Holy Spirit will teach me', should not be condoned. The Holy Spirit's assistance in interpreting the text does not make the need for systematic study redundant, irrelevant or unnecessary. On the contrary, it is *as* we study, analyze, meditate and reflect that the Spirit will guide us.

Difficult and laborious as the above-mentioned task of approximating the original meaning of the text may be, we cannot afford to stop there. We need to go *beyond* the original meaning of the text. In addition to the text's original meaning, we need to think through what it means now – today. You may think that I have now jumped to being the second type of reader, who is merely concerned with what the text means for him, but that is not my intention. We need a way of reading that is twofold, taking the best from both types of reader.

First, we need to discover as far as we can what the text meant *then* – the recovery of the original, intended meaning of the author. Then, and only then, can we think about what the text means *now* – the rereading, contextualization and the application of the text for today. If we bypass the first step, we may end up with a plurality of meanings that the author never intended, which may fuel wrong beliefs and practices. So in order to let John's Gospel be relevant for today, we first need to dig the author's intended meaning out of the text, hence the title of this book: *Excavating John's Gospel: A Commentary for Today*. This may be a rather unusual and lengthy rationale for this book, but I believe it is of the utmost importance to understand how we can or should read a text since that will shape our thinking and praxis.

Finally, as we try to understand the original meaning of the text and its relevance we may still arrive at varying conclusions and different 'versions' of the original meaning of the text, but this may actually be advantageous. None of us knows as much as all of us together, and hence, if we humbly bring our views of the text into the community of faith (or even beyond), there will be an opportunity to test and sharpen our views through dialogue with other people.

Setting the Stage

Just as we would set the stage for a play, so we must first familiarize ourselves with certain issues that might help us to understand John's 'play' properly.

Date and Place

For a long time, people thought that John's Gospel was written sometime in the second century to attack a kind of Gnosticism, i.e., a Greek philosophy that focused on secret knowledge and revelations. However, the discovery of certain fragments of John's Gospel that indicate a much earlier date for the Gospel, combined with the fact that Gnosticism only developed during the latter part of the second century, have caused many people to rethink the date of the Gospel. At present, the majority of scholars tentatively put the date for John's Gospel in the period A.D. 80-100. Whether John combated a form of early Gnosticism is not at all certain.

According to tradition, the Gospel was written in Ephesus (in modern Turkey). However, other large centres of Christian activity that also had a significant Jewish population, such as Alexandria (in modern Egypt) and Antioch (in modern Syria), have also been proposed. Hence, John's Gospel was most probably written outside Palestine in a multi-cultural hub in the Diaspora.

Author

The Gospel itself comes to us anonymously, as do the other three Gospels and much other ancient literature. Although most English translations have the title 'The Gospel according to John', the Greek only says 'According to John', and even this phrase was not part of the original text but a later addition of the Early Church. Even so, does this mean that John himself wrote this Gospel or merely that John was a source for this Gospel? And who is this 'John' anyway – John the apostle (the son of Zebedee) or John the Elder (mentioned by the fourth-century historian Eusebius)?

Alternatively, when we consider some of the internal evidence of the Gospel, is the author the so-called Beloved Disciple, i.e., the disciple that Jesus loved (21:20, 24)? John 21:24 may simply mean that the author is testifying to the authenticity of the Beloved Disciple's witness. In this case, the Beloved Disciple is presented as the witness on whose testimony the Gospel is based but not necessarily as its author. Even if the Beloved Disciple were the author, we still have to resolve the problem of his identity – is he a 'fictional' exemplary character or can he be identified as John the apostle?

As you can see, identifying the author is not a simple task. The Gospel came to us anonymously, so perhaps we need not pry too much. In this commentary we shall call the author 'John'.

Audience

The issue of who John's original readers were, is perhaps a more interesting one. Since the 1960s, there has been a growing consensus that John was writing for a so-called 'Johannine community'. Probably based in Ephesus, this community is believed to have consisted of Jewish Christians who had been expelled from the Jewish synagogues because of their stance regarding Jesus, and who had, according to some, become isolated and 'sectarian'.

Those who hold this view say that John's Gospel should be read as a two-level drama in that the retelling of the story of Jesus actually matches the story of the Johannine community. For example, the story of the man born blind in John 9 who was interrogated by the Jewish leaders and who was eventually driven out of their midst is telling the later story of Johannine believers who were thrown out of the synagogue. One problem with this view is that it is hypothetical; there is no real evidence that such a community existed. Another problem with this view is the so-called 'two-level' reading of the text. Such reading goes against the genre of the Gospel; John's Gospel contains the story or biography of Jesus rather than the biography of the Johannine church (see the section 'Genre' below). Moreover, a 'two-level' reading of John's Gospel would reduce all pre-Easter events to mere foils in order to accommodate the history of the post-Easter Johannine community.

At the other extreme is the view that John wrote his Gospel for everyone and that the Gospels were written for general circulation around the churches. Attractive as this view may be, there are two major weaknesses. First, it is unlikely that the authors of the Gospels had the entire Christian community – both in Palestine and in the Diaspora – in mind; more likely, they wrote for a particular audience, a specific subset of Christians. Second, besides John's Gospel we also have John's Letters. Although we cannot be sure that the same author is behind these writings, the similarity of their theology and style seem to indicate that the Gospel and the Epistles, at the least, belong to the same school or tradition. Since the Johannine Epistles are addressed to a church, it is likely that there was such a thing as a Johannine church (just as there were various Pauline churches).

We do not necessarily have to choose between these two positions; perhaps both are in view. The view of this commentary is that John wrote his Gospel for a specific community, which we might call the Johannine community or church, but I do not necessarily read the Gospel as the history of this community. At the same time, I contend that John also envisaged that his Gospel would circulate *beyond* his local community to other churches.

When we think further about John's possible audience, it becomes more complex. If John's Gospel dates between A.D. 80 and 100, it means that it was written in the aftermath of the destruction of Jerusalem and the failed attempt of the Jews to liberate themselves from the Romans in A.D. 66-70. John could partly have intended his Gospel to give comfort and hope to these traumatized and disillusioned non-Christian Palestinian Jews (some of whom might have fled into the Diaspora). Part of John's audience might also have experienced some forms of persecution – either from fellow Jews or from the world – since John emphasizes the concept of opposition and persecution (see especially 15:18-16:4a).

John could also have written for non-Jewish people, or for Jews who were born in the Diaspora and less familiar with Palestinian Judaism, since he has provided explanatory comments about Jewish terms and customs. John explains, for instance, that 'Rabbi' means teacher (1:38), that 'Messiah' means Anointed (1:41; see also 9:7; 20:16), and in 4:9 and 19:40 he clarifies Jewish customs. The explanation of these Jewish terms and customs, as well as the display of accurate topographical and geographical knowledge (3:23; 5:2; 11:18), suggests that John was either a Palestinian Jew himself or at least very familiar with Judaism. Besides, John frequently quotes from or alludes to the Hebrew Scriptures (our Old Testament), and emphasizes the Jewish festivals and the Mosaic Law. Moreover, the symbolism with reference to Jesus, for example, Jesus as the Bread, Light, Shepherd and Vine, is all rooted in the Old Testament. Accordingly, John probably wants his readers to get acquainted with Judaism.

In conclusion, John's original audience might have been a specific local 'Johannine community' in the Diaspora, consisting of Jewish and Gentile Christians. Some of these Johannine believers may have experienced persecution from synagogue Judaism or the world at large. In addition, John may also have intended to reach out to the traumatized non-Christian Jew after A.D. 70, or, if we take John's purpose in 20:31 into consideration (see the section 'Purpose' below) and the global outlook of the Gospel, then indeed, to everyone.

Genre

John's Gospel has increasingly been classified as a Graeco-Roman biography. The significance of this is that the Gospel is not primarily the story of a 'Johannine community' but that of Jesus Christ. The purpose of the ancient biography is to draw out the significance and interpretation of certain historical events rather than to give an objective, factual historical account. No serious scholar claims, for instance, that the Gospels record the exact words of Jesus as he spoke them, or that they record all events in chronological order; those who do have the difficult (if not impossible) task of explaining why there are so many differences in wording and sequence between the Gospels.

This is not to deny a historical substratum to John's Gospel, but, the question of how much is historical need not dominate the debate concerning the extent to which the Gospel is true. In retelling the dialogue between Jesus and, for example, Nicodemus, John's aim was to persuade and convince his readers not of certain historical facts but of significant theological truths. Whether it is necessary in order to accept the truth claim of John 3 that Nicodemus existed, or whether it is necessary that his conversation with Jesus took place exactly as has been recorded, is perhaps a more ambivalent issue.

Nevertheless, I suggest that there is a need for a historical anchor – the existence of Jesus, the crucifixion and resurrection are necessary historical facts for theological truth. Even if many historical facts cannot be precisely reconstructed any more, there still needs to be historical plausibility. For example, it is essential to have some historical reality behind the Nicodemus story, in that it must be historically plausible that such a conversation between Jesus and a Jewish religious leader could have taken place. Since there is ample evidence that Jesus had heated debates with the Jewish religious authorities, I contend that Nicodemus was a historical person who actually had a conversation with Jesus. As such, the burden of proof is on those who believe that John wove a story around an imaginary character, Nicodemus.

We must also bear in mind that all the Gospel authors were 'theologians'; they wrote from a post-Easter perspective and interpreted the pre-Easter events with a specific (theological) agenda in mind. John's primary concern is to assure his readers that his story of Jesus is a true and reliable witness (cf. 19:35; 21:24). John wants to persuade and convince his readers not primarily of the 'basic' historical facts, such as the existence of Jesus, the crucifixion and resurrection (for these were already known), but of their *significance*. This is because John's document is also a 'Gospel', i.e., a *written* proclamation of what was in the first place *spoken*: the 'gospel' or good news of Jesus Christ.

The two literary categories (ancient biography and Gospel) are not mutually exclusive; the genre of John's Gospel may be Graeco-Roman biography in form and a Gospel in content. That is, looking at the existing genres of that time, John's Gospel fits best that of the ancient biography, but, at the same time, its content is so unique that we can create a new genre 'Gospel'. So we arrive at John's purpose for writing his Gospel, that is: a theological narration or interpretation of the significance of Jesus in order to promote belief.

Purpose

The purpose of the Gospel is explicitly stated in 20:30-31 (cf. 1 John 5:13). John 20:30 (cf. 21:25) reveals that John has made a deliberate selection of Jesus' numerous signs for the twofold purpose stated in 20:31: '...so that you may believe that Jesus is the Messiah, the Son of God, and so that through believing you may have life in his name.' It is not clear, in the Greek, whether in the first purpose clause 'believe' means '*to come* to believe (for the first time)' or '*to continue* to believe'. That is, is John's purpose evangelistic or pastoral – is he writing for non-believers to become Christians or for existing Christians to continue in their faith?

I suggest that both are intended. On the one hand, an evangelistic aim is probable for three reasons. First, the purpose of John the Baptist's coming coincides with the purpose of the Gospel. John 1:7, which does not have the grammatical ambiguity of 20:31, asserts that the purpose of John's witness is that people might come to believe for the first time, which may support a similar reading for 20:31. Second, the aim of John 1-12 and John 20 seems to be to lead people to an initial belief-response to Jesus and his revelation (although the work of the Spirit-Paraclete through the witness of the disciples, as recorded in John 14-17, also aims at this). Third, 20:31 emphatically declares that Jesus is the Christ or

Messiah, implying that the fundamental issue is the recognition of the true identity of Jesus; an issue it seems for non-believers rather than believers.

On the other hand, John's Gospel also emphasizes the pastoral aspect of strengthening and deepening an existing belief. An important issue for John is that disciples start following and continue to follow Jesus (see, e.g., 6:66-69; 21:19, 22). John 13-17, especially, emphasizes the need for continuous belief. This aspect might actually be reflected in the second purpose clause in 20:31, '...so that through (continuous) believing you may (continue to) have life in his name.'

In sum, both aspects (evangelistic and pastoral) are reflected throughout the Gospel and summed up in 20:31. It is not that John pursues two purposes but rather that the *single* purpose of John's Gospel is to bring people to initial belief in Jesus *and* to sustain this belief so that they may (continue to) have life. This also coheres with John's intended audience of non-believers and believers alike, as we have described above.

How then did John's Gospel function in practice? Obviously there were not hundreds of copies of John's Gospel available to hand out as 'evangelistic tracts' to non-believers, as we might do today. It is more likely that the Gospel was read out in the (Johannine) church where non-believers were possibly present, or that the believers, being familiar with the text of John's Gospel, used this material as a basis to evangelize non-believers. At the same time, the Gospel would also be used pastorally, to deepen and strengthen an existing faith.

Characteristics

In order to understand John's Gospel better, we shall briefly discuss its main features and how they function.

John and the Synoptics. Looking at all the four Gospels, we notice that the Gospel of John is both similar to and different from the first three Gospels or Synoptics. Similar, in that John also tells the story of Jesus of Nazareth from a post-Easter, theological perspective, but different, in that John employs a different style (long discourses rather than parables) and makes no obvious mention of demons and exorcisms. John also uses a different vocabulary: instead of the common 'kingdom of God' language in the Synoptics, John prefers '(eternal) life' as his main salvific phrase; miracles are called 'signs' in John; and typical Johannine motifs include light, darkness, truth, revelation, witness, abiding, Father and Son, glory, seeing and knowing. Besides, John's Gospel includes certain events that are not found in the Synoptics, such as the miracle of water turned into wine; Jesus' encounters with Nicodemus and the Samaritan woman; the resurrection of Lazarus; and Jesus' so-called 'I am' sayings. Sometimes John uses a different chronology: Jesus cleanses the temple at the beginning of his ministry, but the Synoptics place the incident at the end.

Literary Techniques. John uses various literary techniques such as irony, misunderstanding, metaphor, symbolism, dualism, characterization and double entendre. We must recognize and understand how John uses these techniques or we may miss the point John wants to make.

Irony is the use of language that says the opposite of what one really means in order to make a point; the truth is exactly the opposite of what is being stated. For example, Jesus' statement in 5:39-40 is ironical because the Jewish leaders assume that, from their study of Scripture, they have eternal life; whereas their rejection of Jesus to whom Scripture testifies shows that, actually, they do not have eternal life.

Misunderstanding, in John, is a prominent motif. Characters in the narrative frequently misunderstand Jesus, but John deliberately uses this for the reader's benefit. For the character's misunderstanding often causes Jesus to provide further revelation, preventing the reader from making a similar mistake. John takes the reader into confidence as it were; the reader is an insider who shares the author's knowledge.

Metaphor is a figure of speech in which a word or phrase literally denoting one kind of object or idea is used to represent another. Jesus' assertion of his being the 'living bread' in 6:51, for instance, cannot be taken literally (bread does not live) but is a metaphor for Jesus' ability to provide life.

Symbolism is a broader category than metaphor. Symbols connect two levels of meaning in a story, in that symbols stand for or suggest something else by reason of relationship, association, convention or accidental resemblance. John frequently uses mundane objects such as light, water and bread as symbols for salvation or eternal life.

Dualism considers reality to consist of two opposite modes. Typical expressions of Johannine dualism are light/darkness, from above/from below, Spirit/flesh, God/devil, life/death, free/slave, truth/lie. John's dualistic worldview presents us with two realms: (i) the realm 'from above', or heaven, to which belong God, Jesus, the Spirit, revelation, life, light, seeing, truth and freedom; (ii) the realm 'from below', or the world, to which belong the devil, 'the Jews', flesh, death, darkness, blindness, lies and enslavement to sin. John thus depicts a soteriological dualism, implying that people either accept Jesus and his revelation and enter the realm above, or reject Jesus and remain part of the realm below.

Characterization refers to the description and development of characters, and John uses this technique to achieve his purpose of promoting belief in Jesus. John portrays various characters interacting with the main protagonist, Jesus, and we, as readers, are to evaluate whether these characters give satisfactory responses. Since characterization also creates a sense of being real, it assists the reader to identify with one or more characters and persuades the reader to take a stand – preferably the one the author recommends.

Double entendre is the use of a word that has two meanings, which often causes ambiguity. For example, the Greek word *anōthen* that qualifies the spiritual birth in 3:3 can mean 'again' (as Nicodemus understands it) or 'from above' (as John intends it).

Signs. John calls the miracles that Jesus performs 'signs'. Although John mentions that Jesus did numerous signs (20:30), he narrates only seven of them: the turning of water into wine (2:1-11); the healing of the official's son (4:43-54); the healing of the sick man at the pool (5:1-9a; cf. 6:2); the feeding of the five thousand (6:1-14); the walking on water (6:16-21); the healing of the man born blind (9:1-6; cf. 9:16); and the resurrection of Lazarus (11:38-44; cf. 11:47; 12:18). Sometimes the miraculous catch of fish (21:1-8) is also counted – either as the eighth sign (seven plus one) or as the seventh sign (instead of the miracle of Jesus' walking on the water in 6:19-21). I adhere to the seven signs during Jesus' public ministry as recorded in John 1-12, and consider the sign in John 21 as the first sign to the disciples – a foretaste of things to come (cf. 14:12). John calls Jesus' miracles 'signs' for like signposts, they point beyond themselves. Properly understood, they reveal various aspects of Jesus and his ministry. Therefore, the emphasis is not on the signs *per se* but on their significance.

'I Am' Sayings. In seven passages John records the well-known 'I am' sayings in which the predicate gives a vivid metaphorical description of Jesus: 'I am the bread of life' (6:35, 41, 48, 51); 'I am the light of the world' (8:12; 9:5); 'I am the gate for the sheep' (10:7, 9); 'I am the good shepherd' (10:11, 14); 'I am the resurrection and the life' (11:25); 'I am the way, the truth, and the life' (14:6); and 'I am the true vine' (15:1, 5). These sayings are often accompanied by discourses and serve to elucidate aspects of Jesus' identity and mission. Besides, they show Jesus in sharp contrast to various features of Judaism that he is fulfilling. The 'I am' sayings are Jesus' self-disclosures to people and John probably intends an allusion to Exodus 3:14, which narrates God's self-revelation to Moses. In this case, the Johannine 'I am' sayings do not merely show Jesus' understanding of himself in relation to God – Jesus is on a par with God himself – but, more specifically, reveal how the divine operates among humanity. Jesus is the locus of God's presence and activity, i.e., God is at work in the world through Jesus. He is God's special agent of revelation and acts on God's behalf (cf. 1:18; 3:34-35; 5:17).

The Jews. A typical Johannine characteristic is a group called 'the Jews'. Although John sometimes uses the term in a generic sense to denote the entire Jewish race, it is more often used in a narrower, specialized sense to refer to Jesus' opponents. 'The Jews' consist of those Jews who are hostile and opposed to Jesus, especially from among the religious leaders in Jerusalem (e.g., 1:19; 5:16-18; 6:41, 52; 7:1; 8:31-59; 9:13-34; 10:31-39). Besides persecuting Jesus, these Jewish rulers also instigated religious persecution against fellow Jews who confessed Jesus as Messiah, as the expression 'the fear of the Jews' indicates (7:13; 9:22; 12:42; 19:38; 20:19). This persecution seems primarily to have been the threat of excommunication from the synagogue, and hence of becoming a social outcast (9:22, 34; 12:42), but even murder was in view (16:2). In John, 'the Jews' are characterized as murderers, liars and belonging to the devil (8:44).

Conflict, Opposition and Persecution. John draws a great deal of attention to the themes of conflict, opposition and persecution. He essentially describes the clash between the world 'from above', represented by Jesus, and the world 'from below', represented primarily by 'the Jews'. In the coming of Jesus into the world, heaven has penetrated the earth, the divine has entered into human history, and God's kingdom has broken into a dark world. This causes conflict, opposition and persecution. John 5-12 predominantly narrates the conflict between Jesus and 'the Jews', and their subsequent opposition to and persecution of Jesus. John 13-17 then informs the reader that the same scenario awaits Jesus' followers – whether it is a conflict with post-A.D. 70 Judaism or with the world at large.

Trial Motif. John narrates his story of Jesus within the wider framework of a cosmic trial or lawsuit. In this trial, 'the Jews' accuse Jesus of his divine claims to provide eternal life, to work on God's behalf and to have a unique relationship with him. As in any trial, it is crucial to have credible witnesses and to keep their testimony going lest the case be lost. In this context we see Jesus' appointing his disciples to be his witnesses in the world after his return to the Father. Besides, Jesus forewarns his disciples that, as his representatives in this world, they too will find themselves accused (whether by post-A.D. 70 Rabbinic Judaism or the world at large). For this scenario of an ongoing cosmic trial the Spirit-Paraclete will be the disciples' legal aid – both the term 'Paraclete' and the functions of the Paraclete have strong forensic overtones. At one level, Jesus is on trial and 'the Jews' are the accusers; at another level, however, there is a subversive trial taking place in which the world, its ruler the devil and its representatives will find themselves in the dock with the Spirit-Paraclete as prosecutor and Jesus as judge (cf. 5:22, 27-30; 12:31, 48; 16:8).

The Holy Spirit. John and Paul probably give us most insights about the Holy Spirit in the New Testament. John's Gospel has more to say about the person and work of the Spirit than any of the Synoptic Gospels. With regard to Jesus, the Spirit empowers

Jesus for his salvific mission and functions as the mode of communication between Jesus and God (1:32-33; 3:34). When it comes to people, the Spirit plays a vital role in salvation. The Spirit is the agent of new birth into God's kingdom, and also sustains this salvation by empowering the believer's moral life (3:5-6). In fact, the Spirit helps people understand Jesus' teaching and respond to him in faith so that they may receive eternal life (4:10-14; 6:63; 7:38-39). Although people could experience this life-giving Spirit already during Jesus' ministry, the Spirit will be fully released only after the cross (19:30; 20:22). After Jesus' return to the Father, the Spirit-Paraclete will equip and empower believers for their salvific mission in this world (14:17, 26; 15:26-27; 16:7-15). The Spirit does not merely operate at an intellectual level but also enables a new mode of worship (4:23-24); stirs up emotions (11:33; 13:21); and is expected to influence the believer's motivation, attitude and will.

Women. Contra the culture of his day, John gives prominence to women throughout the Gospel. Jesus' mother is present at the launch of Jesus' ministry at the wedding of Cana (2:1-12); the Samaritan woman in John 4 is portrayed as a paradigm of true discipleship; Martha and Mary gain significance in John 11-12; 18:16-17 mentions a female gatekeeper; and of the five people mentioned at the foot of the cross, four are women (19:25-27). Finally, Mary Magdalene is presented as the first witness to Jesus' resurrection (20:1-18). Hence, female witnesses are present at crucial points in Jesus' ministry, and provide examples of true discipleship.

Feasts. The various Jewish festivals are an important feature or theme in John's Gospel. The Passover is mentioned a few times, the Feast of Tabernacles forms the background for John 7-8, the Feast of Dedication of the Temple is referred to in 10:22, and 5:1 records an unnamed festival. The Jewish feasts fulfil two functions in John. First, they provide a chronological framework for Jesus' ministry. For example, John mentions three Passover celebrations (2:23; 6:4; 11:55 [12:1; 13:1; 18:28, 39; 19:14 refer to the same Passover as 11:55]). Even if John deliberately brought Jesus' action in the temple in 2:13-22 forward for theological reasons, and that 2:13 and 11:55 refer to the same Passover, 2:23 still records the first

Passover in Jesus' ministry. Since John does not record many events of Jesus' life before the first Passover in 2:23, and given that Jesus' passion coincides with the third Passover recorded by John, Jesus' ministry may, at first sight, have lasted just over two years. However, this is not the complete picture. If the Passover occurred in March/April, and if 5:1 refers to the Feast of Weeks (around May/June), then the period between 2:23 and 5:1 is only about two months. This calculation does not correspond to what Jesus says in 4:35. This verse mentions that there are four more months till the summer harvest, celebrated at the Feast of Weeks, which then puts the context of 4:35 around January/February. Therefore, there must have been another, unrecorded Passover between 4:35 and 5:1, and we must add one year to our first estimation. Thus, we conclude that Jesus' ministry may have covered just over three years.

Second, and perhaps more importantly, these festivals provide a topical framework for the Gospel; a backdrop to Jesus' teaching, portraying Jesus as the replacement/fulfilment of what these feasts stand for or signify (see especially the commentary on John 7-8). Hence, through his reference to the Jewish festivals, John is able to show how Jesus supersedes Judaism.

The Old Testament. John frequently quotes from or alludes to the Hebrew Scriptures, our Old Testament (2:17, 22; 6:31, 45; 7:38, 42; 10:34; 12:14, 38-40; 13:18; 15:25; 17:12; 18:9, 32; 19:24, 28, 36-37), in order to show that Jesus is firmly rooted in the Jewish tradition, and how Jesus fulfils the Jewish Scriptures. For us, as modern readers, this stresses the continuity of the two Testaments; the New Testament cannot be fully appreciated (or even understood) without the Old Testament.

Geography. Although John makes little mention of Jesus' travels, some places that he does mention take on theological significance. The two main locations of Jesus' ministry are receptive Galilee in the north and hostile Jerusalem/Judea in the south (see, e.g., 4:45; 7:1). Samaria, between Galilee and Judea, normally avoided and despised by Jews, gets special attention from Jesus. It is the Samaritans' climactic confession of Jesus as the Saviour of the world that stresses the universal scope of Jesus' ministry. At another level, one's 'spiritual location' is either in the world 'from above', which Jesus represents and which one enters through a spiritual birth 'from above', or in the world 'from below', of which everyone is a part through physical birth, and which is dominated by the devil.

Sacramentalism. The majority of scholars, especially among Catholics, contend that John refers to the sacraments of baptism and the eucharist. According to them, the eucharist is in view in John 6 and baptism comes to the fore in John 3, with the reference to a birth of water and Spirit. Attractive as it may be, there are problems with such a view. If John were referring to the sacraments at a primary level, he reduces the characters in John 3 and 6 to mere foils in order to make a theological point for the Johannine community. We can hardly contend that Jesus wanted Nicodemus to understand that he needed Christian water baptism to enter the kingdom of God; or that 'the Jews' in John 6 were expected to partake in the Christian eucharist, since these sacraments had not yet been instituted at that time.

Even if John were referring to the sacraments at a secondary level, problems remain. There are difficulties with the two-level reading of the text which would be required (see the section 'Audience' above). Besides, is John contending that baptism and the eucharist are prerequisites for salvation? Does the mention of water in John 4:10-14 also refer to baptism? Although John clearly uses eucharistic language in John 6, does this imply that he had the sacrament of the eucharist in mind? If sacramentalism was so important to John or the Johannine community, why then do the Johannine Epistles not refer to these sacraments? Even if a reference to sacramentalism were present at a secondary level, it would merely express something that is already there at a primary level. For example, if the eucharist denotes the continual remembrance of and participation in Jesus' death, this meaning would already be suggested by a non-sacramental reading of the text. Similarly, if water baptism denotes the cleansing from sin and is the outward expression of the inner transformation by the Spirit, the reading I shall suggest in the commentary on John 3 already covers this meaning. In sum, although John uses sacramental language, I do not think that he referred to the sacraments as such; and even if John did refer to them, a sacramental reading of the text does not add information to a non-sacramental understanding.

Outline of John's Gospel

John's Gospel starts with a Prologue (1:1-18) and finishes with an Epilogue (21:1-25). In between, we find the so-called Book of Signs (1:19-12:50), which describes Jesus' public ministry, and the Book of Glory (13:1-20:31), which describes Jesus' private ministry to his disciples, and Jesus' passion and resurrection. A more detailed outline may look as follows (for an exhaustive outline, see the Table of Contents):

Prologue (1:1-18)
Jesus' Public Ministry (1:19-12:50)
    John's Testimony (1:19-34)
    The Call to Discipleship (1:35-51)
    From Cana to Cana (2:1-4:54)
        The Wedding at Cana (2:1-12)
        Jesus' Action in the Temple (2:13-22)
        Jesus and Nicodemus (2:23-3:21)
        Jesus' Supremacy (3:22-36)
        Jesus and the Samaritan Woman (4:1-42)
        Jesus and the Royal Official (4:43-54)
    The Opposition to Jesus (5:1-12:50)
        Emerging Opposition to Jesus (5:1-47)
            Jesus and the Lame Man at the Pool (5:1-9a)
            The Accusation and Defence of Jesus (5:9b-47)
        The Bread of Life (6:1-71)
        Family Debates (7:1-10:42)
            Jesus at the Feast of Tabernacles (7:1-52)
            Jesus and the Adulteress (7:53-8:11)
            Jesus and 'the Jews' (8:12-59)
            Jesus and the Man Born Blind (9:1-41)
            Jesus the Good Shepherd (10:1-21)
            The Rejection of Jesus (10:22-42)
        The Resurrection of Lazarus (11:1-54)
        The Last Phase of Jesus' Public Ministry (11:55-12:50)

Jesus' Private Ministry (13:1-17:26)
  The Final Meal (13:1-30)
    The Footwashing (13:1-20)
    Jesus Foretells His Betrayal (13:21-30)
  Jesus' Farewell Discourses (13:31-17:26)
    Interactive Teaching (13:31-14:31)
      The New Commandment (13:31-38)
      Jesus the Way to the Father (14:1-14)
      The Promise of the Paraclete (14:15-24)
      Jesus Concludes the Session (14:25-31)
    Teaching on Discipleship – Privileges, Obligations and Consequences (15:1-16:4a)
      Obedience, Abiding and Bearing Fruit (15:1-17)
      Witness and Persecution (15:18-16:4a)
    Final Teaching (16:4b-33)
      The Work of the Paraclete (16:4b-15)
      Sorrow Turned into Joy (16:16-24)
      Parables and Plain Speech (16:25-33)
    Jesus' Prayer (17:1-26)
Jesus' Passion and Resurrection (18:1-20:31)
  Jesus' Betrayal and Arrest (18:1-11)
  Jesus' Trial (18:12-19:16a)
    Jesus before the High Priest and Peter's Denial of Jesus (18:12-27)
    Jesus before Pilate (18:28-19:16a)
  Jesus' Death (19:16b-42)
  Jesus' Resurrection (20:1-31)
Epilogue (21:1-25)
  The Miraculous Catch of Fish (21:1-14)
  The Restoration and Commissioning of Peter (21:15-19)
  Peter and the Beloved Disciple (21:20-23)
  The Closure of the Gospel (21:24-25)

Let the Play Begin

The aim of this book is to provide a relevant commentary on the Gospel of John that will bring out the original meaning of the text and apply it to today's context. In order to achieve this aim, we employ a text-centred approach that shall critically examine issues both 'in' and 'behind' the text in order to understand the text in its original literary and historical context. We have divided John's Gospel into appropriate sections that present an exposition of the original meaning of the text. In addition, there are also sections, called 'Reflections', which provide conclusions, further implications as well as possible applications of the text for today.

I have deliberately designed the book so that it is accessible to most people, that is, no theological training is required. I have not used footnotes, although it must be made clear that many distinguished Johannine scholars have profoundly influenced my understanding of John's Gospel. I will use my own translations but the commentary can be used with any modern version of the bible. Occasionally I will also refer to so-called 'textual variants', i.e., variant readings of other Greek manuscripts, which most English versions of the bible mention in footnotes.

The stage has been set, the curtains may go up and the play can begin. The following commentary aims to assist our understanding of the Johannine play, and as such it should be seen as an informed guide but not as a substitute for the play itself. This does not mean, however, that we can simply sit back and relax. If I am allowed to bring in the other metaphor of an excavation site to understand John's Gospel, we need, with the help of the commentary, to excavate this Gospel and dig up the author's meaning from the text, which implies mental effort, perspiration and 'dirty hands'. Or, to stretch the other image with which we started, John's Gospel is like a pool in which you can wade, splash, swim or endlessly dive (as long as you do not remain at the side of the pool). I hope that this commentary will enhance your 'swimming' and 'digging' skills.

COMMENTARY

Prologue (1:1-18)

Many books start with a preface, containing the introductory remarks of the author, stating, for instance, the subject, scope and purpose of the book. John is such an author. The preface or so-called 'Prologue' introduces the protagonist and main themes of the story to follow, and as such sets the stage for the entire Gospel. It presents topics or themes such as light/darkness, life, witness, knowing, believing, spiritual birth, acceptance/rejection of Jesus, glory, truth and revelation. These topics or themes are then picked up and developed in the rest of the Gospel. The significance of the Prologue, therefore, is that it determines how the entire Gospel should be read and understood.

The Prologue may have been derived from an ancient hymn or poem, and subsequently adapted by John. John's use of the concept 'Word' or 'Logos' (the Greek word *logos* means 'word') has caught the attention of many scholars. Various possible backgrounds have been suggested. In Greek philosophies, such as Stoicism and Gnosticism, *logos*, light, truth and life were common categories, and Logos was the principle of existence or the realm through which everything was created (cf. v.3).

John, however, seems to have been immersed in Judaism rather than Stoicism or Gnosticism, as indicated in the Introduction above. In fact, most scholars today contend that John was more influenced by Jewish thinking and that a Jewish background of Word or Wisdom is preferable. Psalm 33:6, for example, mentions that God created through his Word (cf. the apocryphal books Wisdom of Solomon 9:1 and Sirach 42:15). Similarly, Wisdom's role in creation and her intimacy with God are prevalent throughout the Jewish Wisdom literature (e.g., Proverbs 3:19; 8:22-31; Sirach 1:1-10; 24:1-12; Wisdom of Solomon 7:22-9:18).

There is also a parallel between the so-called 'V-journey' of Wisdom and that of Jesus: the Jewish apocalypse *1 Enoch* speaks of divine Wisdom, who pre-exists in heaven, coming to earth, to

God's people to find a dwelling place, but having found none, she goes back to heaven (*1 Enoch* 42:1-2). The apocryphal book of Sirach, however, says that heavenly Wisdom found her dwelling place in the Law (Sirach 24:1-23). John's Gospel reflects a similar journey: the Prologue narrates the first two stages – the pre-existent Logos descended to earth and dwelled among us (1:1-2, 14) – and the third stage, Jesus' return to the Father via the cross, is revealed in the rest of the Gospel. In fact, 16:28 summarizes the entire journey and in this commentary we shall see that John regularly depicts Jesus as Wisdom.

The Prologue can be divided into four parts: (i) the introduction to the Word (1:1-5); (ii) John the Baptist as a witness to the Word (1:6-8); (iii) the reactions to the Word (1:9-13); (iv) the incarnation of the Word (1:14-18).

The Introduction to the Word (1:1-5)

It is no coincidence that John 1:1 parallels Genesis 1:1 ('In the beginning'). John deliberately takes us back to the very start of everything. The pre-existent Logos was God in essence and instrumental in the creation of everything. More specifically, what came into existence in or by the Logos was life (vv.3-4). In his Gospel, John uses two Greek words for life: *zōē*, which is the divine, eternal, indestructible life, and *psuchē*, the human, physical, transient life. *Zōē* is used here in verse 4, and the rest of the Gospel is, to put it simply, a commentary on how there is eternal life in the Logos. In fact, *zōē* or '(eternal) life' is one of the most important concepts in John's Gospel because it is shorthand for 'salvation'.

Verse 5 is expanded in verses 9-11, and reveals that the life-giving Logos-Light shines in this dark world but the world cannot grasp it. The Greek word used for 'to grasp' is an example of John's literary technique of double entendre (see the section 'Characteristics' in the Introduction); it has the sense of both 'to overcome, to overpower' and 'to understand, to perceive'. Thus, this dark world was neither able to overpower nor did it understand the Logos. We shall see that the latter theme of understanding/misunderstanding is very important for John since understanding Jesus and his message will enable a person to express adequate belief but misunderstanding Jesus will be a hindrance to belief.

John the Baptist as a Witness to the Word (1:6-8)

This little section introduces John the Baptist. The first thing we notice is that the description of John the Baptist in the Synoptic Gospels is quite different from the description in this Gospel. However, the few references to John's baptizing ministry in 1:25-33 and 3:23 assure us that the same person is in view. In this Gospel, John is never called 'the Baptist' because John's role is exclusively that of a witness.

As we mentioned earlier, John's Gospel is designed in such a way as to portray a cosmic trial, in which Jesus is accused of his claims to give life and to judge, which are divine prerogatives. As Jesus is on trial, he needs witnesses to testify on his behalf. In this Gospel, John functions as the witness *par excellence* to Jesus. Verse 8 also reveals, right at the outset, that John is subordinate to Jesus; John himself is not the Light but 'merely' witnesses to the Light. Important as John's function is, the spotlight is on someone else. The purpose of John's witness is not just 'to defend' Jesus but to lead people to believe in this Jesus (v.7).

The Reactions to the Word (1:9-13)

In verse 9, we may have the first reference to the incarnation since the verses that follow describe the reactions of people to the incarnate Logos-Light. The coming of the Logos-Light to this world essentially caused two reactions – negative (vv.10-11) and positive (vv.12-13). Negatively, even though the world was created through the Logos (cf. v.3), when the Logos came to the world, people neither knew nor accepted him. The sadness and irony of John's assertion is striking: the creature did not recognize or receive its Creator. Verse 10 homes in on the essential problem – *people do not know God*. This lack of knowledge of God probably caused them to reject God when he came to them as the incarnate Logos (v.11).

Positively, there were people who did accept the Logos, who did believe in him, and these became children of God through a new birth. This birth of God will be further explained in 3:3-8 as a birth of water and Spirit. 'To believe in his name' is shorthand for believing (and understanding) aspects of Jesus in terms of his identity, character, mission and intimate relationship with God.

Thus, John's dualistic worldview is already apparent in the Prologue. The world as a system or environment is dark, does not know God, and fails to recognize or accept the incarnate Logos. But those from the world who do accept him become part of God's family. Although the characters that John will present to us in his Gospel have various responses towards Jesus, since they operate within John's dualistic worldview (cf. the section 'Characteristics' in the Introduction), their responses will eventually boil down to two: acceptance or rejection of Jesus.

The Incarnation of the Word (1:14-18)

The pre-existent Logos became 'flesh', i.e., a human being, and 'lived' among us (v.14). This is the greatest miracle in the history of humankind: the Creator entered his creation by becoming a creature! In verse 14, the Greek word we have translated 'to live' actually means 'to dwell, to tabernacle', and alludes to the Old Testament tabernacle as the dwelling place of God among his people. So, the idea here is that, in Jesus, God 'tabernacled' among us. Jesus is the locus of God's presence and glory. This Jesus, the Logos incarnate, is the protagonist of John's story. Verse 15 then records John's first testimony about Jesus, revealing Jesus' superiority because he was 'first' – both in importance as well as time (an example of double entendre).

Verse 16, which can be translated, 'we have all received from his fullness, namely, grace *anti* grace', presents us with a difficult interpretative decision because the Greek word *anti* can mean 'instead of', 'against' or 'upon'. A glance at the next verse may offer a solution. Verse 17 contains more allusions to the Old Testament through the reference to Moses and the Law: The Law was *given* through Moses (at Mt Sinai) but 'grace and truth' (alluding to God's 'lovingkindness and faithfulness' in Exodus

34:6) *came (into being)* through Jesus. The implication is that Jesus supersedes Moses.

Returning to verse 16, we can then evaluate the three options. The first option, 'grace instead of grace', denotes a replacement theology in which Jesus replaces Moses and the Law. The second option, 'grace against grace', sets Jesus and the Mosaic Law in contrast. The third option, 'grace upon grace', denotes that more grace is given by Jesus in addition to the gracious gift of the Mosaic Law. The third option seems preferable for two reasons. First, the Mosaic Law actually functions as a witness to Jesus (5:39, 46). Second, the idea in 2:1-22, and later, behind John's treatment of the Jewish feasts in relation to Jesus, does not so much indicate a replacement or contrasting motif but rather a fulfilment motif. Thus, God's gift of the Law through Moses was grace, but the 'gift' of Jesus and what comes through him (grace, truth, life) is additional grace. For John, Jesus fulfils, and hence supersedes, what Judaism looked forward to. Nevertheless, the concept of Jesus being the fulfilment of the promises of Judaism includes an element of replacement since the old order has given way to the new one.

Verse 18 sums it up: no one has ever seen God; but the Son of God, who is intimate with the Father (literally 'who is in the bosom of the Father'), has made God known to us – *as Father*. The idea is that what Jesus did was not simply to reveal God but more precisely the fatherhood of God. Verse 12 already implied this when it said that the consequence of belief in Jesus was to become children of God, i.e., an entry into the family of God. We must be aware, however, that the concept of God as Father also exists in the Old Testament (Deuteronomy 32:6; 2 Samuel 7:14; Psalms 68:5; 89:26; Isaiah 63:16; 64:8; Jeremiah 3:4, 19; Malachi 1:6; cf. the names Abiel [1 Samuel 9:1], Eliab [1 Samuel 16:6] and Abijah [1 Samuel 8:2; 1 Kings 14:1], meaning 'God is my Father').

From the Greek verb *exēgeomai* ('to make known' or 'to reveal') in verse 18 we have derived the word 'exegesis' – the Son 'exegetes' or interprets God as the Father as it were. The purpose of exegesis is to bring out the meaning of the text, so Jesus brings out the 'meaning' of God, or, alluding to the title of this book, Jesus 'excavates' God.

Reflection

Right at the outset of his Gospel, John sets the stage and agenda for what is to follow. Thus, the author prepares the reader for what to expect. John has a grand opening to the story of Jesus, and yet, we cannot escape the sad undertone of his prelude. The framework John wants us to adopt is as follows: this world is a world enveloped in spiritual darkness; it does not know God; but by divine initiative, God came to this world as a human being – Jesus. Jesus came to reveal God (as Father) and to share the divine life that is in him. The world did not applaud when the Creator entered his creation – even worse, it did not even recognize him! There was no warm welcome for Jesus – instead the world and its people rejected him, forming a hostile environment for him. Nevertheless, there were some who accepted and believed in Jesus, and these people were subsequently drawn into God's family.

Looking around today, it seems that not much has changed. The world still, largely, rejects the person and message of Jesus, and remains enveloped in darkness. Jesus is still on trial and people still struggle with his exclusive claims and unique person. However, like John the Baptist, we should continue to witness to this Jesus so that some may come to a saving knowledge of him. The tone set by John in the Prologue is sober and yet hopeful. We need to be realistic about the human condition from God's perspective, which will not make us popular when we proclaim it because many people do not (want to) believe their grave situation. At the same time, we can present the 'remedy' – Jesus, God incarnate, who provides divine life to those who accept him.

Is there a greater miracle, a humbler act, than that of the Creator becoming what he created? This God that John presents to us, stooped to our level and entered into our dark existence. But the world at large has not recognized this magnificent gesture; people have not embraced him. How great and dim is the darkness that envelops the world, but how great and bright is the Light that shines – even the darkness could not get it! Because Jesus has an intimate relationship with his Father, he is able to reveal God as Father. This God is a personal God who desires to dwell among his people, to have an intimate relationship with them, and to be known to them as Father. Have we embraced God as Father and found that intimate place – in his bosom? What is our understanding of the fatherhood of God? We cannot excavate enough to discover the depth of our heavenly Father.

Jesus' Public Ministry (1:19-12:50)

The first half of the Gospel, chapters 1-12, is an account of Jesus' public ministry, which lasted just over three years, (see the section 'Characteristics' in the Introduction). John presents it as one that is characterized by words and works, discourses and signs. The setting alternates between receptive Galilee in the north and hostile Judea in the south.

Characters such as John the Baptist, Nicodemus, the Samaritan woman, the royal official, the lame man at the pool, 'the Jews', and so on, come on stage and interact with Jesus. Although John presents a wide spectrum of individual reactions towards John's chief character Jesus, they fluctuate between the absolutes of acceptance and rejection that John's dualistic worldview has created. As readers, we need to examine John's evaluation of their responses towards the main protagonist. John is not neutral in his evaluations because his overall aim is to persuade people to make an adequate belief-response to Jesus.

Setting the Stage (1:19-51)

John 1 has two more sections – the witness of John (1:19-34) and the calling of Jesus' disciples (1:35-51) – that lead up to the proper launch of Jesus' public ministry, which commences in John 2. Just as the Prologue set the stage for the entire Gospel, so 1:19-51 sets the stage for Jesus' public ministry.

John's Testimony (1:19-34)

This section elaborates the role of John the Baptist as a witness, which has already been mentioned in the Prologue (1:6-8, 15).

Divided into two parts, it describes John's testimony before the Jewish religious leaders (1:19-28) and before Israel (1:29-34).

John's Testimony before the Jewish Leaders (1:19-28)

As we mentioned in the Introduction, 'the Jews' in John's Gospel often refers to those Jews who were hostile and opposed to Jesus, especially from among the religious leaders from Jerusalem, the religious capital of Judaism. In addition, we learn from other sources that the Jewish religious leaders and Jewish aristocracy often collaborated with the Romans and caused oppression for the common Jew. These Jewish leaders, we read, sent a delegation to find out who John was (v.19). They had several questions for him, but behind these questions were the doubts: Was he going to be a threat to them? Was he going to start a revolutionary movement against the Romans? According to the Jewish historian Josephus, king Herod certainly thought John capable of causing a rebellion (*Antiquities* 18.5.2).

The situation in first-century Palestine under Roman rule was very volatile and characterized by oppression, injustice, conflict and resistance. Although this resistance was mostly non-violent, occasionally there were violent outbursts. After the death of king Herod in 4 B.C., there were widespread, popular revolts, aimed at overthrowing Herodian and Roman domination. The Romans subdued these movements, although with difficulty. Thereafter, the Jewish religious leaders were always on the lookout to see whether such leaders and movements might arise, afraid that their own position and status might be endangered. Hence, it was imperative that they knew this John and his intentions.

John's response is to deny that he is an important end-time figure like the Messiah (v.20), Elijah (cf. Malachi 4:5) or the Prophet like Moses (cf. Deuteronomy 18:15-18) (v.21). He describes himself in terms of Isaiah 40:3: the prophetic herald announcing Israel's coming restoration (v.23). However, John is not the Restorer himself. The delegation does not give up easily; they now want to know why, and on what authority, John is baptizing if he is not an eschatological figure (v.25).

Baptism was not unknown in Judaism. There was, for instance, proselyte baptism for Gentiles who wanted to embrace the Jewish faith, but that would not explain why *Jews* would undergo John's baptism. At the time of Jesus, Judaism knew of various groups who believed that they were the faithful remnant, the true, righteous people of God. The Qumran community, for example, believed that they were (or would be) the recipients of God's eschatological salvation, and water baptism initiated a candidate into this community of the eternal covenant.

John's baptism may have served a similar purpose. Although 1:31-33 explains that the primary purpose of John's baptism is the revelation of the Messiah to Israel, baptism would naturally evoke the concept of cleansing or purification. The dispute about cleansing/purification in 3:25-26 surrounding the baptizing ministries of Jesus and John in 3:22-23, shows that this aspect of baptism has indeed not been entirely removed. Moreover, it is natural to assume that John's baptism is related to his understanding of himself as the herald of Israel's coming restoration in verse 23. Therefore, it is probable that John considered his baptism as necessary or prepatory for Israel's future salvation (cf. Josephus, *Antiquities* 18.5.2; Mark 1:4; Matthew 3:11; Luke 3:3).

This being the case, it is not strange that the Jerusalem delegation wanted to know which group John belonged to (he may even have been part of the Qumran community at one time); and why he thought it necessary that Jews must undergo his baptism. Surely 'the Jews' in Jerusalem assumed that they belonged to the true people of God.

Interestingly, John does not give a straight answer (although 1:33 shows that John is very well aware of his authority – *God* had sent him to baptize) but makes a christological statement that stresses the importance of Jesus (vv.26-27). He is simply the prophetic herald, announcing someone more important – the one who will bring about Israel's restoration.

Perhaps the phrase, 'among you stands one whom you do not know', in verse 26 echoes the sad assertion of 1:10-11; Jesus came to his own creation but it did not know him. Lack of knowledge will lead to misunderstanding and eventually rejection, as John's story will reveal. Since the problem of humanity is that it does not know God, the solution to understanding, belief and hence salvation, according to John the Evangelist, is knowledge: the saving knowledge of God that Jesus will bring.

John's Testimony before Israel (1:29-34)

The next day, John sees Jesus approaching and exclaims, 'See, the Lamb of God who takes away the sin of the world!' (v.29). There are three possible backgrounds for the title 'Lamb of God': (i) the Suffering Servant of Isaiah 53 who makes a guilt offering for the atonement of sin; (ii) the Passover Lamb of Exodus 12 as the means of escaping God's judgement; (iii) the victorious Lamb of the apocalyptic traditions that will destroy the evil forces (*1 Enoch* 90; Revelation 5:12; 6:16-17; 17:14). We may not need to choose; perhaps all three ideas are in view. It is important to recognize the *salvific function* of this Lamb of God, namely, to take away the sins of the world.

In verse 30, John reiterates his own subordinate position in relation to Jesus (1:15; cf. 1:27), which anticipates the section 3:22-36 on the supremacy of Jesus. As John explains in verse 31, the whole purpose of his baptizing ministry is to reveal the identity of the awaited Messiah to Israel. John himself does not know who the Messiah is, but God has made known to him that the identity of the Messiah would be revealed by the coming of the Spirit upon him. Then, in turn, John could reveal him to Israel.

The coming and remaining of the Spirit on Jesus in verse 32 probably alludes to Isaiah 11:2 which describes the Messiah as being empowered with the Spirit of wisdom, understanding and liberating power. The promise that Jesus will also be the Spirit-Baptizer (v.33), however, is more puzzling. Many Christians perceive 'the baptism in the Holy Spirit' as a technical term for a so-called 'second blessing', i.e., an empowerment for mission that believers need to receive in addition to salvation (the so-called classical Pentecostal position). However, such a position effectively creates two classes of Christians, causing various pastoral complications. Besides, John probably had something else in mind anyway. First, Judaism did not know of a messiah who would bestow the Spirit on others but simply as one who himself was endowed with the Spirit in order to carry out his divinely ordained task. In addition, baptism usually had the connotations of cleansing or purification from sin or moral defilement.

The following picture then emerges: the coming and remaining of the Spirit upon Jesus empowers him with gifts of wisdom, understanding and liberating power in order to carry out his public ministry. As such, Jesus will baptize people with the Holy Spirit, in that Jesus will cleanse and save people *by means of* the Spirit. The original text allows for this interpretation since the Greek preposition *en*, in 'he is the one who baptizes *en* Holy Spirit' (v.33), can mean either 'in' or 'with, by means of'.

This passage, then, provides a concise description of the launch of Jesus' salvific ministry. God reveals the identity of the Messiah to John, who in turn reveals this Jesus to Israel as the Lamb of God who takes away the sin of the world. The Spirit will be the powerful, divine means by which Jesus carries out his salvific ministry. Hence, 'to baptize with the Holy Spirit' is not a technical term for a one-off experience in addition to salvation but shorthand for Jesus' entire programme of salvation for Israel (and indeed the entire world).

Reflection

In countries where a Christian minority faces oppression or persecution (e.g., North Korea, Saudi Arabia, Vietnam, Iran, Bhutan, Myanmar [formerly Burma], Somalia), the religious and/or political leaders of the country may send a delegation to enquire about these Christians and what they do. In such a milieu, where Christianity is already perceived as a threat, will Christians shrink back or will they be able to testify about Jesus without aggravating the authorities? It is important to pray for suffering and persecuted Christians in such countries, and stand with them in whatever way we can. The issue can be quite complicated. In India, for example, where religious persecution has increased since 1998, Christians understand 'freedom of religion' as the right to propagate their faith and invite others to this faith. But in the eyes of many Hindus, the same freedom should allow them to remain within their own religion without being persuaded to convert to another religion. In other countries, where there is true freedom of religion, people may visit churches or approach believers to find out what Christianity is all about. What will our witness be, how will we reply to their questions, and how will we define ourselves?

John's entire ministry can be summed up in one word: witness. His whole life was geared towards being a witness for Jesus. John never sought to be in the limelight but merely pointed to him who was to take centre stage. John did not suffer from an inferiority complex; he knew exactly what his mission was and where he stood in relation to Jesus. May we have the same clarity as John and be messengers of Jesus in this world, heralding the good news of him who took away the sins of the world. In many Christian ministries, sadly, one may often wonder who enjoys the spotlight. That our function is to be a witness for Jesus rather than to draw attention to ourselves, does not put us in a derogatory role. Our greatness or importance is not determined by ourselves or other people; it depends on the extent to which we are able to carry out the task that God intends us to do. John's greatness lay in his pointing away from himself to the one who was greater. Besides pointing to Jesus, an additional challenge may be to point to others who are more gifted, more skilled or better equipped than we are.

The Call to Discipleship (1:35-51)

John 1:35-51 contains two sections – the calling of the first disciples (vv.35-42) and the calling of other disciples (vv.43-51) – but the remarkable parallels between the two invite us to treat them as one unit.

Let us first look at the similarities. First, both passages open with, 'the next day' (v.35 and v.43). Second, both contain an understanding of the call to follow Jesus as a disciple (v.37 and v.43). Third, the invitation 'come and see' is found both in verse 39 and verse 46. Fourth, we learn that Andrew finds Peter (v.41) and Philip finds Nathanael (v.45). As an aside, verse 43 translates literally, 'The next day *he* wanted to go to Galilee and *he* found Philip. And Jesus said to him, "Follow me."' Since the subject 'he' is not explicitly specified, it could be either Jesus or Andrew.

Perhaps the latter is preferable because it makes sense of the 'first' in verse 41, so that Andrew *first* found Peter and *then* Philip.

Fifth, the finder (Andrew, Philip) has some perception about Jesus' identity, which he then reveals to the person found (v.41 and v.45). Sixth, Jesus provides revelation about the person found (v.42 and v.48); although only in the case of Nathanael does John record the response to Jesus' revelation (v.49). In fact, Nathanael professes that Jesus is the Messiah – 'the king of Israel' is a messianic title – and Jesus approves of Nathanael's confession in that he labels it as belief (v.50).

Why does John record the calling of the disciples in two incidents with such striking similarity? One reason may be that through this parallelism John wants to draw the attention of the reader to some important aspect of discipleship. Though by no means exhaustive, we can draw some principles of discipleship from these two episodes. First, people are invited to come to Jesus; then to follow and remain with him as disciples. John seems to have invested the verb 'to remain, to abide' with theological meaning in his Gospel. Therefore, 'they remained with him' in verse 39 means more than a casual stay; perhaps it indicates the continual need to abide or stick with Jesus. Next, they are to witness to others and simply bring them to Jesus, and Jesus will do the rest.

There is, in fact, a whole chain of testimony: John witnesses to Andrew and another disciple; Andrew witnesses to Peter and possibly Philip; Philip in turn witnesses to Nathanael. There seems to be a correlation (if not an identification) between a disciple and a witness, in that a true disciple will bear witness to other people about Jesus.

One important point remains, namely, Jesus' reply to Nathanael in verses 50-51, which reveals a significant aspect of Jesus' identity. In verse 51, we have an allusion to Genesis 28:12, which describes Jacob's remarkable vision of God at Bethel. Jesus' allusion to this event is meant to indicate that he is the mediator or point of contact between heaven and earth, the two realms that are otherwise mutually exclusive in John's worldview. In Jesus, the divine and human intersect. As a result, people will experience 'greater things', i.e., greater or more revelation of God (and Jesus) because Jesus has open access to the heavenly realm.

The concept of revelation turns out to be important for John. For John, knowledge of God or saving knowledge is not something that can be acquired by human reason but by divine revelation – a revelation that is available in and through Jesus. That is, Jesus is both the Revealer and the revelation of God.

Interestingly, Nathanael confesses Jesus as 'Son of God' (v.49) whereas Jesus himself employs the title 'Son of Man' (v.51). In John's Gospel, the title 'Son of Man' is used exclusively by Jesus, mostly in reference to his death (3:14; 6:62; 8:28; 9:35; 12:34).

Reflection

John (the Baptist) remains an exemplary witness. We should note that John continues to point away from himself to Jesus (v.36), and that he does not seem to be worried when two of his disciples left him (v.37). Reading verses 35-37, we can picture John standing with two of his disciples. As Jesus passes by, John looks straight at Jesus (the Greek word used in v.36 denotes an attentive look or fixed gaze) and exclaims, perhaps with a pointed finger, 'Look, the Lamb of God!' John's disciples were probably reminded of what he had said the previous day: that this Lamb of God was the one who would take away the sins of the world (v.29). They may even have witnessed the revelation of the Messiah to Israel by John. Whatever it was, John's exclamation causes the two disciples to leave their master and follow Jesus, their new master. It is noteworthy that John did not attempt to keep his disciples with him, most likely because he knew what his sole function was. Do we have the same attitude as John, or do we sometimes try to 'protect' our ministry and prevent people from going to others, perhaps even to Jesus? If we truly are witnesses to Jesus, we will be keen to send our 'disciples' to the one who is greater than we are. Surely, we would like people to follow Jesus rather than us, would we not?

What is also remarkable in this passage is the simplicity of witness. No complicated programmes, persuasive strategies or extensive arguments. Simply sharing with others what we have experienced and understood of Jesus, and then bringing them to

Jesus may be all that is required. Jesus will then do what is necessary to bring them to an adequate belief-response. Perhaps a gentle 'come and see' is more inviting and persuasive than a lengthy discourse on our doctrinal beliefs.

John stresses the importance of divine revelation. We cannot obtain knowledge of God, which humankind is in need of, by human reason or effort but by revelation. This revelation of the divine is not only available through Jesus but essentially in Jesus. He is both the Revealer and the revelation of God, and hence the key to saving knowledge and salvation. Remember the Prologue, where John asserts that no one has seen God; no one knows God in the sense of having a saving knowledge of him. But Jesus, who is intimate with the Father and who is the mediator between heaven and earth, has come as the revelation of God to reveal him as Father.

Although human mental effort may not give us saving knowledge of God, we should not ignore our cognitive faculties. We shall see that understanding Jesus' revelation is necessary to come to an adequate belief-response. John advocates people to have an intellectual grasp of Jesus' identity, his mission and the nature of his relationship with his Father. In fact, even acquiring such understanding needs divine assistance – from the Spirit. The Christian faith, then, is an understanding faith, and no blind leap into the dark or the unknown. In Johannine terms, faith is a coming out of the dark into the Light (cf. 3:19-21).

From Cana to Cana (2:1-4:54)

There are various indications that John 2-4 is one literary unit, which is sometimes called 'from Cana to Cana'. First, Jesus sets out from Cana in Galilee (2:1-2). Then, after his visit to Jerusalem (2:13-3:21) and Judea (3:22-4:3), he heads back, via Samaria (4:4-42), to Cana in Galilee (4:46). Furthermore, it is during the wedding that Jesus performs his first sign (2:11) and the healing of the official's son is described as Jesus' second sign (4:54). Finally, the theme of 'water' is prominent throughout John 2-4: in Cana, Jesus turns water into wine; to Nicodemus, Jesus talks about a birth of water and Spirit; in 3:22-30, John's water rite sparks off a discussion on purification; and to the Samaritan woman, Jesus offers 'living water'. John often (but not always) uses water as a symbol for salvation, which is not strange since water possesses purifying abilities and naturally evokes the idea of cleansing.

The 'Cana to Cana' section may, approximately, span the first one and a half years of Jesus' ministry. Jesus' initial time in Galilee, covered in 1:43-2:12, may have been a couple of months. Then, from Passover in March/April (2:23) until Weeks in May/June (5:1) is about one year and two months since the information provided in 4:35 (four more months until the harvest in May/June) requires that we include another, unrecorded Passover between 4:35 and 5:1.

John's narrative of Jesus' journey from Cana to Cana can be structured as follows:

2:1-11	the wedding at Cana
2:12	narrative bridge
2:13-22	Jesus' action in the temple
2:23-3:21	Jesus and Nicodemus
3:22-36	the supremacy of Jesus
4:1-42	Jesus and the Samaritan woman
4:43-54	Jesus and the royal official

Jesus Supersedes Judaism (2:1-22)

John 2:1-22 can be divided into two sections: the wedding at Cana (2:1-11) and Jesus' action in the temple (2:13-22). Verse 12 functions as a bridge; it logically connects 2:1-11 and 2:13-22 since it explains Jesus' journey from Cana to Jerusalem via Capernaum. It also invites us to connect the two episodes theologically, though it is not immediately clear how the wedding at Cana relates to Jesus' action in the temple. We will come back to this issue after we have expounded both incidents.

The Wedding at Cana (2:1-12)

The actual story of the wedding at Cana only comprises verses 1-11, marked off by 'in Cana of Galilee' in verses 1 and 11. In the Greek, verse 12 starts a new paragraph and, as we mentioned, connects this story with Jesus' action in the temple.

The statement that Jesus' mother makes, 'they have no wine' (v.3), is actually a request for Jesus to do something about it. Jesus' reply in verse 4a is perhaps a little startling. To address one's mother as 'woman' may sound rude, but it may have been affectionate; although a mild rebuke is probably intended. Then we have Jesus' somewhat enigmatic reference to his 'hour' that has not yet come (v.4b). On the one hand, Jesus says more than once that his 'hour' has not yet come (2:4; 7:30; 8:20); on the other hand, he states that the 'hour' has come (4:23; 5:25; 12:23; 13:1; 17:1). On closer examination, I suggest that Jesus' 'hour' has two different referents. In 2:4; 4:23 and 5:25, the 'hour' refers to the hour of Jesus' messianic ministry; whereas the 'hour' in 7:30; 8:20; 12:13; 13:1 and 17:1 refers to the hour of Jesus' glorification. This needs more explanation.

When Jesus says that his 'hour' has not yet come in verse 4b, he probably refers to the hour of the messianic age, i.e., the new age of justice and peace ('salvation') that God would start through his Messiah. At the same time, however, I suggest that Jesus' subsequent action of turning water into wine actually removes the 'not yet' of the messianic hour. That is, the story of the wedding at Cana symbolizes Jesus' inauguration of the messianic age, and hence the fulfilment of what Judaism was expecting. It marks the start or opening ceremony of Jesus' messianic ministry. This launch of the messianic age is also confirmed by the phrase 'an hour is coming, *and is now*' in 4:23 and 5:25, in which Jesus announces the present availability of a new kind of worship and of eternal life respectively.

The seeming paradox between Jesus' assertion that the hour of the messianic age has not yet come and his subsequent action of turning water into wine, which demonstrates the opposite, can be readily explained. For John, Jesus is in control: his opponents cannot catch him (7:44; 8:59; 10:39); he determines when to lay down and pick up his life (10:17-18); though Pilate wrongly assumes that he has authority over Jesus (19:10-11). Likewise, in this story, Jesus is in full control from the beginning: not even his mother can tell him what to do; only at his time and discretion, Jesus launches his messianic ministry.

In contrast, the other 'hour' did not come during the period of Jesus' public ministry (7:30; 8:20) but only towards the end (12:23; 13:1). This 'hour' refers to the hour of Jesus' glorification, i.e., the time of his death, resurrection and ascension (12:23, 27-28; 13:1; 17:1, 5). Although we differentiate between these two uses of 'hour', we should be careful not to dichotomize Jesus' ministry and his glorification as if Jesus' public ministry was exempt from glory. On the contrary, in verse 11 of the present passage John indicates that Jesus' miracle revealed his glory; the resurrection of Lazarus results in glorification (11:4, 40); Jesus asserts that during his ministry he has glorified his Father (17:4), and in turn, Jesus has received glory through his disciples (17:10). Hence, Jesus' public ministry is one of glory and glorification, but in a narrower sense, Jesus' glorification refers specifically to his death, resurrection and ascension.

Back to the wedding at Cana. Interestingly, the story does not tell us *when* the water changed into wine. Was it during the filling of the water jars (v.7), during the drawing (v.8) or during the tasting (v.9)? Apparently this is unimportant; what is important is *that* it was miraculously transformed. The emphasis is not so much on the miracle *per se* but on the *significance* of the miracle. That is why John calls Jesus' miracles 'signs': the miracles point beyond themselves to what they signify, namely something about Jesus' identity and mission (see the section 'Characteristics' in the Introduction).

The important thing, therefore, is to discover what Jesus' miracle revealed about himself and his work. One clue is given in verse 6 where the water jars used for Jewish purification rites represent the old order of Judaism. Through the miracle of turning the water into wine, Jesus indicates that he will replace the old order with a new one. Next, when the master of ceremonies tastes the water turned into wine, he remarks that this wine is of superior quality and wonders why it was kept until the end (v.10). This superior wine exemplifies what Jesus has to offer; something which supersedes what Judaism can offer, and has been kept until now, until the coming of Jesus.

A clearer picture now emerges. The wedding at Cana symbolizes the messianic banquet described, for instance, in Isaiah

25:6 (cf. Revelation 19:9, 17-18). The miracle was a prophetic act of Jesus, symbolizing the start of the new messianic age – the coming of the kingdom of God. What Jesus has to offer is superior to what Judaism can offer. This event characterizes the start of Jesus' life-giving ministry, which supersedes the old order of Judaism.

Based on this sign, Jesus' disciples believed in him (v.11). The Greek in verse 11 allows for either '…and he [Jesus] revealed his glory' or '…and it [the miraculous sign] revealed his glory'. Although most English translations adopt the former translation, I prefer the latter one because, for John, the signs are revelatory; they reveal aspects of Jesus' identity and mission. As such, John appropriately marks this miracle – that reveals the start of Jesus' glorious ministry – as the first of Jesus' signs.

Jesus' Action in the Temple (2:13-22)

The Jewish festivals are an important theme in John's Gospel (see the section 'Characteristics' in the Introduction). They help us with timing Jesus' ministry and also provide a thematic framework for the Gospel. The first festival John mentions is the Passover (v.13), one of the three pilgrim festivals that required every male Jew to go to the temple in Jerusalem (the others are Weeks and Tabernacles).

There is a growing consensus among scholars that there was only one cleansing of the temple, which took place at the end of Jesus' ministry (as recorded in the Synoptics), but which John put in the beginning for theological reasons (which we shall discover below).

When Jesus enters the temple and sees what is going, he radically intervenes (vv.14-16). Jesus' actions do not display a negative attitude towards the temple (otherwise the quotation of Psalm 69:9 in v.17 does not make sense) but towards the way the temple was being used, namely, as a marketplace rather than a place of worship. His driving people out (literally 'throwing out') of the temple in verse 15 perhaps foreshadows his 'throwing out' the devil in 12:31, and possibly matches the 'throwing out' that the Jews intended for those who believed in Jesus as the Messiah (9:22, 34; 12:42; 16:2).

The reaction of the Jews in verse 18 is an implicit question about Jesus' authority: On what authority could Jesus regulate practices in the temple? Rather than a straightforward answer, Jesus' reply in verse 19 (and John's explanatory comment in v.21) reveals that he himself is the new temple and therefore the new locus of God's presence (cf. 1:14, 18). The temple, along with the Sabbath, the Law and the land, made up the pillars of Judaism. In the Prologue, we saw that Jesus surpasses the Mosaic Law; now we learn that he supersedes another aspect of Judaism by virtue of his being the new temple.

There is perhaps a secondary inference to be made, however, if we connect Jesus' statement in verse 19 with the symbolism of the Passover festival. The Passover commemorates Israel's deliverance from bondage in Egypt, symbolized by the ritual of slaughtering an unblemished lamb and smearing its blood on the doorposts. Verse 19 may then allude to his sacrificial death that delivers people from the bondage of sin (cf. the function of the Lamb of God in 1:29). Thus, Jesus' prophetic action in the temple and his statement in verse 19 reveal that he is the fulfilment of aspects of Judaism.

In verses 20-21, John uses the literary tool of misunderstanding (see the section 'Characteristics' in the Introduction). The Jews misunderstand Jesus' reply (v.20), leading to further clarification (v.21), which eventually benefits the disciples – albeit only after the resurrection (v.22). John frequently uses the misunderstanding of characters in the story to provide subsequent explanation, either by Jesus or by himself, which ultimately benefits the reader.

The Greek verb used in verse 17 and in verse 22 with regard to the disciples is in the passive voice, so that we literally have, 'his disciples were reminded that…'. This implies that an agent would cause the remembrance or calling to mind rather than the disciples themselves. When we come to 14:26, we shall see that one of the tasks of the Spirit-Paraclete will be to bring to memory the words of Jesus, and 2:22 may well record one such instance (12:16 refers to another incident). As a result of the remembrance of Jesus' words (and undoubtedly the better understanding), the disciples responded in belief (v.22).

Reflection

We are now in a position to see how 2:1-11 and 2:13-22 are theologically connected. The two accounts have a christological focus, so that in both episodes Jesus' prophetic actions vividly demonstrate that he supersedes Judaism and will fulfil what Judaism promises and stands for. The miracle at Cana demonstrates that Jesus surpasses the old order of Judaism and inaugurates the new age. Likewise, Jesus' action in the temple symbolizes his superiority over the temple and his words hint at his being the new temple – one of the pillars of Jewish belief (cf. 1:17, which suggests that Jesus supersedes the Mosaic Law, another pillar of Judaism). Besides, both passages end similarly – with a belief-response from the disciples (v.11 and v.22). These common features in both passages would explain why John brought the cleansing of the temple forward.

Have we recognized and experienced the surpassing greatness of Jesus? He is the fulfilment of all God's promises to his people; he is the bringer of salvation, and the locus of God's presence. Jesus' ministry, empowered by the Spirit, promises to be refreshingly new and to exceed all that we have known and experienced. At the same time, Jesus is no 'softy' or pushover when it comes to his mission and his Father's affairs. At the wedding, he chides his own mother not to interfere with his mission and instead mind her own business. In the temple, he acts radically, decisively and violently – perhaps not the picture we usually have of Jesus.

John's narrative poses two challenges to us. First, a word on miracles. It sometimes seems that big 'healing campaigns' and 'miracle crusades' are geared towards the spectacular and people can easily be carried away by what happens on the platform. John reminds us that the focus should not be on the miracles themselves but on the one they point to. This does not mean that we are to reject or be negative towards miracles; on the contrary, if properly understood, miracles can lead to faith (v.11). The second challenge comes from the instruction of Jesus' mother in 2:5, 'Do whatever he tells you!' No conditions, no arguments; just a straightforward call to obedience. Who can fail to be challenged by this?

Jesus and Nicodemus (2:23-3:21)

We now come to John's famous dialogues or discourses in which various characters interact with Jesus. The first character we encounter is Nicodemus. Although many of us know the story of Jesus and Nicodemus, remember we are here to excavate and discover new things. John expects his readers to observe, assess the various characters, and learn from their interaction with Jesus. We divide the passage into three parts: (i) the setting of the stage (2:23-3:1); (ii) the dialogue between Jesus and Nicodemus (3:2-15); (iii) John's commentary on the incident (3:16-21).

Setting the Stage (2:23-3:1)

Most English translations start the story of Jesus and Nicodemus at 3:1, but, for the following reasons, I suggest that the story really begins at 2:23. First, 3:2 literally reads, 'He came to him at night and said to him...'. The 'he' clearly refers to Nicodemus in 3:1, but for the antecedent of 'him' we must go back to 2:24, where Jesus is explicitly mentioned. Second, the phrase 'the signs that you are doing' in 3:2 is an echo of the same phrase in 2:23. Third, there is a threefold repetition of the Greek word for 'man' in 2:25-3:1 causing a particular rhythm, which most English translations have been unable to preserve: '[2:25] he needed no one to witness about *man*; for he knew what was in *man*. [3:1] Now there was a *man* from the Pharisees...'.

What do we know about this man? In 3:1, we learn that Nicodemus belongs to the sect of the Pharisees, who were regarded as experts on the Mosaic Law. Second, Nicodemus is called a 'ruler of the Jews', which means that he was probably a member of the Jewish Council, the Sanhedrin. Third, in 3:10 Jesus calls him 'the teacher of Israel', in which 'teacher' is equivalent to 'rabbi'. So, Nicodemus was one of the leading Pharisaic rabbis and a member of the Jewish Supreme Court. In modern terms, Dr Nicodemus was one of the top theologians of his time.

The following picture of the setting emerges. When Jesus was in Jerusalem, he performed miraculous signs, which caused many people to believe in him (v.23). But Jesus did not entrust himself to them (literally 'did not believe them') because he knew every human being and their motivations, and so questioned their belief-response (vv.24-25). Although the text does not indicate in what way the people's belief-response was defective or deficient, their belief was nevertheless inadequate. Since 3:1 flows from 2:23-25, the implication is that Nicodemus was part of this group of people – not socially, but in the way he was attracted to Jesus and responded to him. What was lacking in the people's response to Jesus is then spelled out in the subsequent story of Nicodemus, because he belongs to this group and speaks for them.

What bearing does this have on the story? When we realize that the story starts in 2:23, then Nicodemus does not appear suddenly, but has specific features. By placing Nicodemus in the right context, we give him 'flesh' as it were. As Nicodemus knew where Jesus had come from (3:2), so we now know where Nicodemus came from. Thus, John 2:23-3:1 sets the stage for the entire Nicodemus story.

The Birth of the Spirit (3:2-15)

Nicodemus came to Jesus 'at night' (v.2). This may partly reflect the rabbinic custom of conducting theological discussions in the evening, but is perhaps also indicative of Nicodemus' spiritual condition: he is still in the dark. His reason for coming to Jesus is that he has seen Jesus' signs (2:23; 3:2) and wants to find out more about this miraculous teacher. The questions in Nicodemus' mind may have been, 'What are his credentials?' and 'Where was he educated?' Jesus, however, ignores the hidden agenda behind Nicodemus' statement in verse 2, and instead starts to talk about entry ('to see' is 'to enter' as v.5 explains) into the kingdom of God; and the need to be born 'from above' in order to enter salvation (v.3).

The Greek word *anōthen* can mean 'from above' or 'again/anew'. Nicodemus opts for the latter meaning (v.4). The meaning 'from above', however, is more likely to be in view because: (i) born 'from above'/of the Spirit (3:3, 5) parallels 'born of God' (1:13); (ii) Jesus is portrayed as the one who came 'from above' (3:2, 13, 31); (iii) as part of John's dualism, the birth 'from above' is contrasted with the natural birth of the flesh in 3:6 (cf. 1:13). In any case, 'from above' would encompass the meaning 'again' since a birth 'from above' is also a re-birth. So, when Jesus talks about entering into salvation through a spiritual birth, Nicodemus misunderstands Jesus, and thinks that he is referring to a second, physical birth.

In order to clarify Nicodemus' misunderstanding, Jesus explains that a person needs to be born of water and Spirit in order to enter into the kingdom of God (v.5). The parallelism between verses 3 and 5 provides clues for understanding this miraculous birth. 'To see' the kingdom of God is to enter into it, and the birth 'from above' is a birth 'of water and Spirit' (cf. the birth from God in 1:13). The grammatical construction, in Greek, of the metaphorical birth of water and Spirit suggests that only one birth is in view, in which the two elements 'water' and 'Spirit' are combined. Since verses 7 and 10 show that Jesus expected Nicodemus to be able to grasp something of what he was saying, we must look at the Hebrew Scriptures (the Old Testament) for the meaning of this birth of water and Spirit.

Two texts come to mind. One is Isaiah 44:3, where 'water' and 'Spirit' are mentioned. However, they are in parallel rather than in series (as we have it in 3:5), and hence water and Spirit interpret one another rather than functioning together. The more likely text is Ezekiel 36:25-27, which reads:

> [25] I [God] will sprinkle clean water upon you [Israel], and you shall be clean from all your uncleannesses, and from all your idols I will cleanse you. [26] A new heart I will give you, and a new spirit I will put within you; and I will remove from your body the heart of stone and give you a heart of flesh. [27] I will put my Spirit within you, and make you follow my statutes and be careful to observe my ordinances.

In this passage, we have God's promise that he will restore Israel by cleansing her from moral impurity by means of water (v.25) and cause an inner transformation (v.26; the 'new heart' and 'new spirit' are metaphors for Israel's transformation at the core of her being). Moreover, God promises to put his Spirit within Israel's 'inner being' so that she can relate correctly to him, i.e., the Spirit will be the inner force that directs Israel to live as God's renewed covenant people (v.27). I understand the 'in you' in verse 27 primarily in relational terms, i.e., God will put his Spirit amongst or in the midst of Israel – at the centre of Israel's life/existence. If we then read Ezekiel 37:1-14 (in my view, throughout this passage the Hebrew *rûach* refers to the divine Spirit rather than 'breath' [contra the NRSV and NIV]) in the context of Ezekiel 36:25-27, it becomes clear that the entire process of restoration is caused and sustained by God's Spirit. Thus, God will renew Israel by means of his Spirit and this 'indwelling' Spirit will be the primary force enabling a renewed Israel to keep her covenant obligations. With this understanding, we return to our passage in John.

Against the backdrop of Ezekiel 36-37, the Johannine birth of water and Spirit becomes a metaphor for entering salvation through the cleansing and renewing work of the Holy Spirit. Moreover, the Spirit, besides being the agent of the new birth, will also be the one to sustain this salvation. The Spirit shall 'indwell' the renewed person and be the primary moral force directing her/him to live as one who truly belongs to the kingdom of God (cf. v.6b). [For an explanation concerning the non-sacramental reading of the text, see the section 'Characteristics' in the Introduction.]

In verse 6, John's dualism comes to the fore through the contrast of 'flesh' and 'Spirit'. 'Flesh' represents the realm from below and 'Spirit' the realm from above, so that the intended contrast is between the two realms. A birth 'of the flesh' is a physical birth into the natural world, whereas a birth 'of the Spirit' is a spiritual birth, which allows one to enter into the heavenly realm of God. These two realms are mutually exclusive. Hence, a mere birth of the flesh does not qualify one for entrance into salvation – only a birth of the Spirit does.

In addition, we suggested that in 3:5 (understood against the background of Ezekiel 36-37) the Spirit does not merely cause the new birth but also sustains the new life because the Spirit 'indwells' the believer. This resultant spiritual transformation, at the core of one's being, then explains the phrase 'what is born of the Spirit is Spirit' in verse 6b: The Spirit, at the centre of the believer's life/existence, directs one's life in such a way that one can behave/live as a worthy citizen of the realm from above, into which one has been born.

In verse 8, there is a play on the double meaning of *pneuma* – 'wind' or 'Spirit'. The point of the pun is that, like the wind, the Spirit is invisible and outside human control. But again, as with the wind, the *result* of the Spirit's sovereign activity is noticeable, namely, a person born of the Spirit. Sadly, however, just as one does not know where the wind comes from, Nicodemus does not know the origin of the Spirit – that it comes 'from above'.

The implication of Jesus' revelation in verses 3-8 is that being born a Jew is not a sufficient qualification for entry into the kingdom of God and hence for belonging to the true Israel, the people of God. The Spirit has now become the identity-marker of the true Israel, and the metaphorical birth of the Spirit is now the necessary condition for entering into salvation. This must have been shocking for Nicodemus, who would naturally assume to be an insider by virtue of his birth as a Jew. His foundations are suddenly shaken and it is no wonder, then, that Nicodemus asks, 'How can this happen?' (v.9).

Jesus rebukes Nicodemus for failing to grasp the spiritual reality of what he was saying, in spite of being a leading theologian (v.10). In verses 10-12, Jesus essentially points out that Nicodemus' problem is a cognitive one; as the top theologian of Israel, he should have done better.

John's use of the plurals 'we' and 'you' in verse 2 and again, verses 11-12, probably indicates that, in the story world, Nicodemus came with his disciples to have a public discussion in the evening with Jesus and his disciples, rather than a scenario in which Nicodemus secretly meet Jesus in the night. In the world of the reader, however, this incident typifies those who are attracted to Jesus, but are still in the dark, and their encounter with Jesus and those who already belong to him.

In verse 13, Jesus reveals his identity: he is the heavenly Revealer who came from the realm above to the realm below, to witness about divine realities (cf. 1:51; Proverbs 30:4). Finally, in verses 14-15, Jesus provides an answer to Nicodemus' question in verse 9. Alluding to the story of the serpent in the wilderness in Numbers 21:4-9, Jesus explains that everyone who looks at him in faith, when he is lifted up on the cross, will be saved. This means that when people understand the significance of his life-giving work at the cross and believe in this crucified Jesus, they will experience a birth of the Spirit, which brings them into the family of God and gives them eternal life.

If we recognize John's allusions to the Jewish wisdom literature, particularly the apocryphal book Wisdom of Solomon, we may probe further *how* this understanding of the cross and the consequent spiritual birth will come about. First, as Wisdom shows Jacob the kingdom of God (Wisdom of Solomon 10:10), so Jesus shows Nicodemus the way to the kingdom of God in verses 3 and 5. Second, John 3:12 finds a parallel in Wisdom of Solomon 9:16: if 'earthly things' are already difficult to understand, how much more 'heavenly things'? Wisdom of Solomon 9:17-18 goes on to explain that Solomon will only be able to understand the 'heavenly things', and hence experience salvation, if God sends Wisdom and the accompanying Spirit. Coming back to John, if the Spirit is the agent of the birth 'from above', and if this birth requires a true understanding of the cross, then it follows that the Spirit might also provide such saving knowledge (cf. the commentary on John 4 and 6). In sum, I suggest that the Spirit facilitates a true understanding of the cross and subsequently a birth into the realm from above.

John's Commentary (3:16-21)

First, there is the issue of where exactly Jesus' words end – at verse 12, 15 or 21? A bible that has 'the words of Jesus' in red print cannot be taken as authoritative – it simply reflects the particular interpretation of the editorial team behind it. I contend that Jesus' conversation with Nicodemus ends at verse 15 and that verses 16-21 are John's commentary. I say this because verses 13-14 use the title 'Son of Man', which Jesus exclusively applies to himself, whereas verses 16-21, including the use of the title 'Son (of God)', reflect the language of the Prologue and hence of John himself.

In these verses, John succinctly states the problem of humanity and the divine solution. The fundamental problem of humankind is that people love the darkness, do evil deeds and are afraid of being exposed. The divine solution is that God sent his Son to save the world that he loves. In fact, God loved the world and its people so much that he *gave* his only Son to be put to death on a cross in order to provide eternal life. The cross is where God ultimately reveals his love for the world. As the Prologue and subsequent passages also mention, there are ultimately only two choices: unbelief in Jesus, which results in immediate judgement and ultimately death; or belief in Jesus, which results in escaping God's judgement and in eternal life.

Reflection

Our analysis of the dialogue between Jesus and Nicodemus has made clear the deficiency or inadequacy of the 'belief' of the people in 2:23, including Nicodemus: they had not been 'born from above' (cf. v.7). Nicodemus is attracted to Jesus because of the signs he performs. He even believes that Jesus is 'from God', but he fails to grasp the significance of the signs and of Jesus being 'from above'. Ultimately, Nicodemus neither accepts nor rejects Jesus; he shows interest but there is no commitment of faith, and hence he remains in the dark – an outsider. Interestingly, Nicodemus gradually fades out of the conversation – his verbal contribution reduces dramatically from verse 2, through verse 4, to verse 9, after which he says no more – so we are left wondering about his response to Jesus. This gradual fading away of Nicodemus adds to his ambiguity – having briefly come to the Light, he disappears into the shadows or twilight zone from where he came.

Nicodemus, then, is representative of people with an inadequate belief-response to Jesus. Such people are attracted to him on the basis of his miraculous signs, but because they only operate at an earthly level, they are unable to accept or grasp Jesus' revelation. Thus, they remain in the dark, as outsiders. John intends that Nicodemus' misunderstanding and dullness should serve as a warning to the reader not to remain ambiguous and uncommitted. Instead, John urges us to believe in Jesus – as the one whose death provides eternal life. No one can experience salvation and be part of God's family except through a birth of the Spirit. This birth of the Spirit occurs when we understand and accept that the cross is God's solution to the problem of sin. What is our response to this revelation of love, to this crucified Jesus? Have we accepted him and experienced this spiritual birth?

In 3:13, we find an implicit warning about the futility of human efforts to understand divine realities. In the time of Jesus, some groups tried to obtain revelation about and access to the divine realm through various means including heavenly visions and asceticism (fasting, abstinence). Today, in many non-western religions and western New Age movements (the latter are actually a revival of ancient and primitive religious beliefs and practices) the same holds true. The use, for example, of mediums, tarot cards, transcendental meditation, the practice of astrology, divination, palmistry, witchcraft and magic, are all popular means of receiving revelation from other realms that are not naturally accessible to us. All these efforts are needless, even redundant, because the one from heaven has come down to tell us about the heavenly realm. Jesus' revelation of God and the divine realm is sufficient and neither should we bypass it nor have to go beyond it.

Jesus' Supremacy (3:22-36)

Jesus' Supremacy over John (3:22-30)

This passage describes in a wonderful way John's testimony about Jesus, and Jesus' supremacy over John. Both John and Jesus were baptizing people (vv.22-24, but note the correction in 4:2), which led to a discussion about purification between John's disciples and a Jew (v.25). John's disciples were concerned about the growing success of Jesus' baptizing ministry over John's, and came to their master for clarification (v.26). John responded by reiterating his role and position in relation to Jesus' (vv.27-30).

John was apparently unconcerned about building a name or kingdom for himself. He was not threatened when people began to go after Jesus. In fact, John urged his own disciples to follow Jesus (1:35-37). Why did John do this? How could he? First, John knew his mission: God had specifically called him to witness to Jesus (cf. 1:6-8, 15, 19-34). Second, John was clear about his own position in relation to Jesus: He was a shining lamp but not the

Light himself (1:8; 5:35); he was the friend of the bridegroom but not the Bridegroom himself (v.29). John was categorical that he had to decrease whereas Jesus had to increase (v.30). He was content to define his own role and status as subordinate to that of Jesus (cf. 1:27, 30).

Jesus' Supremacy over All (3:31-36)

John 3:31-36, like 3:16-21, is a commentary by the author, stressing Jesus' supremacy over all. John's dualistic worldview is evident in verse 31, where he contrasts the two mutually exclusive realms – the heavenly realm from above and the earthly realm from below. Humanity, naturally, belongs to the realm from below and is limited to this realm, but the one from the heavenly realm (Jesus) is superior to everyone. We know from 1:51 and 3:13 that this Jesus is the mediator or point of contact between these two realms. As such, Jesus brings revelation from above, witnessing to what he has seen and heard in that divine realm, but no one accepts it (v.32; cf. 1:11; 3:19).

Verse 34b presents an interesting issue to be resolved. It reads, 'for he gives the Spirit without measure', raising the question, 'Who is the giver of the Spirit – God or Jesus?' Some scholars think that verse 34b refers to the anticipated Spirit-baptism of Jesus in 1:33, and conclude that verse 34b speaks of Jesus' giving the Spirit to people. However, there are a few problems with this view. First, as we argued in 1:33, John the Baptist did not envisage Jesus' giving the Spirit to people but was referring to Jesus' carrying out his ministry by means of the Spirit. Second, John could hardly be saying, 'Jesus speaks the words of God because *Jesus* gives the Spirit to people'. It is more likely that God is the subject, so that 'Jesus speaks the words of God because *God* has given *Jesus* the Spirit without measure'. In that case, 3:34 does not refer back to 1:33 but to Jesus' endowment with the Spirit in 1:32. This would also dovetail nicely with 3:35, which states that the Father has given 'everything', i.e., the entire revelation, into Jesus' hands.

Looking at the nexus of ideas communicated in 1:32, 1:51, 3:13 and here in 3:31-36, we are in a position to understand precisely what the Prologue (1:18) means when it states that Jesus can reveal God. Jesus is sent by God to speak the words of God because God has endowed him with the Spirit and given the entire revelation to him. Jesus' empowerment with the Spirit, then, is primarily an empowerment of revelatory wisdom in order to reveal God. Whereas Old Testament prophets brought some revelation of God, Jesus *is* the ultimate revelation of God, bringing eternal life to those who accept him but judgement upon those who reject him, as verse 36 clarifies. Again, John leaves us with two basic choices: acceptance or rejection.

As an aside, I contend that John (the author) did not primarily see Jesus as one who came to earth with all pre-existent knowledge of God and himself (although we do not deny this possibility), but more as one who was provided with this revelatory knowledge *by the Spirit*. I suggest that it is primarily through the Spirit that Jesus reveals what he has seen and heard from the Father. This would also explain other comments of Jesus, asserting that he only speaks what he hears the Father saying and does what he sees the Father doing (5:19-20; 8:26-28, 38; 14:24; 15:15). On one extreme, we could have the view that, prior to the incarnation, the Son and the Father 'sat around the table' and decided, in detail, everything the Son was about to do during his mission on earth. In contrast, I prefer to believe that during his earthly ministry Jesus was in constant communion with his Father through the Spirit, and received information/guidance regarding what to do and say. In sum, the Spirit functioned as the channel or mode of communication between Jesus and his Father.

Reflection

John gave Jesus pre-eminence because he knew his mission and his own position in relation to Jesus: He had to become less and Jesus had to become more important. It is a life-long challenge for us to endeavour to decrease so that Jesus can increase. Our interests, our ministry, our name should be subordinate to those of Jesus. Does Jesus truly occupy the most important place in our lives and do we exalt his name above our own? Do we have the desire to let Jesus grow in us at the expense of our own desires and dreams? Paul puts it this way, 'it is no longer I who live, but it is Christ who lives in me' (Galatians 2:20). Like John, let us give Jesus supremacy so that our witness in word and deed might attract others to the Light.

If indeed the Spirit functions as the channel of communication between Jesus and God, we should be greatly encouraged. The Spirit then becomes the driving force of the Christian life: through a birth of the Spirit we enter into the family of God; through the Spirit we understand who Jesus is; through the Spirit we know God as Father and are in communication with him; through the Spirit we are guided in our speech and conduct. If Jesus was the prototypical Spirit-empowered man, then the Spirit-empowered Christian may function in a way similar to him.

Jesus and the Samaritan Woman (4:1-42)

After the intriguing account of Nicodemus, we come to the remarkable encounter between Jesus and the Samaritan woman. As we listen in on this conversation, it will become evident that John wants us to evaluate her response, but also compare it with that of Nicodemus.

Like Nicodemus, the Samaritan woman is an individual character, who is representative of a larger group. Both stories are about belief-responses, and common themes include water, Spirit and witness. Notably, the bulk of the 'from Cana to Cana' section deals with qualifications for entry into eternal life and the obstacles that prevent it. Despite the similarities, Nicodemus and the Samaritan woman stand in great contrast. Nicodemus was a well-known, well-to-do, well-educated Jewish religious leader. The woman, on the other hand, belonged to a community despised by the Jews: she was a Samaritan (cf. v.9). Besides, even her own people probably treated her as a social outcast because of her questionable lifestyle (mentioned in vv.16-18). This may well explain why she came to draw water alone, and at such an unusual time (v.6 says it was noon, the hottest part of the day).

We have divided the pericope as follows: (i) setting the stage (4:1-7a); (ii) the gift of living water (4:7b-15); (iii) the giver of living water (4:16-26); (iv) the responses of the woman, the disciples and the Samaritans (4:27-42).

Setting the Stage (4:1-7a)

We read that Jesus discovered that the Pharisees were aware that his disciples were baptizing more people than John. To avoid any possible confrontation (he may have been aware of John's encounter with the Pharisees, narrated in 1:19-28) he leaves Judea for the more receptive Galilee in the north (vv.1-3). Normally, Jews going from Judea to Galilee would travel east of the Jordan to avoid Samaria (John explicitly mentions in v.9 the estranged relationship between Jews and Samaritans). However, verse 4 seems to indicate that Jesus was under a divine imperative: he *had to go* through Samaria.

As we read the story, we will realize that Jesus did not shrink back from this encounter with a complex character – a Samaritan, a woman and a social outcast. Jesus crossed geographical, ethnic, religious, social and gender barriers in order to meet this woman.

The reader may wonder why John includes so many details in verses 5-7a. I suggest that, by drawing attention to the patriarchs, a well and a woman, John intends to evoke an Old Testament betrothal-type scene, such as we find in Genesis 24 (Abraham's servant [on behalf of Isaac] and Rebekah), Genesis 29 (Jacob and Rachel) and Exodus 2:15-22 (Moses and Zipporah). The significance or effect of this is to create a certain expectation: Will this Samaritan woman also function as a bride, and if so, for whom? In fact, this betrothal imagery will shape the bigger story in which Jesus' dialogue with the Samaritan woman takes place, and in the reflection, at the end, we will come back to this.

The Gift of Living Water (4:7b-15)

Although Jesus starts the conversation with a simple request (v.7b), the woman is quite startled (v.9). This, John explains, is due to the estranged relationship between Jews and Samaritans (v.9b). Jesus then introduces two, related topics: the gift of 'living water' and the identity of the giver (v.10). They form the core of the two halves of the dialogue (4:7b-15 and 4:16-26). The phrase 'living water' only occurs thrice in John – twice here in verses 10-11, and once in 7:38.

Jesus had obviously moved from a literal level (the request for some physical water in v.7b) to a metaphorical level (the offer of 'living water' in v.10); and we are led to ask what this 'living water' refers to. Judaism knew of four possible referents for 'living water': (i) life or salvation (Isaiah 12:3; 35:6-7; 55:1-3; Jeremiah 17:13; Zechariah 14:8); (ii) cleansing or purification (Leviticus 14:5-6; Numbers 19:17ff.); (iii) the Spirit (Isaiah 44:3); (iv) divine wisdom or teaching (Proverbs 13:14; 18:4; Isaiah 11:9). It is likely that all these possible referents are in view so we need not choose between them.

Combining these four referents, I suggest that *'living water' is a metaphor for Jesus' Spirit-empowered wisdom teaching that cleanses and gives life to those who accept it.* We have already surmised that Jesus was endowed with the Spirit in order to speak God's words, i.e., to provide divine teaching, but a quick glance ahead will confirm these thoughts. In 6:63, Jesus explicitly states that his teaching is Spirit-empowered and produces eternal life. Then, in 7:38-39, John identifies the Spirit as the referent of 'living water', and, in 15:3, Jesus confirms the cleansing abilities of his teaching (cf. 17:17).

Like Nicodemus, the woman does not recognize that Jesus is now speaking of spiritual issues. She misunderstands Jesus and thinks that he is talking about literal, running water (v.11). She mockingly asks Jesus whether he thinks he is superior to their patriarchal ancestor Jacob (v.12). The careful reader will detect the irony in such a statement, having just learned in 3:22-36 about the supremacy of Jesus. The woman's misunderstanding provides an opportunity for further revelation: Jesus explains in verses 13-14 that he is the source of 'living water', that this 'living water' is actually *life-giving* water, and that 'drinking' from this water will quench one's spiritual thirst forever. If 'living water' is a metaphor, then 'to drink' from this water would, naturally, be intended metaphorically. 'To drink' the living water, then, is to believe in Jesus and accept his life-giving teaching. Verse 14 goes on to explain that those who have accepted Jesus and his gift of life will, in turn, become a secondary source of 'living water' (Jesus being the primary source).

We can excavate further if we consider the following passages from the apocryphal wisdom book of Sirach:

> She [Wisdom] will feed him with the bread of learning, and give him the water of wisdom to drink. (Sirach 15:3)

> "Those who eat of me [Wisdom] will hunger for more, and those who drink of me will thirst for more. Whoever obeys me will not be put to shame, and those who work with me will not sin." All this is the book of the covenant of the Most High God, the law that Moses commanded us as an inheritance for the congregations of Jacob. (Sirach 24:21-23)

In the first reference, Wisdom promises to give her disciple the water of wisdom to drink, which in John 4 refers to Jesus' wisdom teaching. Comparing the second passage, Sirach 24:21-23, with John 4:13-14, we see that Jesus makes a greater claim than divine Wisdom – those who drink of the divine wisdom that Jesus gives, are permanently satisfied. Jesus, then, surpasses Wisdom, and the Mosaic Law with which Wisdom is identified.

Back to the Samaritan woman. Although verse 15 shows that she makes some progress in understanding – her request shows that she has grasped the superiority of the water that Jesus has to offer – she still remains at an earthly level. Nevertheless, she is responsive and has made more progress than Nicodemus.

The Giver of Living Water (4:16-26)

Seeing that the woman has not fully understood the nature of Jesus' gift, he changes tactics and focuses on his identity. Some scholars think that the two parts of the dialogue are disjointed; they contend that the first attempt having failed, Jesus makes a radical change from the topic of water to that of worship. I find, however, that there is coherence when we recognize the overarching purpose of the encounter. Jesus' aim is that the woman will come to believe by recognizing who he is and accepting his offer of life-giving water. When the woman fails to grasp the nature of Jesus' offer, he starts to focus on his identity, hoping that when she recognizes the true identity of the giver she will also recognize the true nature of the gift. Besides, Jesus has already introduced both topics – the gift and the giver – in verse

10, and simply picks up on the second topic. So, we conclude that the two topics introduced in verse 10 are discussed in verses 11-15 and verses 16-26 respectively, and are governed by the single aim that the woman will make an adequate belief-response.

Therefore, in verses 16-18, Jesus' aim is not so much to discuss the woman's moral life as it is to show his revelatory knowledge, so that the woman would begin to recognize his identity. Indeed, the woman shows some progress: she goes from addressing Jesus as 'Sir' to recognizing him as 'prophet' (v.19); she even introduces the spiritual topic of worship (v.20). Nevertheless, her thinking remains at an earthly level, and hence Jesus still has some more work to do.

In verses 21-24, we learn four important things from Jesus' response to the woman's implicit question about the right place to worship God. First, as the new temple (cf. 2:19-21), Jesus has become the true 'place' of worship. Second, the new mode of worship – in Spirit and truth – is a worship empowered by the Spirit and characterized by truth; or based on Jesus as the Truth (cf. 1:14, 17; 3:21; 14:6). Third, it is a worship of God *as Father*, which naturally requires a new birth into the family of God (cf. 1:12-13; 3:5). This coheres with the purpose of Jesus' coming, namely, to reveal God *as Father* (cf. 1:18). It also implies that we stand in a similar relationship to God as Jesus himself. Fourth, the believer does not have to wait until heaven to experience or participate in this kind of worship; it has become a present reality by virtue of Jesus' coming – the messianic 'hour' has arrived *now*.

The conversation now moves toward the climax. The woman recognizes that Jesus is talking about important issues and brings up the subject of the Messiah who will reveal everything (v.25). In response, Jesus reveals straightforwardly to her that he is the Messiah she is expecting (v.26). Jesus' words in verse 26 literally translate, 'I am, the one who is speaking to you'. This is not one of the seven 'I am' sayings (see the section 'Characteristics' in the Introduction); nevertheless, John may have intended a parallel between Jesus' self-revelation to the woman and God's self-revelation to Moses in Exodus 3:14. Surely, we expect the woman to make a confession at this point, but we are held in suspense because the disciples, who had gone to the village to get some food (v.8), intrude on the scene (v.27). This is no coincidence. John is a skilled storyteller, and we shall see that Jesus' interaction with his disciples in verses 31-38 actually enhances the climax.

The Responses of the Woman, the Disciples and the Samaritans (4:27-42)

In 4:27-42, John describes the varied responses of the woman, the disciples and the Samaritans in the village. Let us first examine the response of the woman. Although the text is not explicit, there are several indications to suggest that the woman responded positively to Jesus, in faith. First, she leaves her water jar behind (v.28), possibly symbolizing that her thirst has been quenched. Then, in verses 28-29, she invites her fellow-villagers to 'come and see' this man, Jesus, who she tentatively believes is the Messiah (cf. 1:46). We can translate the question in verse 29 as 'Is he perhaps the Christ?', cautiously suggesting an affirmative answer rather than serious doubt. Subsequently, many Samaritans believe in Jesus on the basis of the woman's witness (v.39), and their climactic confession of Jesus as the Saviour of the world in verse 42 probably includes the woman's confession. Although the woman struggled for understanding throughout the dialogue, Jesus kindly helped her to progress. This is reflected in the titles she uses for Jesus; she goes from 'a Jew' (v.9) to 'Sir' (vv.11, 15, 19), 'prophet' (v.19), 'Messiah' (v.29) and finally 'Saviour' (v.42).

The intrusion of the disciples does not merely delay the climax of the story but actually heightens it. Jesus' dialogue with the disciples in verses 31-38, like his conversation with the Samaritan woman earlier, starts at a material level and moves to a spiritual or symbolic level. Jesus explains to his disciples that his 'food' is his mission, namely, to do the will of his Father and to complete the task that the Father has assigned to him. He then invites them to participate in his mission. That the fields are 'white' for the harvest may indicate that they are *over*ripe. There is an urgency 'to harvest' those people who are ready to confess faith in Jesus, and bring them into the kingdom of God. Verses 35-36 imply that the disciples can already start with this harvesting process *now*. Ironically, it is the *woman* and not the disciples who participates in Jesus' mission. The disciples do not bring anything from the village, except physical food, but the woman brings the entire village! Thus, the disciples' intrusion in verse 27 and their conversation with Jesus in verses 31-38 actually enhance the reader's understanding of true discipleship.

The response of the Samaritans described in verses 39-42 is impressive. Many of them believed in Jesus because of the woman's testimony (v.39), and many more believed when they heard Jesus for themselves (v.42). The Samaritans' asking Jesus 'to remain' with them reflects John's understanding of what true discipleship is all about: to abide in him (cf. 1:39; 8:31; 15:1-10). This brings us to the climax of the story: Jesus is confessed as the Saviour – not just of the Jews but of the entire world (cf. the universal scope of the Prologue and of God's mission in 3:16).

Reflection

John's skill as a storyteller is evident in the story of the Samaritan woman. It is one that contains many lessons. The Samaritan woman herself provides a lesson on true discipleship: She witnesses and brings people to Jesus (cf. 1:35-51), and actualizes the challenge of participating in Jesus' mission we saw in 4:35-38. Remarkably, she achieves what the leading theologian Nicodemus was unable to accomplish (to confess belief in Jesus) and what the 'professional' disciples were unable to do (to participate in Jesus' mission). The outsider becomes an insider whereas the supposed insiders either remain in the dark (Nicodemus) or are outclassed (the disciples). As Christians, let us not be slow to understand spiritual realities; instead, let us be eager to participate in God's mission in this world. Nevertheless, it should not surprise us if, at times, God uses an outsider to teach us a lesson.

In addition, Jesus' offer to the woman is instructive. Stagnant water eventually starts to stink, but fresh, running water brings life and refreshment. Let each of us be a spring bubbling over with water that can bring life to others. Has the 'living water' in us already started to (over)flow and water other lives? Remember the universal scope of Jesus' mission: everyone is invited to come to Jesus and drink of the 'living water'.

Jesus crossed many barriers to meet this Samaritan woman. In today's world, where societies are becoming increasingly pluralistic, the challenge is to associate with others who are very different to us. Rather than sticking to our own group, John's Gospel challenges us not to be ethnocentric but to build bridges. Let us be open and reach out especially to the marginalized, the people whom we sometimes perceive as outsiders: the homeless person, the single parent, the ex-convict, the divorcee, the (ex-)alcoholic, the prostitute, the eunuch or transsexual, and so on. How do we relate, for example, to Muslims (especially after 9/11), homosexuals and people with HIV/AIDS without immediately stigmatizing or condemning them as sinners whom we should avoid? Are our churches open to all these people or do we not know what to do with them? The world is full of needy, broken and hurting people. May we be the hands, feet and mouth of Jesus by building up relationships with them, witnessing to them and bringing them to Jesus.

The need for Christians to cross barriers becomes imperative if one looks at Hinduism, the majority religion of India, which is home to a sixth of the world's population. Hinduism divides society up into discriminating, mutually exclusive, hierarchical castes or social groups, and is inextricably linked to principles of relative purity and pollution. In the caste hierarchy, the Brahmins are at the top and the Untouchables or Dalits (who account for a sixth of India's population) are at the very bottom —outside the caste system (which explains the alternative term 'Outcasts'). Despite the fact that the Indian Constitution forbids untouchability and discrimination on the grounds of caste, in practice it is still operative; in fact, the caste system (or Hindu **apartheid***) pervades all religious and social structures. This is in sharp contrast to Jesus' frequent association with the 'outcasts' of his day that we see in John's Gospel.*

Coming back to the betrothal imagery in 4:5-7a, we are now in a position to see that Jesus indeed functions as a sort of bridegroom (there was already a clear allusion in 3:29) and the Samaritan woman as a bride – in that the woman's confession of faith in Jesus symbolizes a spiritual betrothal. It is through this bigger story that John provides a significant corrective to Jewish thinking that the Jewish people are the people of God, envisaged as the 'bride' of God (Isaiah 62:5; Jeremiah 13:10-11). John radically subverts this understanding. First, in John 3, we saw that a spiritual birth, rather than physical birth as a Jew, determines who belongs to the true Israel. Second, here in John 4, we have, instead of a Jewish 'bride', a Samaritan one: the betrothal between Jesus and his people is not based on ethnic but on spiritual birth. The Spirit-born disciples of Jesus are the real bride. The book of Revelation, perhaps not written by John himself but certainly standing in the same tradition, beautifully picks up on this imagery in its portrayal of the future wedding between the Church and Jesus (Revelation 19-22).

Even today, many still think that regular attendance of church or being born in a Christian home is sufficient to enter the wedding hall of heaven. Although these are important privileges (just as being born a Jew was a privilege), it is a birth of the Spirit and a confession of faith, based on an adequate understanding of Jesus and the cross, that ultimately qualifies for salvation. What people need is a life-transforming encounter with the living Christ and a taste of the 'living water' in order to be part of his future bride.

Jesus and the Royal Official (4:43-54)

After his two-day stay with the Samaritans (v.40), Jesus leaves for Galilee (v.43), resuming the journey he started in 4:3. Verse 44 presents some difficulty because it is uncertain what the word 'hometown/homeland' in the phrase 'a prophet has no honour in his own hometown or homeland' refers to. If it refers to Nazareth as Jesus' hometown or to Galilee as Jesus' homeland, it contradicts the welcome he receives from the Galileans in verse 45. A more likely choice would be Jerusalem (as hometown) or Judea (as homeland). John 7:41-42 indicates that the Messiah was expected to come from Bethlehem in Judea rather than from Galilee; and John 5-12 will show that hostility towards Jesus mainly comes from Jerusalem and Judea. Therefore, the purpose of verses 44-45 seems to be to show the contrast between a hostile Judea in the south and a receptive Galilee in the north.

Verse 46 reveals that Jesus has come full circle since 2:1 with his return to Cana, where he had turned water into wine. John immediately introduces the next character: in nearby Capernaum lived a certain royal official whose son was sick and close to death.

We must bear in mind that the focus is on the official and not on his ill son. John uses the boy's healing, significant as it is, simply as a foil for the response of the royal official to Jesus.

The identity of the royal official is unclear. He could have been a member of the royal family or someone in service of the king – a palace official or even a Roman centurion. He was clearly a prominent person since verse 51 mentions that he had slaves. Although we cannot be certain, this 'royal official' was probably in the service of or related to king Herod Antipas (ruler over Galilee from 4 B.C. to A.D. 39). Since the Jewish aristocracy often collaborated with the Romans, this man (if he were a Jew) would also be considered a collaborator and shunned by the populace.

But Jesus does not turn his back on him; on the contrary, he assures the official that his son is alive (v.50). The man simply believes Jesus on the basis of his word, and, on his return home, his faith is honoured or validated when his servants bring him the good news of the child's recovery (v.51). When the official realizes that his son got better at the precise time/moment that Jesus had spoken, he and his entire family put their faith in Jesus (vv.52-53). The official's 'belief' in verse 50 may simply have been to trust or to take Jesus at his word, whereas the 'faith' in verse 53 may denote a saving belief.

Like the Samaritans in 4:41-42, the royal official also believes in Jesus because of his word – without a drawn-out struggle for understanding. If this is the case, Jesus' critical remark in verse 48, 'Unless you see signs and wonders, you will never believe', can hardly have been directed towards the official – especially since the 'you' in Greek is plural! Who, then, is Jesus addressing in verse 48? I suggest it is his Galilean audience. But why was Jesus so exasperated? Verse 45 states that the Galileans had seen everything he had done in Jerusalem, probably referring to the miraculous signs mentioned in 2:23. However, we know from 2:24-25 and the story of Nicodemus that the 'belief' that people showed in Jesus on that occasion was somehow deficient. Therefore, despite the welcome they gave Jesus, the Galileans' 'faith' was also lacking. Consequently, Jesus seems to encourage these people towards a belief that is less dependent on signs.

Reflection

We are at the end of the section 'from Cana to Cana' and have seen various characters, the most important of whom are the disciples, Nicodemus, the Samaritan woman and the royal official. The disciples, though not always quick to understand (remember 4:31-38), nevertheless stand firmly at the side of Jesus from the outset (1:35-51; 2:11, 22). In Johannine terms, they have chosen to follow Jesus and remain with him throughout.

Looking at the characters of Nicodemus, the Samaritan woman and the royal official, we observe the following: Nicodemus, the top theologian of Israel and presumably the insider, is outclassed by two despised outsiders: a female Samaritan outcast and a royal official, who may have been a Roman-collaborator. After their respective encounters with Jesus, both the Samaritan woman and the royal official witnessed to others, who in turn came to a saving belief in Jesus. The royal official seemingly had no difficulty taking Jesus at his word. He could have said, 'Hold on a moment Jesus, how can you be so sure that my son is alive? I think it would be better if you came home and laid your hands on him.' But no, the official simply believes Jesus' word and goes home (cf. the challenge 'do whatever he tells you' in 2:5).

On the scale of religious prominence there is a downward movement: from the prominent Jewish theologian, to a Samaritan woman, and finally, a possible traitor (perhaps even a Gentile). On the scale of belief-responses, however, there is an upward movement: from ambiguity, to a slow progression towards faith, and finally, to an instant belief based on Jesus' words. John's painstaking organization of characters may subvert our worldview: those we least expect, respond the best. Besides, those the world has marginalized or sidelined may be prominent or exemplary in the kingdom. Have we recognized ourselves in one or more of the Johannine characters so far?

In the section 'Characteristics' in the Introduction, we clarified the nature and purpose of 'signs' in John's Gospel, but, in the light of Jesus' critical remark in 4:48, more needs to be said. First, an adequate or saving faith, for John, is one that has understood something of Jesus' true identity, character, mission and *relationship with God. The question follows whether miracles can provide sufficient basis for such faith. On the one hand, signs can evoke belief – Jesus himself endorses a belief based on signs (10:37-38; 14:11) and even John asserts that signs are expected to produce saving belief (20:30-31). On the other hand, not every 'belief'-response to Jesus' signs seems to be adequate or even authentic (2:24-25; 6:14-15, 26-27). What Jesus seems to be critical of, then, is not miracles per se (otherwise he would not have performed so many) but of people's attitudes towards them.*

As long as we understand miracles to reveal something about Jesus' true identity, character, mission and relationship with God, they can be a valid and sufficient basis for faith. It is when the miracles are misunderstood and attention is diverted from Jesus to miracles for miracles' sake that the responses are deemed insufficient. There is a danger of misrepresenting miracles in today's 'healing campaigns' and 'miracle crusades', but when correctly understood they can elicit saving faith. Therefore, although 'signs-faith', i.e., a belief based on miracles, is not necessarily negative, John tries to get people beyond that. While Jesus' signs can be a sufficient basis for saving faith, it seems that his word is a better and more solid basis (cf. 20:29).

The Opposition to Jesus (5:1-12:50)

Leaving the section 'from Cana to Cana' behind, we come to another major section, which can be called, 'The Opposition to Jesus'. John 5-12 describes how 'the Jews', a group of people largely from among the religious leaders in Jerusalem, increasingly oppose Jesus. The Prologue has prepared us for the negative reactions of people towards Jesus (1:10-11), but until this point Jesus has not faced much hostility and conflict. That situation is about to change.

In Jerusalem/Judea, the hostility leads to several threats to kill Jesus (5:18; 7:1, 19; 8:37, 40; 10:31-33; 11:53), threats that are ultimately realized when Jesus is crucified. Except John 6:1-7:9, which describes Jesus' ministry in Galilee, and 10:40-11:6, when Jesus briefly takes refuge across the Jordan river, all events in John 5-12 take place in or near Jerusalem. Jerusalem was the centre of the Jewish religious establishment and hence of hostility. Although Jesus also meets with opposition in John 6 (though not from the Galileans but again from 'the Jews'), he does not encounter the kind of persecution or receive the death threats he does in Jerusalem/Judea (cf. 4:44-45). Nevertheless, Jesus' opponents are unable to carry out their threats before Jesus' appointed time (7:30, 44; 8:20, 59; 10:39).

In the section 'Characteristics' in the Introduction, we explained the importance of Jewish festivals for John and how they provide a sense of time during Jesus' ministry. The first reference to a festival is in the 'Cana to Cana' section (2:13, 23) but all other references to the Jewish feasts occur in John 5-12 (5:1; 6:4; 7:2; 10:22; 11:55/12:1). We inferred that the 'Cana to Cana' section covered approximately one and a half years of Jesus' ministry. John 5-12 would then account for the remaining one year and ten months – from the Feast of Weeks (May/June) in 5:1 to the second Passover (March/April) in 6:4 to the final Passover in 11:55/12:1. This would bring the length of Jesus' ministry to three years and a few months (cf. the section 'Characteristics' in the Introduction).

It is more important to notice, however, that the various Jewish festivals form the backdrop for Jesus' teaching. They show how Jesus replaces or fulfils what these feasts stand for; and hence how he supersedes Judaism (cf. 2:13-22). Since Jerusalem is the centre of 'the Jews' and the religious capital of Judaism, Jesus' conflict with his opponents in Jerusalem amounts to a conflict with Judaism as a religious institution.

John's narrative style is very skilful. He shows how Jesus' presence in Jerusalem, the religious-political headquarters of his opponents, and his engaging in theological disputes, cause controversy and mounting tensions. It leaves the reader wondering what it will lead to.

Emerging Opposition to Jesus (5:1-47)

The leading players in John 5 are Jesus, an invalid man and 'the Jews'. The narrative is characterized by accusations, betrayal and counter-attack. The chapter can be divided as follows: (i) the encounter between Jesus and the lame man at the pool of Bethesda

(5:1-9a); (ii) the accusations of 'the Jews' (5:9b-18); (iii) Jesus' twofold defence (5:19-40); (iv) 'the Jews' being accused (5:41-47).

Jesus and the Lame Man at the Pool (5:1-9a)

The story in John 5 is set within the context of an unnamed Jewish festival (v.1). A textual variant mentions 'the Feast', meaning the Feast of Tabernacles, but this variant has no strong textual support. Besides, John 7 explicitly mentions the Feast of Tabernacles, making it likely that another festival is in view here in John 5. The Passover festival, mentioned thrice in John, is also unlikely. The only other festival that requires a pilgrimage to Jerusalem is Weeks or Pentecost, fifty days after Passover. Originally, Weeks celebrated the wheat harvest but over time this festival came to be associated with the giving of the Mosaic Law (*Jubilees* 6:15-22; Babylonian Talmud *Pesahim* 68b [the Talmud is a commentary on the Mishnah, the primary law code of Rabbinic Judaism]). If we are right, this would also cohere with the latter part of the story where Moses is mentioned (5:45-46).

More important than the festival, is the new character presented to us: a man who has been ill for thirty-eight years (v.5). His illness is not specified, but, in the light of verses 8-9, it seems that he was paralyzed; perhaps the result of a childhood illness or accident. In any case, his illness has kept the man from participating in socio-religious activities for thirty-eight years. According to Jewish law, he was probably not even allowed to worship in the temple (Mishnah *Hagigah* 1:1 [compiled around A.D. 200 but reflecting earlier rabbinic tradition]). He was a social outcast.

Apparently there was a pool in Jerusalem, called Bethzatha or Bethesda, which had the reputation of having mystical healing powers. The footnote to verse 3, included in most English translations, contains the tradition that an angel would come at certain times to stir up the water, and the first person who got in would be healed immediately. Although this verse 4 is not considered part of the original text, the explanation it gives may not seem so strange when we consider verse 7, which shows that something mystical did happen when the water was stirred up.

As with the Samaritan woman and the royal official, Jesus reaches out to this marginalized person. At first glance, Jesus' question to the man, 'Do you want to become better?', seems absurd, but perhaps Jesus wishes to know what the man really wanted. Perhaps, after thirty-eight years the man had become comfortable or secure with his illness, or even resigned to it. Healing would mean new, perhaps unwanted, responsibilities. Nevertheless, Jesus probably takes the man's reply in verse 7 as an implicit request for help, and heals the man of his illness. By now we should be sufficiently conditioned by John to look for the man's response to Jesus and to evaluate it, but no response is recorded – at least not at this point – the man simply walks away. Only the next passage records his response to Jesus.

'The Jews' Accuse Jesus (5:9b-18)

This section opens with the loaded phrase 'Now that day was a sabbath', and describes the first serious clash between Jesus and the Jewish religious leaders. 'The Jews' readily notice that the healed man is carrying his mat on the Sabbath, which they consider an offence (v.10). The oral tradition of the Pharisees painstakingly spells out what can and cannot be done on the Sabbath. This oral tradition, reflected in the Mishnah, mentions thirty-nine things one is not allowed to do on the Sabbath: 'The generative categories of acts of labor [prohibited on the Sabbath] are forty less one: ... (39) he who transports an object from one domain to another' (Mishnah *Shabbat* 7.2). In response, the man quickly shifts the blame, saying that the man who healed him had commanded him to take up his mat (v.11). However, since the man does not know the identity of Jesus (v.13), 'the Jews' cannot not pursue the issue at that moment.

Later, however, Jesus seeks out the man in the temple, and says to him, 'See, you have been healed, sin no longer so that nothing worse may happen to you' (v.14). This implies that there had been some relation between the man's illness and (his) sin, so Jesus advises him to sin no more. This does not imply, however, that illness is always caused by one's personal sins. Jesus, in a later episode, explicitly objects to such an oversimplification, denying a relation between a man's blindness and (his) sin (9:1-3). But in John 5, in the specific case of this man, there seems to have been such a link and Jesus gives a corrective advice.

The man, seemingly unable to accept Jesus' reprimand, and perhaps out of spite, goes to 'the Jews' and reports that Jesus is the man who healed him (v.15). That we should interpret the man's action negatively is clear from the following verse: 'And for this reason "the Jews" started persecuting Jesus...' (v.16). The man's betrayal of Jesus to the Jewish religious authorities seems to have sparked off this persecution. The issue was not so much that Jesus had performed a miracle but that he had done it *on the Sabbath*. Jesus' reply to the charges brought by 'the Jews' is that if his Father 'works' on the Sabbath, so does he (v.17). This further infuriates 'the Jews' since Jesus was implying that he is equal to God; and incites them to plot his death (v.18).

Coming back to the man at the pool who was healed by Jesus, we see that his response to Jesus was negative. First, Jesus had to tell him after his healing that he should stop sinning, and then the man, unable to take in Jesus' correction, betrayed him to the officials. In fact, we can only fully appreciate this story if we recognize that John wants us to compare the response of the man at the pool with that of the man born blind in John 9.

If we are permitted a quick glance forward in the Gospel, we see that there are many parallels between the two stories: (i) both men had been disabled for a long time and unable to participate in the socio-religious life of that day; (ii) both men were healed by Jesus on the Sabbath; (iii) in both stories there is mention of a pool; (iv) on both occasions, 'the Jews' investigate the healing; (v) in both accounts, Jesus later finds the two healed people in order to provide spiritual healing too.

Despite these remarkable resemblances, the two men respond rather differently – both to the Jewish authorities and to Jesus. The formerly invalid man betrays Jesus to the authorities, whereas the man in John 9 defends Jesus before the authorities (to the extent that he also is persecuted). The lame man seems rather unresponsive; he is unable to take in Jesus' warning and does not progress in his knowledge of him; the text gives no indication that the man came to faith in Jesus. The resolute stance of the man born blind before the Jewish religious leaders, however, caused him to progress in his knowledge of Jesus, and, when Jesus later found him, he was keen to respond in faith. Both men needed physical and spiritual healing, but whereas the man who was formerly blind also gained spiritual sight, the man who was formerly lame gave a 'lame' response to Jesus.

Jesus' First Argument – His Work (5:19-30)

The remainder of chapter 5 contains a monologue of Jesus, consisting of a twofold defence (5:19-30 and 5:31-40) and a counter-attack (5:41-47). The first part of Jesus' defence is a nice unit bracketed by Jesus' saying that he can do nothing by himself (v.19 and v.30). Replying to the charges of 'the Jews', Jesus will now elaborate on his statement in 5:17 and explain why he can do what he is doing. Jesus' first argument essentially emphasizes two points. First, the Son is doing the Father's work. Second, the Son's work is primarily to give life and to judge.

John has cleverly constructed Jesus' reply. Verses 19-20 parallel verse 30, stressing Jesus' total dependency on the Father: he can only imitate what he sees the Father doing and repeat what he hears the Father saying. This is possible because the Father loves the Son and reveals everything to him (v.20; cf. 3:35); and the Son seeks to do the will of the Father (v.30; cf. 4:34). We know from passages such as 1:32-33 and 3:34-35 that Jesus is able to do what he sees and hears from the Father because he is endowed with the divine Spirit, who is the channel of communication between him and the Father.

Verses 21-23 parallel verses 26-27, emphasizing the Son's authority to give eternal, divine life (the Greek word *zōē* and its verbal derivative are used) and to judge. These two functions are divine prerogatives in the Old Testament – no one could give life and judge except God – and with this assertion, Jesus puts himself on a par with God. Interestingly, John uses the verb 'to give (eternal) life' only three times: once the subject is the Father (v.21), once the Son (v.21) and once the Spirit (6:63). The Son has the authority to impart this divine life to others because he has this life (in) himself – Jesus is the source of eternal life (cf. 1:4; 4:14).

Besides, Jesus has the authority to judge because he is the Son of Man, the point of contact between the heavenly and earthly realms.

Finally, verses 24-25 parallel verses 28-29, but there is also a subtle contrast since they speak of different time frames: verses 24-25 contain a present or realized eschatology, whereas verses 28-29 convey future or unfulfilled eschatology ('eschatology' refers to the doctrine of the last things). Verses 24-25 talk about a time that is *present* ('an hour is coming and is *now*') in which the dead will hear the Son's voice and will live. These 'dead' must be the 'spiritual' dead, the people who have not yet heard Jesus' words and experienced the life that is available in him. If they hear the Son's word and believe, i.e., understand and accept Jesus' teaching, they will receive eternal life (cf. the sheep hearing the voice of the Shepherd in John 10). In contrast, verses 28-29 speak of a time that is *future* ('an hour is coming [but is *not* now]') because it talks about people coming out of their graves. This, very likely, refers to the bodily resurrection of the dead at the end of time; a resurrection which for some will lead to eternal life and for others will result in eternal judgement.

So, Jesus' defence for his action on the Sabbath is that his work is God's work. To put it differently, in Jesus, God himself is at work. This is the case because Jesus is entirely dependent on his Father and seeks to carry out the Father's work on earth, in the power of the Spirit. Jesus' actions again imply that he supersedes Judaism: in this case, he is Lord of the Sabbath (cf. the story in Mark 2:23-28, and its parallel in Matthew 12:1-8 and Luke 6:1-5, which makes a similar point).

Jesus' Second Argument – His Witnesses (5:31-40)

Scholars have recognized that John presents his Gospel as a cosmic trial in which Jesus is charged for the kind of claims he makes in verses 17, 21 and 27. As in any defence, it is crucial to have witnesses. Verse 31 reflects Jesus' knowledge of the Mosaic Law, which requires that a defendant needs at least two witnesses (Deuteronomy 17:6; 19:15). On this occasion, Jesus calls forward no less than four witnesses.

One witness who is summoned is John the Baptist (vv.33-35). Although John was not the Light himself, as a shining lamp he testified to the Light. From John 1 and 3 we have learned that John's sole mission was to witness to Jesus. The second testimony in his defence is provided by Jesus' own works (v.36). Jesus often uses 'works' to refer to his miracles, which are essentially God's works (7:21; 9:3-4; 10:32, 37-38; 14:10-11; cf. the previous passage 5:19-30). Besides, we know that John (the author) labels Jesus' miracles 'signs' because they point to Jesus and witness to his identity and mission. However, Jesus' 'works' may also refer to his entire ministry (4:34; 17:4). God the Father is the third witness (v.37), who may also be in view in verse 32, where 'another' probably refers to God himself. In turn, Jesus also witnesses about the Father since no one has heard or seen him (cf. 1:18). The final witness is provided by the Hebrew Scriptures (the Old Testament), which testify that Jesus is the one who can give life (vv.39-40). Jesus ironically points out that 'the Jews' study the Scriptures because they presume to find eternal life in them but they reject the one who the Scriptures say is able to give the life they are searching for.

Despite the number and credibility of the witnesses that Jesus puts forward in his defence, he knows that his accusers, 'the Jews', will remain unconvinced because God's word does not abide in them (v.38) and because they are not willing to come to him to have life (v.40).

'The Jews' Accused Instead (5:41-47)

After his twofold defence, Jesus launches a counter-attack and turns the tables on 'the Jews'. He points to the essential problem of his accusers in verses 41-44. Having said in verse 38 that 'the Jews' did not have God's word in them, Jesus, in verse 42, asserts that God's love does not indwell them either. In verse 44, he puts his finger on the essence of their problem and the reason for their unbelief: they accept glory from people. They seek after the glory of people rather than the glory of God, and this attitude prevents them from belief in and acceptance of Jesus (see also 7:18; 12:42-43).

Jesus does identify the problem of his accusers, but does not, in turn, bring charges against them. Verses 45-47 essentially elaborate the irony in verses 39-40. Jesus points out to his accusers that Moses, in whose writings they trust, will eventually be their accuser. That is, the Scriptures that they study so devotedly will eventually witness against them. Suddenly, from being the accusers, 'the Jews' find themselves standing accused – not by Jesus but by Moses, their hero of the faith.

It must have been very difficult, even impossible, for 'the Jews' to imagine that Moses, the giver of the Law, would eventually become their accuser. Essentially Jesus' argument goes like this: If 'the Jews' had believed Moses' words, they would be expected to believe Jesus' words too because those very writings witness about Jesus. Implicitly, Jesus indicates that he is greater than Moses because his testimony is greater. As readers, we have already been prepared for that by John (1:14-18; cf. 2:1-22), but for 'the Jews' this would be difficult to take in. 'The Jews' assume that the Scriptures and Moses are their witness but they witness to Jesus instead. Rather than being on the side of the accusers, the Scriptures and Moses are on the side of the defence and put the accusers on the stand. Whereas 'the Jews' accuse Jesus in 5:9b-18 of breaking the Law, Jesus points out in 5:39-40, 45-47 that it is actually 'the Jews' who 'violate' the Law because they do not believe the Mosaic writings.

Reflection

John 5 has several implications that we might want to reflect on. First, if Jesus' divine work is primarily to give life, one may ask how it relates to the healing of the lame man. Perhaps we could look at it like this. The lame man was in a pitiful condition: he was not merely physically disabled, but also a social outcast, economically dependent (perhaps survived by begging), and in need of spiritual healing. Jesus initially healed him at a physical and socio-economic level – the man could walk again, gain economic independence, go to the temple and participate in worship. Unfortunately, he was unable to receive the spiritual healing that Jesus also offered him. This story demonstrates that Jesus has a holistic view of people and their needs. Jesus does not only offer an everlasting life but also a qualitatively better life (cf. the promise of abundant life in 10:10), encompassing all aspects of human existence. Perhaps we need to realign our approach to match that of Jesus; to have the same holistic outlook on people and their needs. What is more, we see Jesus' utter dependence on his Father, and his desire is to carry out the Father's work on earth in the power of the Spirit. The challenge for us is to be 'in tune' with our heavenly Father and do what he desires from us with the help of the same Spirit that enabled Jesus.

Once again, we see that instead of recognizing Jesus as the saviour, the one sent by God to give life, the world rejects and persecutes him. Jesus is put on trial and accused of the divine claims he makes. More importantly, this trial has not been concluded till date; the case is ongoing and witnesses are continuously needed. Not only are his claims brought into question, but his life as well. One only needs to read Dan Brown's controversial novel The Da Vinci Code (New York: Doubleday, 2003), suggesting that Jesus was married to Mary Magdalene; or Theodore W. Jennings Jr., The Man Jesus Loved: Homoerotic Narratives from the New Testament (Cleveland: Pilgrim Press, 2003), arguing that Jesus was an active homosexual, to realize that Jesus is still in the dock. Or look at the various religions: in the diverse pantheon of Hinduism, Jesus is merely a god besides many other gods; according to Islam, Jesus is merely a prophet but not the Son of God. John calls us to be witnesses in this cosmic lawsuit to support the case of Jesus in this world. Are we among those witnesses? It is no easy task. From John we learned that we have to point away from ourselves, and let Jesus be in the limelight rather than putting ourselves there; that we must decrease so that he can increase. In his farewell speech in chapters 14-16, Jesus will say much more about the task of a witness but the challenge is already before us.

Our testimony, of course, is not simply what we say, but also what we do. St. Francis of Assisi once said, 'Preach, preach, preach, and if necessary use words' and on another occasion, 'It is of no use to walk somewhere to preach if not the walking is our preaching'. People around us observe our lifestyle; watch what we say and do, how we treat others. They may be our neighbours, colleagues at work, friends and family. Sometimes it can be hardest to be a witness to those who know us best. It may be hard, but Jesus has given us his Spirit, he has also set us an example to follow, and we have the help of other witnesses (the bible, fellow believers and miracles). Let us also remember our brothers and sisters across the world, who are persecuted because of their faith (see the reflection on 1:19-34). Pray that they will be able to remain strong witnesses for Jesus.

The lame man, with his lame response, serves as an example of what we must avoid. He showed ingratitude, shifted the blame when confronted, could not take correction and finally betrayed Jesus to the authorities. Let us think of how we would react if Jesus did something so great for us; or when Jesus corrects us. How do we react when people accuse or mock Jesus?

Think also about the attitude of 'the Jews' – they preferred the glory of people to the glory of God. It is human, is it not, to desire human recognition and praise? But often it becomes the driving force, creating problems and turning us into people-pleasers rather than God-pleasers. Jesus was wholly focused on glorifying his Father, who, in turn, glorified him. There is nothing wrong with receiving human recognition and praise; but it is important to have a sense of balance and priority.

There is also nothing wrong with the study of the Scriptures per se; on the contrary, the Scriptures do contain life in that they point to the one who is able to give life. However, there was some flaw in the way 'the Jews' studied the Scriptures, and hence in their search for life. This should serve as a warning. Let us reflect on our own use and study of the bible. Do we read and study the bible for its own sake or because we believe it contains the revelation of God and his dealings with humankind, which is ultimately revealed in Jesus? As a witness, the bible reveals and points to the one who gave his life to give us life. Unfortunately, some study the bible merely for its history, philosophy or morality. For example, Mahatma Gandhi, one of India's greatest leaders, was attracted more to Jesus as a teacher of ethics than to Jesus as the saviour from sin and death. Our study of the bible is not an end in itself but should lead us to a (deeper) personal relationship with the Father and the Son.

The Bread of Life (6:1-71)

We consider 6:1-71 one literary unit with a single theme: Jesus is the true bread from heaven who gives life to the world. This theme is developed against the backdrop of God's miraculous providence of manna during Israel's journey through the wilderness. Hence, this chapter provides a concrete example of how Moses wrote about Jesus (5:46). This may be the rationale behind John's placing this material here. We divide the narrative into four episodes: (i) the sign (6:1-15); (ii) an interlude (6:16-21); (iii) the bread-of-life discourse (6:22-59); (iv) people's responses (6:60-71).

The Feeding of the Five Thousand (6:1-15)

We suddenly find ourselves in Galilee again. The large crowd of people that 'followed' Jesus because of his miraculous signs (v.2) reminds us of a similar crowd in 2:23-25. Consequently, this crowd could potentially put their faith in Jesus and, considering the use of the verb 'to follow', become his disciples. John thus creates a certain expectation: Will the crowd come to faith in Jesus and become true followers? What is important for John is that people not only come to Jesus but also stay with him: people must confess their faith in Jesus but also stick with him in discipleship. We will examine the crowd's responses as the discourse progresses. Verse 4 completes the setting for this narrative, and the reader is now prepared to interpret the coming miracle and the subsequent discourse in the light of the Passover and all that is stands for.

Before Jesus tests the crowd which keeps 'following' him, he first tests his disciples (vv.5-9). They have been with him for at least two years (between 2:23 and 6:4, which mention the Passover, there was another, unrecorded Passover [see the section 'Characteristics' in the Introduction]); they have seen Jesus performing several miracles; and they have heard most of his teaching. So, Jesus' question to Philip in verse 5 is a challenge to think in terms of Jesus' identity and potential. Philip, it appears, has not progressed that far. His reply in verse 7 reveals that, according to him, this situation has no solution – to feed the crowd would be impossible. Although Andrew is more resourceful, he also approaches the challenge from a human perspective (vv.8-9). Both Philip and Andrew think merely in terms of human possibilities rather than miracles; whereas Jesus challenges his disciples to approach problems from a divine perspective. Indeed, it is a challenge to think 'from above'.

The crowd could easily have comprised about 10,000 people, since the Greek only says that Jesus made 5,000 men sit down (v.10); most likely women and children were also present. Jesus' aim was not simply to provide a free meal. Rather, Jesus performs this miracle in order to reveal something of his identity and mission, namely that if he can miraculously provide physical food he can also provide spiritual nourishment. The crowd makes a promising start when they recognize something of Jesus' identity – he is the Prophet like Moses of Deuteronomy 18:15-18 (v.14). However, their desire to make him some sort of national leader (perhaps expecting that he would deliver them from the Roman-Herodian oppressors) is too worldly – still 'from below' – and causes Jesus to withdraw (v.15).

An Interlude (6:16-21)

The narrative about the disciples' going to the other side of the Sea of Galilee and of Jesus' miraculously walking to them on the water probably forms part of the Christian tradition (cf. Mark 6:45-52). It functions as a break between the miraculous sign and the subsequent discussion about its significance. Some scholars think that this incident fits the Passover imagery, in alluding to the crossing of the Red Sea, but this is perhaps somewhat far-fetched.

Some have interpreted verse 19 as 'they [the disciples] saw Jesus walking *along* the sea,' meaning along the shore. This is unlikely for several reasons. First, the primary meaning of the preposition *peran* in verse 17a is 'across', implying that the boat was travelling to the other side of the sea rather than along its circumference. Moreover, between 'and as it became evening [after or around sunset but before night]' (v.16) and 'darkness had already come' (v.17), a considerable amount of time has passed.

This coheres with the distance that the boat has already covered: 25 or 30 stades is between 4.7 and 5.7 kilometers (v.19). Hence, the boat would have been in the middle of the sea, about five kilometers from the shore (the Sea of Galilee is about 11 kilometers across). Finally, had Jesus been walking along the shore, would the disciples have been terrified?

Jesus' reassurance to the disciples – 'I am' – in verse 20 does not belong to the seven 'I am' sayings (see the section 'Characteristics' in the Introduction), but an allusion to Jesus' divine control over nature is perhaps intended (cf. 4:26). To reassure his disciples further, Jesus uses the imperative 'Fear not' (v.20). Note the other miracle: although the boat was about five kilometers offshore in the midst of a storm, when the disciples wanted to take Jesus into the boat, they *immediately* found themselves ashore (at the precise point they were headed to) (v.21).

The Bread-of-Life Discourse (6:22-59)

After the sign and interlude, we arrive at the bread-of-life discourse itself, which is an exposition of the miraculous feeding. We divide this discourse into the following parts: (i) the true bread (6:22-33); (ii) the bread of life (6:34-40); (iii) the giving of the bread (6:41-51); (iv) the consumption of the bread (6:52-59).

The True Bread (6:22-33)

The crowd keeps following Jesus (vv.22-25), which appears commendable, but Jesus knows that their intentions are still very worldly – they simply want another free lunch (v.26). Even to have continued seeking Jesus because of his signs, as they initially did (v.2), would have been more spiritual; hence, their faith seems hardly 'faith' at all. Typically, Jesus moves from a material to a spiritual level (v.27), but the crowd misunderstands the term 'to work', as being human achievement (v.28), to which Jesus replies that 'to work' means 'to believe' (v.29). Jesus' explanation preempts any idea that he teaches a doctrine of salvation by works. God only demands one 'work' from people to receive eternal life: to believe in his Son who provides true spiritual nourishment.

The crowd, unable to follow Jesus any longer, is stuck at an earthly level, thinking of Jesus merely as a miracle worker (v.30). They do not grasp that the physical feeding was a sign of Jesus' ability to feed them spiritually. Nevertheless, the crowd makes some progress in understanding, by setting the feeding and the bread within the theological framework of the manna in the wilderness (v.31). However, the crowd demands from Jesus a greater miracle than the one they had witnessed, implying that while Moses gave their ancestors bread from heaven, Jesus just gave ordinary bread.

In verses 32-33, Jesus corrects the crowd's misinterpretation of Israel's experience in the wilderness. First, it was not Moses but God who gave bread from heaven. Second, God's provision of bread is not a thing of the past but a present reality – it is given now. Third, Jesus rather than manna is the true bread from heaven. Fourth, the true Bread gives life to the world. The real contrast, then, is between two kinds of bread: manna and the *true bread* from heaven.

Verse 33 contains an example of John's use of double entendre (a word with two meanings) where the audience often chooses the wrong one, which then provides an opportunity for further revelation. In 3:3, for example, Nicodemus chooses the meaning 'again' whereas 'from above' was intended, and the Samaritan woman understands 'living water' in 4:10 as 'running water' rather than life-giving water. The Johannine ambiguity in verse 33 lies with the subject: should we translate, 'he [Jesus] who comes down' (NIV) or 'that [the bread] which comes down' (NRSV)?

The Bread of Life (6:34-40)

The crowd continues to think at an earthly level and merely desires a continual supply of this miraculous bread (v.34). This wrong expectation of the crowd is precipitated by John's deliberate ambiguity in verse 33 outlined above. Like Nicodemus and the Samaritan woman, the crowd opts for the wrong meaning – 'that which comes down'. Since the crowd still does not understand the nature of the true bread from heaven, the only solution is to provide a simple and straightforward revelation. Jesus explains that he is the bread of life who will sustain those who believe in him (v.35). Jesus is not the *giver* of the bread of life, as the crowd expects (v.34); he himself *is* the bread of life.

Verse 35 introduces the first of the seven so-called 'I am' sayings in John's Gospel (see the section 'Characteristics' in the Introduction). Every 'I am' saying is a divine self-revelation of Jesus, echoing God's self-revelation to Moses. The use of 'I am' puts Jesus on a par with God himself, and the predicate or proposition that follows reveals a particular aspect of Jesus' identity and mission. In this case, Jesus' divine self-revelation is that he is the giver and sustainer of eternal life (again the word *zōē* is used), satisfying the seeker's spiritual quest.

Jesus' revelation conjures up images of Wisdom, who invites people to come to her banquet:

> She [Wisdom] has slaughtered her animals, she has mixed her wine, she has also set her table. She has sent out her servant girls, she calls from the highest places in the town,...'Come, eat of my bread and drink of the wine I have mixed' (Proverbs 9:2-3, 5).

> 'Come to me [i.e., Wisdom], you who desire me, and eat your fill of my fruits...Those who eat of me will hunger for more, and those who drink of me will thirst for more' (the apocryphal book Sirach 24:19, 21).

To 'eat' and 'drink' of Wisdom are metaphors for accepting God's teaching, which leads to life. Personifying Wisdom in the Old Testament and Jewish writings of the intertestamental period was a way of describing how God was present and acting among his people. Jesus, however, transcends the offer of Wisdom: His invitation promises a once-for-all satisfaction of hunger and thirst of those who accept him and his teaching. This also reiterates the promise of 'living water' that quenches all thirst in 4:14. Jesus invites people to come to his banquet and have table-fellowship with him; the food that he has to offer promises to fulfil the spiritual needs of people.

Jesus perceives that the crowd, tragically, will not accept his invitation (v.36; cf. 2:24-25), and this verse anticipates the negative responses in verses 41 and 52.

Verses 37-40 essentially reveal the priority of divine initiative over human response; those who are 'given' to Jesus by the Father are those who come to Jesus and respond in faith. To put it differently, the initiative for salvation lies with God, and then people are enabled to respond. Hence, it would be inappropriate to read into the text a doctrine of predestination.

The Giving of the Bread (6:41-51)

In verse 41, the 'grumbling' of the people in response to Jesus' words, reminds us of the grumbling and murmuring of the rebellious Israelites in the wilderness (Exodus 16:1-12). They grumble because they are offended by Jesus' claims to have a divine origin. These people think they know his origins (v.42).

It is important to notice that the term 'the Jews' is used from now on instead of 'the crowd'. It is a possibility that this crowd consisted of 'the Jews', but it is more likely that from among the crowd a group of 'the Jews' became openly hostile towards Jesus. The crowd, portrayed by John as dull in understanding and as following Jesus with the wrong intentions, disappears into the background, whereas 'the Jews' come to the foreground. From this point on, 'the Jews' become increasingly antagonistic towards Jesus and ultimately reject him.

Jesus asserts that no one can come to him unless drawn by the Father (v.44), reiterating that God's initiative precedes that of humankind, as mentioned in verse 37 (cf. Jesus' drawing people to himself in 12:32). Jesus' saying that all who have heard from the Father and understood will come to him (v.45b) is puzzling if we compare it with 5:37b, which denies such a possibility. In the light of Jesus' quotation from Isaiah 54:13 (v.45a), perhaps he means that those who *want* to hear and learn from the Father come to Jesus. In other words, God will instruct his people through his Son. This also makes sense of Jesus' reminder in verse 46, which echoes 1:18.

Verses 48-51 are an exposition of verse 33, explaining *how* Jesus will give life to the world. The life-giving bread is given to the world and effects life for the world, *on the cross* (the giving of his 'flesh' in v.51 refers to the cross). In death, Jesus will give his own life in order to provide eternal life to the world. Thus, the 'bread of life' is not simply a metaphor for Jesus as the one who gives life, but, more precisely, for *Jesus crucified*. Ultimately, life comes from this death (cf. 12:24); it is the giving of the bread on the cross that provides life. People appropriate this eternal life when they 'eat' of this bread, i.e., when they believe in the crucified Jesus (v.51).

This ties in with John 3, which puts the cross at the centre of the Christian faith. It is the place where God ultimately reveals his love for this world, deals with sin, and offers reconciliation and eternal life through his son Jesus (cf. 12:32). For those who understand this event and respond in faith to the crucified Jesus, it opens the way to have a life-giving relationship with God who wants to be known as 'Father'.

The Consumption of the Bread (6:52-59)

'The Jews' get seriously upset over Jesus' offensive invitation to eat his flesh (v.52). They continue to have a view 'from below' and misunderstand Jesus completely. As verses 48-51 are an exposition of verse 33, so verses 53-55 explain verse 35.

If the 'bread of life' is to be understood metaphorically, then we must also interpret its consumption metaphorically. Needing a metaphorical interpretation and seeing the parallel between verses 53-55 and verse 35, it would appear that 'to eat his flesh' and 'to drink his blood', are metaphors for coming to and believing in Jesus, respectively. In the light of 'the bread of life' being a metaphor for the *crucified* Jesus, it would be more accurate to say that 'eating' Jesus' flesh and 'drinking' his blood denote coming and believing in the one who is lifted up on the cross (cf. 3:14-15).

The result of a proper consumption of Jesus' flesh and blood is a life-giving relationship with Jesus of mutual indwelling (v.56). The parallelism between verse 54a and verse 56 indicates that eternal life essentially consists of the remaining of the believer in Jesus and vice versa. Verse 57 reiterates that Jesus is the source of eternal life, i.e., the divine life that the Father and Son share (cf. 5:26; 14:10; 17:21). Verse 58 is a repetition of verses 48-50, contrasting the manna of the past that was not able to sustain life, and Jesus as the true life-giving bread from heaven.

The majority of Johannine scholars contend that verses 51-58 refer to the eucharist or the Lord's Supper, but we are cautious of taking such a view (cf. the section 'Characteristics' in the Introduction). First, if John intended to communicate to his *post-Easter* audience that it is essential to partake in the eucharist, it would reduce Jesus' audience in the narrative to a mere foil – we can hardly expect 'the Jews' to have understood this *before* the cross. Second, although John uses eucharistic language, it does not necessarily mean that he had the sacrament of the eucharist in mind. For if sacramentalism was so important to John or to the Johannine community, why do the Johannine Letters not refer to the sacraments? Third, even if John intended a reference or allusion to the eucharist, at a secondary level, it would merely express something that is already there at a primary level. The sacrament of the eucharist denotes the continual remembrance of and participation in Jesus' death; but we have already suggested this meaning by our non-sacramental reading of the text.

People's Responses (6:60-71)

This section speaks of a sifting of Jesus' disciples. First there was the scandal over Jesus' origin and identity (vv.41-42), then came the invitation to 'eat' Jesus' flesh and 'drink' his blood (v.52). Even many of Jesus' disciples seem to find his teaching hard and difficult to accept (v.60). Jesus replies that if this has offended them, how much more they would be offended if they were to see the Son of Man ascend to where he was before (vv.61-62). Jesus is referring here to his return to the Father, which would start at the cross (cf. 3:14) and finish with the ascension (an event John frequently refers to [7:33; 14:28; 16:5; 20:17] but does not record).

Jesus foreknows those, even among his disciples, who do not believe (v.64; cf. v.36 and 2:24-25); and indeed many of his disciples reject him and become 'non-disciples' – no longer following him (v.66). When Jesus challenges the Twelve, Peter, as a spokesman for them, confesses adequate belief and commitment to discipleship (vv.67-69). Nevertheless, from among the Twelve, one (Judas) will eventually turn his back on Jesus (vv.70-71).

Again, the problem with the crowd and the disciples seems to be a cognitive one – they are slow to understand. Note the cognitive vocabulary in this passage: to hear, to know, to 'see' (perceive), and to believe. Jesus' words cause offence, are hard to accept and cause defection, precisely because (but especially when) they are not properly understood (cf. vv.41-42, 52, 60, 66). But they are life-giving to those who understand and accept them (vv.63, 68-69).

We need to say a little more about verse 63, which translates: 'The Spirit is the one that gives life, the flesh does not benefit anyone; the words that I speak to you are Spirit and life.' That the Spirit gives life (v.63a) has already been observed in John 3-4, where we learned that the Spirit facilitates entry into eternal life through a spiritual birth and empowers Jesus' life-giving teaching.

Verse 63b, 'the flesh does not benefit anyone', is more puzzling because the referent of 'flesh' is uncertain. It could be argued that it refers to the human, unbelieving mind. Like the contrast in 3:6 between 'flesh/human' and Spirit, verse 63b may refer to the unbeliever who is locked in his/her 'fleshly' or human thinking, whereas the life-working activity of the Spirit illuminates the human mind. Plausible as it may sound, there are two reasons why I suggest that 'flesh' refers to Jesus' life, in particular to the giving of Jesus' life in death on the cross. First, in verses 51-58, 'flesh' also refers to Jesus' death. Second, verse 62 refers to Jesus' ascent, starting at the cross, and verse 63 sheds further light on this event.

If 'flesh' in verse 63b refers to Jesus' death on the cross, how do we explain that this is of no benefit to people? In the light of verse 63a and our understanding of John so far, I suggest that one needs to understand the significance of the cross before Jesus' death can be life-giving. Many may 'believe' that a man called 'Jesus' died on a cross almost two thousand years ago, but it may not be the kind of saving, life-producing belief that John has in mind. Only when Jesus' death on the cross is understood as the supreme expression of God's love for this world, as God's way to deal with sin and provide eternal life, *only then* Jesus' death is of benefit.

What is more, it is the Spirit who facilitates this understanding in a person, mediating the significance of the Christ-event on the cross. Consequently, verse 63c also becomes clear: Jesus' words are Spirit and life in that the Spirit reveals the meaning and significance of Jesus' life-giving teaching. In sum, the Spirit gives life particularly in his role of a cognitive agent – facilitating people's understanding of Jesus and his teaching and hence assisting them to produce an adequate belief-response that will result in a life-giving relationship with Jesus.

Reflection

John 6 tells again the story of Jesus' identity and mission: he is the bread of life who will give life to the world through his death on the cross. This picture of Jesus' death fits the context of the Passover (see v.4) where an unblemished lamb is sacrificed to escape God's judgement (cf. 1:29; Exodus 12). What is more, John 6 is essentially an invitation to Wisdom's 'banquet'. The various belief-responses to Jesus' invitation, however, confirm the tragic story of the rejection of Jesus, to which the Prologue has already hinted.

The main characters that interact with Jesus are the crowd, 'the Jews' and Jesus' disciples. The crowd initially shows (signs-)faith and some indication of discipleship, but follows Jesus for the wrong reasons. As a crowd, they fail to believe (v.36). From within the crowd, 'the Jews' emerge as an openly hostile group. Offended by Jesus' revelation of his identity and mission, they reject him and become increasingly alienated from him. A major sifting also takes place among Jesus' disciples, and many of them abandon him. The Twelve, Jesus' inner circle of disciples, however, make a confession of adequate belief and a commitment to discipleship. However, even among the Twelve there would eventually be a defector. It is evident that discipleship is a dominant theme in John: it involves coming to Jesus, and then remaining as a follower.

We see the attitude of the crowd and realize that even today, people have different concepts of Jesus and different motivations for seeking him, but Jesus is quick to burst balloons. An encounter with

Jesus, who knows what is going on inside us, can be unnerving, but our wrong expectations and misconceptions of Jesus must be exposed before we can understand and appreciate who he truly is.

As for Philip, Jesus was essentially challenging him to think 'from above'. Such a challenge may come to us too when we are faced with a situation that is impossible to solve with mere human resources. What is important is our attitude; the problem remains the same but our approach may make the difference. Do we tend to despair or do we think of what is possible with God? The sheer impossibility of the situation should drive us to think 'from above'. Jesus challenges his followers to see problems from a divine perspective (cf. the concept of setting one's mind on divine things in Matthew 16:23; Mark 8:33; Colossians 3:2).

We have seen that Jesus is the giver and sustainer of divine life, satisfying all our spiritual needs. How can we come to Jesus' banquet and feed on him? By faith – the one who believes in him will never ever be hungry again. Jesus often uses mundane objects like bread, water and light to teach spiritual truth about himself and his mission. Let us not be dull in our understanding and hardened in our hearts. To recognize the true identity of Jesus and grasp the meaning of his words, requires an open mind, enlightened by the Spirit. Perhaps we should pause and reflect on our desires and mindset. Do we crave material things and earthly recognition above spiritual nourishment? Jesus' words are Spirit-and-life. Which of Jesus' words or commands do you find most difficult to accept or perhaps even offensive? Reflect also on Peter's reply, 'Lord, to whom can we go?'; for him, defection was not an option.

John seems to advocate an understanding faith, i.e., a belief that has truly grasped something about Jesus' identity, mission and his relationship with the Father. Such understanding does not come naturally to people; indeed, it can only come 'from above'. It is the Spirit, the agent 'from above', who reveals the meaning and significance of Jesus' teaching to people, and as such facilitates a saving understanding and belief-response.

John's understanding of salvation would exclude three extreme views that are seen in certain quarters of today's Church. One view is that salvation is only propositional knowledge, such as 'I believe that Jesus died for my sins' or 'I believe that Jesus is the Son of

God'. Another attitude, which sometimes results from the previous one, is that a person can enter into a saving relationship with Jesus 'with no strings attached'. Third, some have an anti-intellectual attitude towards salvation, expressed in statements like 'you do not need to understand; just believe' or 'take a leap in the dark'. John would certainly question these attitudes and advocate a belief that involves our intellect as well as our will, motivation and attitudes. We must understand something of Jesus' true identity, mission and relationship with his Father. Besides, we must commit ourselves to Jesus and stick with him in life-long discipleship.

Family Debates (7:1-10:42)

John 7-8 and John 9-10 are two literary units, which substantiate the increasing hostility towards Jesus. Both sections end on the same note: the attempt of 'the Jews' to kill Jesus (8:59; 10:31-39). In the light of the intense conflict between Jesus and 'the Jews' which finally leads to Jesus' death, and the negative portrayal of 'the Jews', some scholars have labelled John's Gospel as anti-Jewish, but such a conclusion is unnecessary. Rather, John most often uses the term 'the Jews' to denote a specific subset of the Jewish race, namely, the Jewish religious leaders from Jerusalem who are hostile and opposed to Jesus (see the section 'Characteristics' in the Introduction). 'The Jews' in John function as a character-type, embodying a particular response towards Jesus. As such, 'the Jews' should be distinguished from other Jewish characters, such as the crowd, Nicodemus, John the Baptist, the disciples, the lame man and the man born blind.

If John is not anti-semitic, how do we explain the intensity of this conflict between Jesus and 'the Jews'? A good suggestion has been made to label these clashes as 'family debates'. We can understand this as follows. 'The world', for John, denotes a system or environment that is hostile to Jesus, and its people are in darkness and produce evil (1:10-11; 3:19). However, this evil, dark and hostile world is the object of God's love and saving activity (3:16-17) – he sent Jesus into the world to bring light and life. 'The Jews' are identified with 'the world' (8:23); they belong to the world and represent it. They are a microcosm of the world as it were. Consequently, 'the Jews' embody the hostile response to Jesus and yet, are also the object of Jesus' saving mission. One normally does not argue at length with someone one does not care about. However, it is not uncommon to have disputes between family members. Therefore, being a Jew himself, Jesus came to his own family as it were, in order to discuss the house rules.

At the same time, Jesus redefines the concept of family. Who belongs to the family of God? What is involved in belonging to God's family? Who are your father and family? These fundamental issues already came to the fore in 1:12-13 and 3:3-8, but are discussed at greater length here in John 7-10. Hence, at the core of the conflict between Jesus and 'the Jews' is the issue of family. In keeping with John's dualism, there are two families and their respective fathers: Jesus constitutes a new family that has God as Father, whereas the devil, the ruler of 'the world', is the father of those who belong to 'the world'. Between these two families exists a long-standing feud. Thus, John's Gospel creates a tension. At one level, Jesus came to his own people to discuss family issues, but, at another level, Jesus' coming brought the reality of two mutually exclusive and opposing families into sharp focus.

Jesus at the Feast of Tabernacles (7:1-52)

The setting of John 7-8 is the so-called Feast of Tabernacles or Booths. This was one of the three great Jewish festivals that required Jews to make a pilgrimage to Jerusalem, and it lasted for seven days. The people were to live in temporary huts or booths to recall the days when Israel lived in huts during the Exodus from Egypt (Leviticus 23:42-43). This festival was originally a harvest festival and was an occasion for great rejoicing. The festival was associated with the symbols of water and light. John draws on these symbols in chapters 7 and 8 respectively: in 7:37-39, Jesus claims to be the source of life-giving water; in 8:12, Jesus presents himself as the life-giving light. Thus, John uses the Feast of Tabernacles as the backdrop for Jesus' self-revelation as the source of salvation.

John 7 can be divided into five sections: (i) Jesus goes to the feast (7:1-13); (ii) Jesus' first discourse (7:14-24); (iii) Jesus' second discourse (7:25-36); (iv) Jesus' invitation (7:37-39); (v) people's responses (7:40-52).

Jesus Goes to the Feast (7:1-13)

The violent intentions of 'the Jews' cause Jesus to stay in Galilee rather than to go back to Judea (v.1). However, as the Feast of Tabernacles approaches, Jesus' brothers challenge him to go to Judea to manifest himself more publicly (vv.3-4). They may have alluded to Jesus' performance of miracles before the people in Jerusalem in 2:23. Or, perhaps they have the wedding at Cana in mind, urging him, as Jesus' mother did, to move to the centre stage. Anyway, John's aside in verse 5 reveals that verses 3-4 are probably a mockery rather than a serious request.

Jesus' brothers are unable to perceive that Jesus does in fact operate at centre stage – even a cosmic one – revealing himself to the world (cf. 1:18, 50-51; 3:17). In fact, Jesus' ultimate public revelation of himself (and the Father) is to happen shortly at Golgotha (cf. 12:32). It must have been painful for Jesus to realize that even his own brothers do not understand him and his mission.

As in Cana, Jesus remains in control and tells his brothers that his time has not yet arrived (v.6; cf. 2:4). Verse 8 has a textual variant, 'I am not *yet* going to this festival' (see the footnote in your English version of the bible), which is probably the original reading, and also matches the 'not yet' in verse 6. Hence, Jesus remains in Galilee. After his brothers have gone, Jesus also goes to Jerusalem, but on his own initiative and not in the manner his brothers suggested (v.10).

Ironically, the feast is a commemoration of God's goodness but 'the Jews' are looking for a way to kill the Son of God (vv.1, 11). The grumbling that we saw in 6:41 continues here among the crowds (vv.12 and 32). Typically, the crowd is divided and unable to decide who Jesus is, but they are too afraid of their leaders to discuss this issue publicly (vv.12-13).

Excursus: 'The Fear of the Jews'

'The fear of the Jews' was a dominant factor in the lives of many people in Jesus' time. This fear, a constant theme in John, affected common people (7:13), the parents of the man born blind (9:22), some Jewish authorities (including perhaps Nicodemus) (12:42), Pilate (19:8), Joseph of Arimathea (19:38) and the disciples (20:19). Neither the fear nor the threats should be underestimated. Those professing openly that Jesus was the Messiah were in danger of excommunication from the synagogue (9:22; 12:42; 16:2), making them social outcasts; or worse, followers of Jesus were in danger of being killed (16:2). History shows that, across the globe, Christians repeatedly face such threats and persecutions from opponents of Christianity, up to the present day. These threats and the resultant persecution should not be disparaged – then or now.

John 15:18-16:4a shows that Jesus took the threats of the Jews very seriously. He warns his followers of what will happen to them, but, at the same time, he encourages them to continue to witness, promising them assistance in the form of the Paraclete. In other words, Jesus' commands his disciples to continue in their discipleship – 'You shall also witness...' (15:27). In the context of a cosmic trial, if the disciples ceased to witness during times of persecution, they would not only fail as disciples but also the case where Jesus is on trial would be weakened or lost. We would not be too wide of the mark if we were to suggest that Peter's denial of Jesus in John 18, which was a discontinuation of his discipleship (even though it was temporary), was caused by this fear of the Jews. Precisely to prevent these kinds of situations, Jesus will send the Paraclete to assist the believer (14:16-18; 15:26-27). Moreover, Jesus' followers have the assurance of his peace to withstand fear and persecution (14:27; 16:33; 20:19-21).

In his Gospel, John implicitly challenges his readers not to give in to fear and to threats of persecution. In his Letter, John gives further reassurance that perfect love will cast out fear (1 John 4:18).

Jesus' First Discourse at the Feast (7:14-24)

For the first few days of the feast, Jesus remains 'hidden', but halfway through the week he starts teaching in the temple (v.14). 'The Jews' are startled by Jesus' understanding of the Scriptures because they are aware that he has not been taught by anyone (v.15). It literally reads, 'How does he know the writings', and so John probably intends an echo of 5:47 where Jesus accuses 'the Jews' for not knowing Moses' writings.

Similarly, verse 18 harks back to 5:44, indicting 'the Jews' for seeking praise for themselves. 'The Jews', as Moses' disciples, study his writings and presume to understand them, but John points out ironically that in reality they have not grasped the essence of Moses' writings because they do not believe the one who truly understands Moses' writings. They are in danger of missing the point (read 'salvation') completely. Jesus' assertion that his teaching is not his but God's (v.16) does not come as a surprise to the careful reader, who will remember texts such as 3:34 and 5:19, 36.

That Jesus has resumed the debate of 5:39-47 is clear from the explicit reference to Moses and from Jesus' accusation that none of his opponents keeps the Law (v.19). Then, Jesus questions them about their reasons for wanting to kill him. The crowd appears to be taken aback at Jesus' question and wonders where he got the idea from that someone wants to kill him (v.20). The crowd may be oblivious of the murderous intentions of 'the Jews' (although see v.25) but they come dangerously close to being on the side of 'the Jews'. Their accusation that Jesus is demon-possessed reveals their incomprehension and aggravation.

Jesus reminds his audience in verses 21-23 of his healing of the lame man at the pool on the Sabbath, an act that 'the Jews' had unjustly condemned. He points out that if a small 'work' (circumcision) is allowed on the Sabbath, then how much more a greater 'work' (the healing of an entire person – the lame man at the pool). His action, he claims, was justified; in fact, it was an act of social justice. Jesus' challenge literally translates, 'are you furious with me because I healed *the whole person* on the Sabbath?' (v.23b), and reminds us again of Jesus' holistic outlook on humanity (cf. Jesus' treatment of the Samaritan woman).

In verse 24, Jesus exhorts the crowd: 'Do not judge according to appearance but according to right judgement.' 'The Jews' had misjudged Jesus' action on the Sabbath, and based on this poor judgement, they persecuted him and even sought to kill him (5:16-18). Despite their intensive study of the Scriptures, they were unable to evaluate Jesus' action on the Sabbath correctly. How could they? Remember the prerequisite for making a right judgement is to seek God's will rather than one's own (5:30). That is why Jesus declares that he can do nothing on his own but only does what he sees and hears from God. This was exactly the problem: 'the Jews' were not seeking God's will but speaking on their own, seeking their own glory and hence unable to make correct judgements (vv.17-18; cf. 5:44). The crowd is also in danger of misjudging Jesus (cf. vv.12, 20).

Jesus' Second Discourse at the Feast (7:25-36)

The crowd is puzzled. Their religious leaders want to kill Jesus but are not taking any action. This makes the people wonder whether their leaders have concluded that Jesus is really the Messiah (vv.25-26). In verse 27, Jesus' listeners claim to have knowledge: (i) they claim to know Jesus' origin (cf. 6:42); (ii) if Jesus were really the Messiah, no one would be able to know his origin; (iii) therefore, the implicit conclusion is that Jesus cannot be the Messiah.

Jesus, however, points out their lack of knowledge – of God and hence of himself (vv.28-29). In fact, Jesus punches a whole in their syllogism (a reasoning in which a conclusion is drawn from two propositions): since the crowd does not know God, they do not know the one who comes from God, and hence their first proposition of knowing Jesus' origin is proven to be a wrong one.

This is not the first instance of people wrongly presuming to have knowledge of divine things. In 3:2, Nicodemus claims to have knowledge of Jesus but it proved to be rather insufficient. In 5:39-47, Jesus tells 'the Jews' that their knowledge of the Scriptures is not as thorough as they think; otherwise they would not reject him. In 6:41-42, 'the Jews' also assume they know Jesus' origins and are offended by Jesus' claim to have come from heaven. Each time Jesus points out what their problem is and what they need to do, but their response is not encouraging. Similarly, on this occasion, the people react negatively and try to arrest him, but Jesus remains in control – his 'hour', i.e., the time of his arrest and passion, had not yet arrived (v.30).

It becomes increasingly clear that most of Jesus' audience has a cognitive problem – they do not understand Jesus and his teaching – and a hostile attitude. Yet, there are glimmers of hope. Many people in the crowd do believe in him, reasoning that Jesus' miraculous signs prove him to be the Messiah (v.31). Others, however, especially 'the Jews', remain persistent in their misunderstanding of Jesus and in their hostile attitude (vv.32-36).

When 'the Jews', identified here as Pharisees and chief priests, hear the grumbling of the crowd (see vv.25-27), which perhaps poses a danger to their authority, they send temple guards to arrest Jesus (v.32). This confirms Jesus' evaluation of 'the Jews'; they are caught up in their desire for human praise and react violently towards potential threats to their authority.

Jesus' habitually enigmatic replies throw his audience off balance and are regularly misunderstood – as is the case here in verses 33-36. Jesus refers to his imminent departure to his Father, but his opponents mockingly suggest that perhaps he plans to go into the Diaspora and teach the Gentiles (the word can mean either 'Greeks' or 'Gentiles'). Little do 'the Jews' know that the Gentiles will come to Jesus (12:20-21).

Another irony is that his opponents' search for him will be fruitless (v.34). 'The Jews' search for Jesus that they might kill him, an endeavour in which they eventually succeed, but they do not search for Jesus as the saviour and the revealer of God. For John, the quest for Jesus, expressed by the words 'to seek' and 'to find', is essentially a quest for life/salvation. The disciples have embarked on the right quest (1:38; 6:68-69); the crowd is sometimes/often on a wrong quest (cf. 6:24-26); but it is 'the Jews' who are on an entirely erroneous quest: they seek to kill Jesus (5:18; 7:1) and seek the glory of people (5:44; 7:18).

Jesus' Invitation (7:37-39)

The last day of the feast was the great day, when there was a ceremony in which water was carried from the pool of Siloam to the temple and poured out as a libation to secure rain (cf. Mishnah *Sukkah* 4:9-10, which says that this water pouring ritual even happened every day of the feast). During the ceremony, people sang the words of Isaiah 12:3, 'With joy you will draw water from the wells of salvation' (see the Babylonian Talmud *Sukkah* 48b). Against this symbolic background, Jesus invites people to come *to him* to receive life-giving water.

As the footnotes in your English translation of the bible indicate, the punctuation of verses 37-38 is not entirely clear. Related to this issue is the difficulty of identifying the subject in the line, 'out of his innermost being...'. One translation would read, 'Let anyone who is thirsty come to me, and let the one who believes in me drink. As the scripture has said, "Out of his [Jesus'] innermost being shall flow rivers of living water."' Another reading goes like this, 'Let anyone who is thirsty come to me and drink. The one who believes in me, as the scripture has said, "Out of his [the believer's] innermost being shall flow rivers of living water."' Hence, the question is, 'From whom will the "living water" flow – Jesus or the believer?'

I suggest that the latter option is preferable. Both interpretations do assert that Jesus is the primary source of 'living water' (cf. 4:14), but the latter interpretation makes the believer an *additional* or *secondary* source of 'living water'. As Christ is the source of 'living water' for the believer, this water will keep on flowing from within the believer – this life-giving water is the Holy Spirit, as verse 39 clarifies. Thus, after the believer has drunk from the source of living water (Jesus), the life-giving water (the Spirit) will become in her/him a spring of water welling up to eternal life. As a result, the believer becomes a source of living water for others. We saw this process, for example, with the Samaritan woman in John 4. She 'drank' from Jesus and in turn became a secondary source of living water for her fellow-villagers. The challenge John presents to his readers seems clear: have we drunk from the living water? Is the living water in us flowing to others?

John's comment in verse 39 also presents a problem. It explains that, in verse 38, Jesus was referring to the Spirit, which believers would receive in the future for as yet there was no Spirit. For a full explanation we must wait until we reach 20:22, but we shall try to explain the somewhat puzzling phrase 'for the Spirit was not yet' in verse 39. John can hardly be saying that the Holy Spirit did not exist for we know that Jesus was endowed with the Spirit, and people had already started to experience this Spirit through Jesus' teaching (cf. 1:32-34; 3:34; 4:10-14; 6:63). However, the Spirit was limited to the person of Jesus and would only be fully released, i.e. made available, to people after the cross and resurrection. By the phrase, 'the Spirit was not yet', John may mean something like 'the Spirit was not yet fully available' or 'the Spirit was not yet working in people in a way that would be possible only after Jesus' glorification'. Jesus' glorification is thus a prerequisite for the giving of the Spirit (16:7 mentions another prerequisite).

People's Responses (7:40-52)

Jesus' invitation in verses 37-38 appears attractive, and yet, it causes division in the crowd (vv.40-43). It causes some to believe that Jesus is the Prophet like Moses (cf. Deuteronomy 18:15-18); others that Jesus is the Messiah; and still others to argue that Jesus cannot be the Messiah. As we already observed in verses 12, 25-27 and 31, the crowd seems unable to make up its mind and remains divided about who Jesus is. The crowd is a microcosm of humanity, and the reactions and divisions in the crowd represent the responses of acceptance and rejection that humankind can make (cf. 1:10-13; 3:18, 36).

Jesus' words/actions at the festival caused the Jewish religious leaders to send the temple guards to arrest him (v.32) but they are apparently unsuccessful (vv.44-45). The Pharisees and chief priests are obviously unhappy that the guards have not arrested Jesus, and question them about their failure to capture him. Their reply, 'Never has anyone spoken in this way!' (v.46), may reveal their admiration of Jesus or their sheer inability to arrest Jesus because of his authority (cf. v.15).

The meeting now turns sour. First, the excuse of the temple guards for failing to arrest Jesus angers the authorities. They attack the guards, accusing them of being deceived by a man in whom none of the religious authorities believed (vv.47-48). Second, the religious leaders condemn the crowd: the crowd does not know the Law but is under a curse; thereby implying that it is susceptible to deception (v.49). Third, the authorities turn on one of their own. Nicodemus, a respectable, prominent leader, challenges his colleagues on the apparent injustice being adopted (vv.50-51). However, he is mocked and overruled, and, as in his discussion with Jesus, fails to participate further and, once again, disappears from the scene (v.52). The irony, of course, is that the religious authorities who presume to know the Law and have discernment are the ones who do not sufficiently understand the essence of the Law. They deceive themselves regarding Jesus and are not able to judge correctly (cf. 5:39-47; 7:19-24).

Reflection

Jesus' injunction to judge correctly and not by outward appearance (v.24) poses a challenge for all of us. How often have we misjudged situations or people? From our discussion it becomes clear that in order to judge correctly we must have the right priority: to seek God's will first, which requires that we be in tune with God.

Some people reasoned that Jesus' miraculous signs were proof that he was the Messiah – and they believed (v.31). In John's Gospel, 'signs-faith', i.e., a belief on the basis of miracles, is not necessarily negative, although John encourages people to go further than that. As long as miracles are seen to reveal something about Jesus' true identity, character and mission, they can be a valid and sufficient basis for faith. It is when the miracles are misunderstood and attention is diverted from Jesus to the spectacular that people's responses are insufficient. We saw such responses in 2:23-24 and in 6:25-26 but this should not lead us to think that miracles have no value. Miracles can elicit faith if they are correctly understood (cf. the reflection on 4:43-54).

In this chapter, more than previously, the character of the crowd comes through. The crowd is divided (vv.12-13, 20, 25-27, 30-31, 40-43); it cannot make up its mind about Jesus and hence represents the two basic reactions of humankind. Some from the crowd believe; others remain undecided or side with 'the Jews', falling back into rejection and remaining part of the hostile world. In John 12, we shall encounter the crowd again. The challenge before us is to determine whether we are still part of the crowd or have already stepped out and made our position clear. A crowd is often a comfortable place because one can remain anonymous and uncommitted; but Jesus' teaching functions like a sword, dividing the crowd, forcing people to make up their minds.

Some people remain part of the crowd because they are afraid to discuss issues in the open, afraid to be identified and be persecuted. The implicit warning to these people is not to be controlled by their fears, realistic as they may be. When in fear, people often choose between 'fight' or 'flight', but the better option is to face up to your fear. In Johannine terms, fear should not result in lack of confession and commitment (flight) nor in accusation (fight) but in open confession and identification with Jesus (facing up).

Jesus and the Adulteress (7:53-8:11)

The footnote in your English translation of the bible mentions that the oldest Greek manuscripts we have do not contain this passage, so this story is almost certainly a later addition (the first evidence of such addition comes from as late as the fifth century). We may encounter two opposing attitudes: (i) to discard the information regarding the history of the passage; or (ii) to discard the passage because it was not part of the earliest form of the Gospel. Both attitudes are naïve and essentially ignore the possibility of the Gospel being written or edited/composed over a period of time by more than one person. Instead of ignoring the passage or its history, I suggest that we take both seriously.

As a starting point, I suggest that we accept the text as we have it today without ignoring the process by which it reached its final form. For example, we allow for the possibility that John's Gospel was not written in one sitting but is the result of various editions, drawn out over a period of time. As it is part of the bible, we regard this passage as authoritative, but we also take its history seriously. This means we shall have to reason why this story found its way into the Gospel as we have it today, and how the story fits in with the surrounding text. Such an attitude does not compromise a doctrine of divine inspiration or the authority of the bible; but does take into account that the bible – even some of its individual books – was written over a long time by several authors. This obviously means more explanatory work, and with this in mind, we turn to the story itself.

While Jesus was teaching in the temple, on another occasion, his opponents bring to him a woman who was caught in the act of adultery (vv.2-3). Posing as observers of the Mosaic Law, Jesus' opponents ask his opinion on the matter (vv.4-5; cf. 5:39ff.). However, since the Mosaic Law requires that both the adulterer and the adulteress be stoned (Leviticus 20:10; Deuteronomy 22:22-

24), one wonders where the man is! In fact, verse 6 reveals they have brought the woman to Jesus, not because they are concerned about justice but because they want to trap Jesus. Besides, the issue here is not whether the woman is guilty or not – Jesus' command to sin no longer in verse 11 implies her guilt – the issue in this passage is one of right judgement.

A few days earlier (in the time frame of the Gospel at least), Jesus had accused his opponents of not keeping the Law and also challenged them to judge rightly instead of judging according to outward appearance (7:19-24). In this story, the scribes and Pharisees seem unwilling or unable to judge rightly. Their aim is to bring charges against Jesus; by setting a trap for him, they hope to find grounds to accuse him. Instead, when Jesus challenges them, they find themselves in no position even to judge the adulterous woman (vv.7-9). Jesus' challenge to his opponents in verse 7 is radical and goes beyond the requirement of the Mosaic Law, which states that the witnesses should be the first to execute the death penalty (Deuteronomy 17:7). It serves as a good illustration that one should not accuse/judge others lightly.

Perhaps, like others, we are curious about what Jesus was writing with his finger in the soil (vv. 6, 8). One suggestion is that, just as God wrote the ten commandments on stone tablets with his finger (Exodus 31:18), Jesus wrote down the ten commandments. Another suggestion comes from a few late documents (ninth and eleventh century), which add to verse 8 the words 'the sins of each of them'. However, these suggestions are speculative and do not carry much weight. Moreover, verse 9 states that Jesus' opponents left because of what they *heard* Jesus say, rather than what they saw Jesus write.

Who then has the right to judge? The one without sin, the guiltless one (v.7), the one to whom God has given authority to judge – the Son of Man (5:22, 27, 30). What is his verdict? A verdict tempered by grace. He does not sentence her but sets her free and commands her to sin no longer (vv.10-11). Who, in the end, stands condemned? It certainly is not the woman. Although they claim to be legal experts, Jesus' opponents did not apply the Mosaic Law with enough care: first, they failed to bring the adulterer; next, they were unaware of the responsibility of a witness. Hence, Jesus' opponents stand condemned. Their leaving the scene is an acknowledgement of their guilt/sin and consequently their disqualification to judge (v.9). They have not given heed to Jesus' advice in 7:24, with the result that once again the accusers have become the accused (cf. 5:45).

This story exemplifies the principle Jesus set out in 7:24: one must judge correctly and righteously. Moreover, since 8:15-16 repeats the same principle, the passage 7:53-8:11 seems to be framed by the commands stated in 7:24 and 8:15. I suggest, therefore, that this story was inserted into the Gospel at a later stage to illustrate the principle stated by Jesus in 7:24 and 8:15.

Reflection

We identify three areas for reflection: (i) biblical interpretation or hermeneutics; (ii) Jesus' attitude towards various people; (iii) principles for judging.

Regarding biblical interpretation, this passage brings up two issues. First, in studying the bible, let us not forget to study its history where necessary. In this case, we took into consideration the fact that this passage was almost certainly a later addition. As a result, we had to address the issue of why this story was inserted into the Gospel and why at this particular place. Although such an approach means more work, it certainly deepens our understanding of Scripture. Second, we should remain within the light of Scripture, i.e., we avoid dubious speculations. More so, when the issue at hand (what Jesus wrote on the ground) is not the most important one. We should expect, if the issue were important, that the author would give more information (cf. the issue of when the water had become wine in 2:1-12). Hence, the emphasis should remain on those issues which the author stresses rather than on those we find interesting. Remember the lesson in the first section of the book: we read John's Gospel primarily to discover what John intended. In this story, the issue is of right judgement.

It is interesting to observe Jesus' dealing with various people. Knowing what goes on in people (cf. 2:24-25; 6:64), he is able to quickly get to the heart of the matter. False accusations rebound, hidden motives are unmasked, balloons are burst, and slippery traps are evaded. Jesus' teaching is such that no one goes unaffected; it causes division as his hearers are forced to make up their minds about who this Jesus is. Those who perceive Jesus' teachings and actions as attacks on their beliefs and status, react sharply – with false accusations, hate, and plans to get rid of him. Jesus is quick to turn the tables on his opponents, but is patient and gracious towards the sinner. Notably, Jesus is less sympathetic to the hypocritical, scheming religious authorities than to a defenceless sinner, because they are supposed to teach and guide the common people, and are expected to judge rightly. To quote Luke, 'From everyone to whom much has been given, much will be required; and from the one to whom much has been entrusted, even more will be demanded (Luke 12:48).

As for judging others, we should judge slowly and rightly. First, we must be slow to judge lest we be judged ourselves (cf. Matthew 7:2). We must first inspect or sort out our life before we judge others (cf. the speck and the plank in Matthew 7:3-5). Second, we should judge rightly/correctly, i.e., in keeping with God's word and with the grace of Jesus. To judge incorrectly, according to human standards and outward appearances, will result in condemnation, slander, gossip, and so on. Remember that Jesus expected those who had the authority to judge, to judge rightly. Many of us may be in similar positions of authority and leadership – pastors, teachers, youth leaders, directors/CEOs, managers and judges – so we need to heed Jesus' teaching. This principle also applies at a macro level: if leaders of nations are not able to judge rightly, corruption, perversion of justice and other malpractices will follow. Unfortunately, we see such situations in many countries, hampering their development and damaging their credibility.

Jesus and 'the Jews' (8:12-59)

This section is undoubtedly the most poignant in the conflict between Jesus and 'the Jews'. The accusations oscillate between 'the Jews' alleging that Jesus is demonized (v.48) and Jesus charging his opponents with being children of the devil (v.44). Not surprisingly, it ends with another attempt to kill Jesus (v.59).

At the heart of this 'family debate' is the issue of which family one belongs to and who one's father is.

We can divide the passage as follows: (i) Jesus the light of the world (8:12-20); (ii) Jesus announces his departure (8:21-30); (iii) liberating truth (8:31-38); (iv) fathers and families (8:39-47); (v) Jesus' supremacy over Abraham (8:48-59).

Jesus the Light of the World (8:12-20)

The Feast of Tabernacles, besides being associated with water, is also connected with light, in that there is a ceremony of light in the women's court of the temple. Moreover, 'light' in the Jewish tradition sometimes symbolizes salvation (e.g. Isaiah 9:2; 42:6; 60:19). Here, in verse 12, Jesus applies the imagery of light to himself: 'I am the light of the world'. This is the second of the seven 'I am' sayings or divine self-revelations of Jesus. Since the phrase 'the light of the world' in verse 12a is paralleled by 'the light of life' in verse 12b, the idea is that Jesus is the life-giving light of the world who dispels the darkness (cf. 1:4-5). Jesus does not have a chance to elaborate on this revelation because his opponents immediately heckle him (v.13), triggering off a ferocious dispute. In the next chapter, however, Jesus returns to the subject of his being the light of the world.

In verse 13, the Jewish religious leaders accuse Jesus of not having a valid testimony because he acts as his own witness. Jesus' reply in verse 14, 'Even if I testify about myself, my testimony is true', is puzzling because it seems a blatant contradiction of an earlier statement, 'If I testify about myself, my testimony is not true', in 5:31. Jesus' opponents seem to have a point and appear to have finally trapped Jesus.

A closer look at verses 14-18, however, will reveal how Jesus works himself out of this apparent impasse. Jesus is well aware of the Mosaic requirement for two witnesses to validate a testimony (v.17). Remember 5:31-37, where Jesus revealed that he has several witnesses who testify on his behalf. One of these witnesses is God the Father himself, and here in verses 14-18 Jesus expands on that idea.

We have already seen that Jesus enjoys such an intimate relationship with his Father, that he is the only one who can reveal God as Father. Moreover, in John 5, we observed that Jesus emulates the Father in what he says and does, and that when Jesus works, the Father is at work. Here, in verses 14-18, Jesus reverts to that principle: when Jesus judges, the Father also judges (v.16); when Jesus testifies, the Father also testifies (v.18). Consequently, Jesus' testimony of himself is accompanied and validated by his Father's testimony. We may even conclude that, due to the unique association of Jesus and his Father, Jesus' testimony is equivalent to or includes the Father's testimony. Thus, Jesus' testimony has the twofold validation of himself and his Father. This fulfils the requirement of the Mosaic Law.

Jesus' opponents fail to recognize Jesus' origin (v.14) and hence his oneness with God (cf. v.19). Consequently, from their viewpoint, Jesus' witness is merely carried by himself, which is not legally valid. However, as Jesus points out, they judge according to 'the flesh', i.e., human standards (v.15), echoing the principle he stated in 7:24, 'Do not judge by outward appearance.' For the Jewish religious leaders do exactly that; they judge according to human standards, looking at outward appearance. The previous story of the adulteress was a vivid example of such a faulty approach to people and situations.

Jesus Announces His Departure (8:21-30)

From verse 21 onwards, the discussion becomes sharper. Jesus goes on the offensive, pointing out that while he is from above, 'the Jews' are from below, i.e., of the world (v.23; cf. 3:31), and that they will die in their sins unless they believe that he is 'I am' (v.24). This means that 'the Jews' (and others like them) will die as condemned people unless they recognize Jesus' true identity and origin (cf. 3:18-19). Jesus' opponents continue to display their inability or unwillingness to understand Jesus and his teachings (vv.22, 27). Indeed, they do not allow the light of the world to enlighten them and hence, fail to think 'from above'.

This, of course, reminds us of the Prologue: the Light that enlightens everyone was coming into this dark world but the world did not understand it (1:4-5, 9-11). From those verses and this passage here, we can gain insight into how Jesus gives life. As the life-giving Light, Jesus illuminates people's minds. Consequently, an adequate understanding of Jesus' identity, character, mission and his relationship with the Father enables people to make an adequate faith-response. To reject this illumination will result in misunderstanding or failing to understand Jesus and his teachings, causing one to remain in darkness and under judgement (cf. 3:18).

Despite the host of insults and negative responses that Jesus receives from 'the Jews', verse 30 surprisingly mentions that many (probably referring to Jesus' opponents) 'believed' in him. However, having studied the attitude of 'the Jews', one wonders whether this 'belief' is authentic and adequate or whether it is questionable (cf. 2:23-24; 6:60-66).

Liberating Truth (8:31-38)

Jesus now turns his attention to those amongst 'the Jews' who 'believed' in him. In verses 31-32, he says, 'If you remain in my word, you are truly my disciples; and you will know the truth, and the truth will set you free.' Thus, remaining in Jesus' word results in knowing the truth – the truth which liberates. This completes the picture that we sketched in 6:63 of how Jesus' teaching is life-giving: *Jesus' words give life because they contain liberating truth*. For 'the Jews' who 'believed' it implies that if they continue to adhere to Jesus' teaching, they will prove that their 'belief' is adequate, saving belief. Remembering 6:60-66, we realize that this indeed is the crux: Will they be able to understand, accept and hence remain in Jesus' teaching, or will they find it too difficult, too demanding, too scandalous and turn their backs on him?

They certainly do not show promise in verse 33, taking offence at Jesus' implicit assertion that they need to be set free. As Abraham's descendants, they claim to be free people who have never been subject to anyone (v.33). This is obviously a lie and ignores the fact that they were subject to the Persians and Greeks in the past, and are now under the oppressive rule of the Romans.

Jesus, however, overlooks this lie and points to their greater enslavement, namely, to sin (v.34). Such slaves do not have a permanent place in God's household; only sons, i.e. children of God, do (v.35; cf. 1:11-12). What is needed, then, is *a spiritual liberation from sin* – liberation that Jesus can provide (v.36). This spiritual liberation will then grant/guarantee an eternal place in the family of God through a spiritual birth (cf. John 3).

'The Jews' who 'believed', however, are unlikely to attain this spiritual liberation as Jesus succinctly points out in verse 37 that 'my word makes no headway in/amongst you.' Jesus' teaching, which contains liberating truth, will neither be understood nor accepted by this group, showing that their belief was not belief in the Johannine sense at all.

Jesus has not finished with them. He challenges them, saying that just as he speaks of what he has seen with *his* Father, so 'the Jews' should do what they have heard from *their* father (v.38 [the italicized personal pronouns are, in fact, textual variants but make good sense]). This somewhat enigmatic saying becomes the core of the conflict in 8:39-47.

Fathers and Families (8:39-47)

This part of the confrontation between Jesus and his opponents cuts to the very heart of the problem of 'the Jews'. Some people consider John to be anti-Jewish because he portrays 'the Jews' in a negative way. The casual reader may also wonder whether Jesus' biting language is appropriate; surely, there must be a better way to win people over. But there is another way of looking at it. Although the term 'the Jews' in John's Gospel sometimes denotes the Jewish people in general, it mostly refers to a specific group of people, namely the Jewish religious leaders from Jerusalem. These leaders, for example the Pharisees and chief priests, were supposed to guide the people in the right interpretation of the Law and in right practice. In practice, however, they were excessively concerned with interpretative issues to the extent that they burdened the common people.

When Jesus appeared on the scene with his radical teaching, which subverted the pillars of Judaism, these leaders perceived

Jesus as a threat. Rather than recognizing and welcoming him as the Messiah, they rejected him and planned to get rid of him. Jesus, however, kept explaining to them the real purpose of his coming, the real condition of people, and the consequences of rejecting him. Heated as these debates were, at times, they were nevertheless debates *'within the family'*. The fierceness of Jesus' language showed his deep concern and compassion for his kinsfolk rather than indifference or hate. Yet, these debates were also about families at another level – a spiritual level – as we shall see in this passage.

'The Jews' assert that Abraham is their father, but Jesus' response is to say that their conduct does not show much affinity with Abraham's (vv.39-40). Jesus' subsequent assertion, 'You are doing the works of your father', in verse 41a, implies that 'the Jews' have a different father from the one they claim. 'The Jews' are furious and reply that they are not bastards (literally, 'We are not born out of fornication') but have God as father (v.41b). They consider themselves part of God's family because they are born of the Jewish race; the natural descendants of Abraham and heirs of the promise given by God to Abraham.

Jesus, however, subverts this view. First, Jesus has revealed in his dialogue with Nicodemus that a spiritual birth rather than an ethnic birth qualifies one for the kingdom of God, and hence, to be part of God's family (cf. 1:12-13). This birth is available to everyone who believes – Jew and Gentile alike. Second, the proverbial sayings 'a tree is known by its fruit' (derived from Matthew 7:15-23) and 'like father, like son' hold true in this case too. One's behaviour says much about the family to which one belongs. 'The Jews' claim to belong to God's family but Jesus points out that their behaviour shows otherwise (v.42).

Jesus laments that 'the Jews' do not know and accept his teaching because they do not comprehend it (v.43). In verse 44, he puts his finger on the essence of the problem: 'the Jews' have the devil, not God, as their father. The devil is characterized as a murderer and a liar, and the lies and desire of 'the Jews' to kill Jesus unmistakably reveal that they belong to his family (v.44). Jesus' opponents will naturally choose to do what their father desires, so it comes as no surprise that they want to kill Jesus. 'The

Jews', then, are instruments of the devil, controlled by him. They can only listen to or produce lies, and are immune to the truth (v.45). Since 'the Jews' do not belong to God's family, they cannot 'hear', i.e., understand, the words of God that Jesus speaks (v.47). As they belong to the devil's family, 'the Jews' do not possess the liberating, saving truth that Jesus provides (vv.31-32, 44).

Jesus' Supremacy over Abraham (8:48-59)

'The Jews' are utterly scandalized by Jesus' words, and insultingly call him a Samaritan (an ethnic group that was despised by the Jews [cf. 4:9]) and say that he is demon-possessed (v.48). This, of course, is very ironic, because Jesus has just pointed out that 'the Jews' were in fact 'demon-possessed' (v.44). The debate goes back and forth until 'the Jews' mockingly inquire, 'You are not greater than our father Abraham, are you?' (v.53). Jesus' reply, 'before Abraham existed, I am', asserts his supremacy over Abraham, in that he existed prior to Abraham, having an equal standing with God (v.58; cf. 3:31). 'The Jews' interpret Jesus' claim as blasphemy, and try to stone him (v.59; cf. 5:17-18). Jesus, however, hides himself and leaves the temple (v.59).

Reflection

As the light of the world, Jesus came to enlighten people about the things of God. Many people today are seeking intellectual or spiritual illumination. New Age movements in the West, rooted in Eastern religions and mystical traditions, are becoming quite popular. This is because they promise peace, enlightenment, freedom of moral absolutes, and the reunification of humanity (whose nature is essentially good and divine) with an impersonal god. Perhaps Christians can offer an alternative illumination or enlightenment to these seekers. Like John the Baptist, Christians are supposed to be lights, pointing to the true and greater light who can give life and disperse darkness (cf. 5:35-36).

For John, people either belong to the family of the devil or the family of God, and the transition from the former to the latter is made through a birth of the Spirit through faith in the crucified

Christ (cf. John 3). Just as 'the Jews' could not rely on their pedigree for salvation, neither can we. Being born in a Christian family is a great privilege (as it was to be born as a Jew) but it does not constitute a birth into the kingdom or family of God. People are enslaved to sin and need liberation, which comes from accepting and adhering to Jesus' teaching because it contains liberating truth.

This kind of radical language has never been popular, and till today many find it offensive. In the West, many people do not believe that humankind is contaminated by sin, under the rule of the devil, and in need of salvation. In the East, Hinduism, for example, can accept Jesus as a god but not the exclusive claims that Jesus is the only way to the only true God. Hence, we need to find a way to communicate to people the reality of the condition of the human race and God's solution to it – without unnecessarily offending them and without compromising the radical nature of the Gospel.

For the believer, the challenge is to live according to the new family code. Being part of God's family, certain behaviour is required of us: to adhere to Jesus' teaching; to stick to him in discipleship; to judge correctly and not according to human standards; to decrease so that Jesus can increase; seeking God's glory rather than that of people; and so on. Since other people observe us, our life-style could be a telling witness. Will people see the resemblance to our heavenly Father?

I have used the term 'liberation' to describe Jesus' salvific action on behalf of humankind, but this may need further clarification. Although Jesus primarily provides a 'spiritual' liberation from the oppression of sin and the devil, he also liberates from physical and socio-economic forms of oppression We can see examples of the latter in the lives of the Samaritan woman, the lame man at the pool and the man born blind (in the next chapter). I therefore use liberation as a synonym for 'salvation', viewing it as the release of people from spiritual oppression in order to have an eternal relationship with God, but also from other forms of oppression in the here and now.

It is sometimes difficult to strike a balance in this concept of liberation/salvation. The tendency is to swing between two extremes: a single-minded concern for people's welfare only in this world, and an over-spiritual approach to life that neglects the here and now. For example, on the one hand, some sectors of the Church emphasize the 'winning of souls' to the extent that sometimes life in the present is downplayed or neglected. As a result, we see a dichotomy between the spiritual dimension and the social, economic and political aspects of life. On the other hand, liberation theologies, with their (often needed) emphasis on social justice and improvement of quality of life in the present world, sometimes seem to neglect the spiritual dimension and the 'there and then'. Liberation theologies are so-called 'bottom-up' theologies, starting from the situation of the oppressed and marginalized upon which a theology of liberation is constructed. Frequently, however, the spiritual dimension, i.e., the oppression of sin and the devil, seems to be secondary to the humanitarian dimension. Instead of the two extremes, I suggest that we need a theology that is both 'top down' and 'bottom up', a theology that is able to maintain a balance between liberation from spiritual oppression as well as other forms of oppression (injustice, poverty, inequalities, diseases) in order to improve the quality and assurance of life – both here and there.

Jesus and the Man Born Blind (9:1-41)

Jesus declared in 8:12 that he is the light of the world, but as we saw, he was not given an opportunity to explain himself. He now gets this opportunity. In 9:5, Jesus reiterates that he is the light of the world and goes on to demonstrate this truth in the healing of the man born blind. The stories of the lame man in John 5 and the blind man in John 9 have a number of similarities and therefore invite comparison. The reactions of the two people who were healed, towards the religious authorities and towards Jesus stand in sharp contrast (cf. the commentary on 5:9b-18).

We divide the narrative into four parts: (i) light for the blind (9:1-12); (ii) the first interrogation (9:13-23); (iii) the second interrogation (9:24-34); (iv) people's responses (9:35-41).

Light for the Blind (9:1-12)

John introduces the main character in this story straightaway: a (nameless) man blind from birth (v.1). The comment of the disciples in verse 2 is indicative of the common notions of that day that the man was blind because either he or his parents had sinned. Jesus corrects their presupposition and says that the man's condition man is simply an opportunity for God's redemptive work to be revealed (v.3). Instead of dwelling on the possible cause of the man's condition, Jesus focuses on what is possible with God. Jesus seems to convey a sense of urgency for his disciples to participate in the work God is doing in the world, while there is still an opportunity (v.4; cf. 4:31-38; 5:17).

Although the physical healing of the blind man in verses 6-7 is a precursor to the broader topic of spiritual blindness and spiritual sight, Jesus is not solely concerned with 'spiritual' issues. He is also eager to deal with realities of life in the here and now. Let us consider this blind man for a moment: his blindness was more than just a physical disability. First, it had forced him to become economically dependent on the benevolence of others – he was a beggar (v.8). Second, Jewish regulations probably restricted his entry into the temple and participation in regular worship. The Mishnah, for example, mentions, 'All are liable for an appearance offering before the Lord except for…the blind' (*Hagigah* 1:1; cf. the Dead Sea Scroll 4Q394 f8 3:19-4:4). Third, the associations between blindness and sin, probably left him stigmatized as a sinner (vv.2 and 34). In short, this blind beggar was an economic, social and religious outcast; living on the periphery of society. Jesus' healing of the blind man will lead to (or is aimed at) his spiritual healing (see vv.35-38). However, his physical healing also had profound implications for his economic, social and religious status, once again showing that Jesus' outlook on humanity is holistic.

The neighbours are quite startled at what they see, but the man is unable to give accurate testimony because he does not know where his benefactor went (vv.8-12). So far, the story of the man born blind closely resembles the story of the lame man in John 5; but this will soon change.

The First Interrogation (9:13-23)

Apparently, the people who knew the blind beggar were not satisfied with the man's explanation, which indeed, was inadequate (vv.8-12), so they bring him to the religious authorities (v.13). John's aside in verse 14 that this healing happened on the Sabbath reminds us of the furore over the same issue last time (5:9b-16).

The investigation is more systematic this time. The religious leaders first question the former blind man himself (vv.15-17). His testimony that Jesus had healed him causes a problem for the Jewish leadership. Some of the Jewish leaders reason that Jesus is not from God because he violated the Sabbath (v.16a). However, others argue that if this is the case – and Jesus is a sinner – then how can he perform such miracles (v.16b). This causes division among Jesus' opponents (cf. the division of the crowd in 7:40-43).

The real cause for the rift, however, is not so much about Jesus being a sinner (they have already established this in their minds) but how their conviction of Jesus can be squared with their other conviction that only someone from God can perform these miracles. Their latter belief could have caused them to revise their opinion of Jesus (cf. 10:38), but unfortunately, Jesus' opponents are stuck in their darkness. Where Nicodemus was able to reason that if Jesus performs such miracles he must be from God (3:2), his colleagues are unable to do so because of their commitment to the premise that Jesus is a sinner.

John wants us to observe how the formerly blind man progresses in understanding Jesus' identity and also as a witness. He starts by saying that the man who healed him is called Jesus (v.11), and now, in verse 17, he identifies Jesus as a prophet. This is quite resonant of the way the Samaritan woman advanced in her understanding of Jesus, and makes the reader curious about how far this man will come in grasping the truth about Jesus. John keeps us in suspense, however, because 'the Jews' now summon his parents to testify to what happened (vv.18-19).

The testimony of the parents in verses 20-23 is disappointing and the anti-thesis of the kind of witness John is advocating. It would be natural to presume that the parents know what their son has told the neighbours in verse 11, which means they know how the miracle happened and who performed it. Instead, the parents claim to be ignorant and suggest that their son can speak for himself (v.21). They eschew the call to be witnesses because of their fear of 'the Jews'. John explains that 'the Jews' had already decreed that anyone who confessed Jesus to be the Messiah would be expelled from the local synagogue, which would mean social exclusion (v.22).

Not only the parents of the man born blind were in the grip of fear, but also the crowd (7:13), Joseph of Arimathea (19:38) and even the disciples (20:19) (cf. the excursus 'The Fear of the Jews' in 7:13). Although this fear was real and not to be minimized, John implicitly criticizes those who give in to it when he contrasts the parents' fearful testimony with their son's bold testimony, to which we now turn.

The Second Interrogation (9:24-34)

After the parents had put the ball back in 'the Jews' court, they summoned the healed man for further questioning. In this second interrogation, the formerly blind man turns out to be a very clever witness to the great annoyance of his interrogators.

'The Jews' begin by clarifying their position regarding Jesus: 'We know that this man is a sinner' (v.24; note the pompous claim to knowledge again). They probably hoped to intimidate the formerly blind man into agreeing with them, but the man courageously questions their presupposition (v.25a). In addition, the man puts forward *his* claim to knowledge, namely, that once he was blind but now he can see (v.25b). When 'the Jews' repeat their question regarding the mechanics of the healing (cf. v.26 and v.15), the man sharply reminds them that he had already given this information, and adds ironically, 'You do not want to become his disciples, do you?' (v.27). His tone upsets his interrogators and they start to insult him: we are disciples of Moses with whom God spoke, but you are the disciple of this man from who-knows-where (vv.28-29).

Instead of being intimidated, the man grows in confidence. He switches gears and goes on the offensive, mocking his interrogators' lack of knowledge regarding Jesus' origins (v.30). The man follows up the mocking attack with a simple syllogism: (i) God does not listen to sinners; only to those who worship and obey him (v.31); (ii) someone who is not from God cannot do such an unprecedented miracle (vv.32-33); (iii) hence, this Jesus must be from God. Although the man only states the two propositions of the syllogism, his implicit conclusion is clear enough to his interrogators, as their reaction shows in verse 34. They accuse him of being born in sin (cf. v.2), mock him for trying to educate them, and eventually expel him (cf. the threat of expulsion from the synagogue in v.22).

People's Responses (9:35-41)

After the religious authorities have excommunicated the man, Jesus comes in search of him (v.35). Once again, we notice Jesus' readiness to reach out to the marginalized. The man is eager to believe in the Son of Man but he does not know who this man is – 'Who is he, sir?' (vv.35-36). Just as he did with the Samaritan woman, Jesus plainly reveals his identity: he is the Son of Man (v.37). The man responds promptly: he confesses, 'I believe, Lord!', and worships Jesus (v.38; cf. Thomas' response later in 20:28). The man's understanding of Jesus has progressed from 'the man called Jesus' (v.11), to 'a prophet' (v.17), 'a man from God' (v.33), to the climactic 'Lord' (v.38). Like the Samaritan woman in John 4, and contra the lame man in John 5, the man born blind reaches adequate, saving belief in Jesus.

In verse 39, Jesus sums up the implications of his coming as the light of the world. Jesus came so that those who lack spiritual sight may receive it, while those who claim to see may become or appear blind. The latter group, which boasts of spiritual insight, consists of those who reject the light when it comes and thus confirm their own blindness.

Some Pharisees reply, 'We are not blind, are we?', revealing that they recognize that Jesus is speaking of spiritual realities, but they assess themselves wrongly (v.40). They place themselves in the category of those who have spiritual sight, but by doing that they actually confirm their own blindness. If they had admitted to their blindness, they would not have sin and would have received spiritual sight. As it is, they claim to have sight, but their rejection of Jesus proves otherwise, and they only stumble further into their darkness (v.41).

The way John contrasts the responses of the man born blind and the religious leaders is striking. As the man opens up more and more and finally makes a full confession of faith, so the Pharisees become increasingly blind to Jesus, leaving them in total darkness. The progressive blindness of the Pharisees is expressed over verses 16, 24, 29, 34 and finally 41. In the end, the man who was blind from birth receives physical and spiritual sight, while the Pharisees are left with complete spiritual blindness.

Reflection

As the light, Jesus came to illuminate this dark world by providing revelation of God as Father. Those who reject or fail to understand him will continue in blindness and darkness. Blind spots in one's worldview (cf. the disciples in v.2) or flawed logic (cf. the reasoning of the Pharisees) prove obstacles to clear vision. However, if we acknowledge our blindness, the light will illumine us and lift the blindness so that we can see. Those who 'see'/understand and accept the light will receive life and enter into God's family.

When a person has had a life-changing encounter with Jesus, people often want to know what caused the change: 'We knew her as such and such; what has changed her?' This provides us with an opportunity to witness, to explain what Jesus has done. Not everyone will accept such testimonies. Some people mock our experience of Jesus in this age of reason and logic, but let us not be afraid of, or intimidated by, people. In other situations, the interrogation may be more severe and persecution may follow. And yet, John encourages us not to shrink back. If people reject us, Jesus will seek and find us. This world as 'world' will remain a dark and hostile place, but we can shine and direct others to the Light.

The biased and turbulent interrogation, countered by the bold witness of the man born blind, is a close approximation of what a believer can expect when s/he takes part in the cosmic trial that Jesus is involved in. In John 14-17 (especially 15:18-16:4a) we will see more of this. The believer as a witness in the face of persecution is a prominent Johannine theme that is very relevant today. In many situations, people are persecuted for their faith (not only the Christian faith). When we look at the 'Persecution List' on the website of Open Doors International, an organization serving persecuted Christians worldwide, we see how relevant John is for today (http://www.opendoors.org).

Although John records only three instances of people who are healed by Jesus (the royal official's son in John 4, the lame man at the pool in John 5 and the man born blind in John 9), he makes it clear that illness was a complicated problem. Beyond the obvious physical dimensions of the disease, there was often socio-religious ostracism (restricted participation in the religious life of their day; often illness was thought of as caused by personal sin); and economic dependency (illness often led to begging). Consequently, although Jesus' healing of the man's physical blindness was aimed at his spiritual healing, it also had profound implications for his economic, social and religious status. The life, the salvation Jesus has to offer is not merely for the 'there and then' but also for the 'here and now'. Jesus' approach is holistic: he wants to restore people's relationship with God, their relationships with one another, and in their relationship with society. We may want to reassess our programmes of evangelism, social action, and so on. Perhaps we should also evaluate our approach to the marginalized in general. Perhaps some of us stigmatize (in thought or deed) the person with HIV/AIDS, the divorcee, the homosexual, and so on, as sinners with whom we should avoid physical and social contact (cf. our reflection on 4:1-42 on building bridges with the marginalized).

Occasionally, disease may even have a global impact. For instance, AIDS, sometimes called 'the leprosy of the twenty-first century', affects all dimensions of life – the individual, family and society. Yet, many people (and governments) deny the prevalence and scope of the epidemic, or underestimate its challenges. According to recent reports from the WHO and UNAIDS, Sub-Saharan Africa is home to more than 60% of people with HIV/AIDS worldwide. In countries like Botswana, Zimbabwe and South Africa, for example, 20-35% of the population is infected, most of them in the age group of 15-49 years. This causes serious socio-economic problems as those in this category, representing the productive workforce and young parents, are dying; leaving millions of children orphaned. The average life expectancy has dropped to below 40 years in nine African countries – Botswana,

Central African Republic, Lesotho, Malawi, Mozambique, Rwanda, Swaziland, Zambia and Zimbabwe.

The AIDS epidemic is also spreading rapidly in Asia. India, for example, currently has the largest number of HIV/AIDS patients in Asia and is second only to South Africa, globally. Current trends indicate that soon India will overtake South Africa in numbers, but its government and the wider society have yet to acknowledge the enormity of the problem. AIDS is a global epidemic: the western world cannot brush it aside as a problem of the non-western world, especially in this day of international trade and travel. It is impossible to quarantine particular continents or countries, so the non-western world needs to wake up quickly to the realities of the epidemic. Sadly, in India, it is not the Church or Christians who are at the forefront of the battle against AIDS, but the Bill and Melinda Gates Foundation, working through local NGOs. In the light of Jesus' example, Christians should not neglect their public duties and respond to the AIDS epidemic in a holistic manner.

We had suggested that the remarkable parallels between this story and the story of the lame man in John 5 require a closer look. The two men underwent similar experiences – they were healed by Jesus on the Sabbath and consequently interrogated by Jesus' opponents – but they reacted and progressed quite differently. So also in life, though many may start with equal circumstances or opportunities, some will respond very differently so that the outcome of their lives will vary greatly. It is not the start that is most important but how one finishes.

Jesus the Good Shepherd (10:1-21)

John 10 introduces a new topic, but not a new audience; Jesus is still speaking to the Jewish religious leaders we met in John 9. The idea of Jesus as the good shepherd may evoke images of a gentle shepherd herding his sheep through idyllic green pastures, flowing with water. Whether John intends such a picture needs to be seen. The passage can be divided into three parts: (i) good and false shepherds (10:1-10); (ii) Jesus the good shepherd (10:11-18); (iii) the response of 'the Jews' (10:19-21).

Good and False Shepherds (10:1-10)

John 10:1-10 covers two related topics: in 10:1-6, Jesus is depicted as the shepherd of the sheep, and, in 10:7-10, Jesus is presented as the gate of the sheepfold. Nevertheless, the overall topic is that of good and false shepherds.

The false shepherds – thieves and bandits (the latter are some kind of militant social activists) – are those who break into the sheepfold, whereas the good shepherd legitimately enters by the gate (vv.1-2). Verse 3 mentions that the (good) shepherd calls his own sheep by name and leads them out. This raises the question, 'Out of what will he lead the sheep?', to which the obvious answer is, 'Out of the sheepfold'. In the light of verse 16, where the word 'sheepfold' also occurs, 'sheepfold' is probably a metaphor for Judaism – more specifically, the kind of Judaism that 'the Jews' propagate. Jesus calls people out of the fold of Judaism into the fold or family of God. When he goes ahead, his sheep will follow because they know his voice (v.4). 'To follow' carries the idea of following Jesus as disciples. However, the sheep will not follow the false shepherd – the stranger (perhaps the thief or bandit who has broken in) – because they do not recognize his voice (v.5).

By implication, Jesus is the good shepherd and the Jewish religious leaders are the false shepherds. The background of this parable seems to be Ezekiel 34 where the leaders of Israel are criticized for not having led, fed and protected 'the sheep', i.e., the people of Israel. Tired of their incompetence, God takes over and promises to appoint a Davidic shepherd to feed his people and to provide safety and abundance. This promised shepherd in the line of David is Jesus, the good shepherd.

Jesus' audience, however, does not understand what he is talking about (v.6). John labels verses 1-5 as a parable or figure of speech (v.6), and this parable is told to the Pharisees, who have just been characterized as being blind (9:40-41). Their blindness probably hinders their understanding. Jesus 'parables' apparently require spiritual or cognitive 'sight' in order to be understood.

In verses 1-5, Jesus is the true shepherd who enters the pen by the gate and leads his sheep out of the fold of Judaism. In verses 7-10, however, Jesus changes the metaphor causing a reverse movement. Now Jesus is the gate, and whoever enters through him (into God's fold) will find salvation (vv.7 and 9). Jesus' 'I am the gate for the sheep' is the third 'I am' saying, revealing that Jesus is the door to salvation. The false shepherds, including the present Jewish religious leaders, brought nothing but destruction and death, but Jesus the good shepherd has come to bring eternal life (*zōē*) in abundance (v.10).

Jesus the Good Shepherd (10:11-18)

Another 'I am' saying or divine self-revelation of Jesus occurs in verses 11 and 14: 'I am the good shepherd.' The 'goodness' of the shepherd is characterized by his devotion or care for the sheep: he lays down his life for the sheep (vv.11, 15). This stands in sharp contrast to the attitude of the hired hand. When the enemy (the wolf probably denotes the devil) comes to attack, the hired worker runs away, leaving the sheep unprotected, because he neither owns the sheep nor cares for them (vv.12-13). Jesus, however, claims ownership; as the shepherd, he knows the sheep in his fold and is willing to sacrifice his life on behalf of his sheep.

The concept of the shepherd's laying down his life is, of course, a reference to Jesus' sacrifice on the cross on behalf of humankind (cf. 3:14; 6:51). Interestingly, when Jesus speaks of laying down his life, the word used for 'life' is *psuchē*, which denotes the human, physical life (cf. the commentary on 1:4). Therefore, what Jesus will lay down on the cross is his human or earthly life not his *zōē*, his divine life. Indeed, the divine life he shares with his Father cannot be laid down.

Verse 15 expands on verse 11: both verses assert that Jesus is the good shepherd, who lays down his life for the sheep, but verse 15 inserts a statement about the reciprocal knowledge between Jesus and his Father, and Jesus and his sheep. Based on, or rooted in, the intimate knowledge between Jesus and his Father, there exists an intimate knowing between Jesus and his sheep. Jesus knows his sheep, calls them by name and leads them; his sheep, in turn, hear and know his voice and follow him (vv.3-4). This relationship based on mutual knowledge also creates trust: the sheep trust in the shepherd. In his depiction of Jesus as the good, caring, reliable shepherd, John may have also had Psalm 23 in mind.

Verse 16 reveals that Jesus' concern stretches beyond the ethnic borders of Israel. In verses 3-4, Jesus is calling people out of the pen of Judaism, but here he says that he also has the task of calling people out of the Gentile pen. This will not come as a surprise if we remember Jesus' stay with the Samaritans in John 4, which ended with the climactic confession of Jesus as the saviour of the world. In fact, John has displayed a universal outlook from the beginning of his Gospel: the world is the object of God's love and hence he sent his Son to save the world.

The result of Jesus' calling people from two pens is not two but one flock. Thus, there will be one shepherd over one flock, consisting of those who have responded to his voice. Jesus came to establish the true 'Israel' made up of Jews and Gentiles alike. As we know from John 3, entry into this new 'flock' or community is not by ethnic birth but by a spiritual birth. This teaching of the one flock and one shepherd parallels the Pauline teaching in 1 Corinthians 12:13; Galatians 3:28; and Ephesians 2:14-16.

In verses 17-18, Jesus leaves us in no doubt that he is in control. No one can take his life from him. He has the authority (i.e., delegated power) to lay down his human life, as well as to take it up again (in the resurrection) (cf. 5:26-27; 17:2).

The Response of 'the Jews' (10:19-21)

Jesus' 'parable' in verses 1-5 was not understood (v.6), so Jesus provides further explanation in verses 7-18. However, Jesus' teaching, once again, causes division among his audience (v.19; cf. 7:43; 9:16). Unlike the Synoptic Gospels, where Jesus' teaching goes for long stretches without much interruption from his audience (e.g., the Sermon on the Mount in Matthew 5-7), John regularly records people's reactions to Jesus and his teaching. As in 8:48, here, in verse 20, many of 'the Jews' insinuate that Jesus is demon-possessed and insane. Others, however, reason that one who is demon-possessed cannot open the eyes of the blind (v.21), as Jesus had done in the previous chapter. 'The Jews', therefore, remain as divided as they were in 9:16.

Reflection

Jesus' allegation that the Jewish religious leaders were false shepherds may serve as a warning for us today. For those of us who are pastors, teachers, elders, deacons and youth leaders, entrusted with 'sheep', the challenge is to take our responsibility of feeding, leading and protecting the sheep seriously. Only if we study the word of God seriously and correctly, can we feed others. Only when we stay close to the good shepherd ourselves and imitate him, will we be able to guide others. Or, if I am allowed to change the metaphor a little, perhaps we should see ourselves more as sheepdogs than shepherds, assisting the one shepherd.

Jesus' 'parables' serve as communication in veiled language that needs to be interpreted, i.e., Jesus' 'parables' require spiritual or cognitive 'sight' in order to be understood. Jesus came to reveal God, i.e., to make him known, because people do not know God (8:55) and are not from God (8:47). However, Jesus' life-giving revelation is not overt; we must 'hear', i.e., understand it before it results in life (cf. 5:24-25). Jesus' revelatory teaching is often enigmatic: the Johannine Jesus uses metaphors, double entendre and symbolism, causing people to misunderstand him. Even when Jesus explains himself in plain terms, people find it difficult or offensive to take in, and hence reject it (6:60-66). Perhaps all Jesus' teachings can be called 'parables' (cf. 10:1-6), because they need to be deciphered before the 'life' they offer can be appropriated (cf. 4:10, 14; 6:63). In fact, people need to be 'healed' of their spiritual 'blindness' so that they understand Jesus' revelation and can enter into eternal life. Some people progress cognitively and spiritually, like the Samaritan woman, the royal official and the man born blind; but others, like Nicodemus and 'the Jews', do not. How much have we grasped of Jesus and his teaching? How many blind spots have been uncovered in the past year?

In this portrayal of Jesus as the good shepherd, we see him as someone who is deeply personal and caring; he calls us by name, goes ahead of us and shows us the way, clearing obstacles that might bring harm. We see immediate associations with Psalm 23. The picture of Jesus as the gate reminds us of the wide and narrow gates we find in the Synoptics. We can enter into the kingdom of

God only through Jesus. *By listening to his voice and following him, we can be sure of participating in the abundant life that the Father and Son share. One thing that is clear is that God views the world impartially: there is only one flock – the Church – in which there is place for everyone, regardless of ethnic and socio-economic backgrounds. In God's family, there is no place for parochialism or ethnocentrism.*

We have talked of sheep and shepherds, but there is also the issue of voices: voices of strangers and false shepherds versus the voice of Jesus, the good shepherd. The voice of Jesus provides life to the spiritually dead (5:25), gives guidance in life (10:3-4), and even causes physical resurrection from the dead on the last day (5:28). We live in a world where many voices try to make themselves heard. Through the media we are persistently told to buy in to consumerism which may silence the other voice which calls us to a life of simplicity. Other, conflicting voices can be heard on issues like abortion, euthanasia, homosexuality, divorce, remarriage, cloning, stem-cell research, war, creation and salvation. We need to have a well-informed opinion on such matters if we want to have a relevant voice or witness in this world. A dogmatic approach may be self-defeating, as we saw, for example, in 7:53-8:11. Sometimes we may discover that certain issues are not as black or white as we thought but are composed of many shades. Life is not simple; it is complex, confusing, nuanced, and, at times, paradoxical and absurd. How then do we find direction, purpose, security, principles and answers? By distinguishing and hearing the voice of the good shepherd.

The Rejection of Jesus (10:22-42)

This passage concludes the bigger section on family debates between Jesus and 'the Jews', which began in John 7. No matter how much Jesus tries to reason with his opponents, they seem to be entrenched in their blindness and darkness, and ultimately embody the response of rejection. We divide the passage into two parts: (i) the unity of the Father and Son (10:22-30); (ii) the response of 'the Jews' (10:31-42).

The Unity of the Father and Son (10:22-30)

Another festival has arrived, namely the Feast of the Dedication (of the temple) or Hanukkah (v.22). This feast commemorated the purification and rededication of the temple in 164 B.C. by the Jewish revolutionary Judas Maccabeus after the Seleucid king Antiochus Epiphanes had defiled it. The apocryphal book 1 Maccabees 4:36-61 narrates this historical event in detail.

As Jesus is walking around in the temple premises, 'the Jews' confront him again (vv.23-24). They demand that he makes a public declaration whether or not he is the Messiah (v.24). Jesus replies, saying that he has already answered their question but they do not believe him (v.25). He then points out that the reason for their unbelief is that they are not his sheep (v.26). In verses 27-29, Jesus implies that if they were his sheep, they would have heard his voice, followed him and received eternal life. As it stands, however, they have not been 'given' to Jesus by the Father.

This does not imply a doctrine of predestination. It simply reveals that the initiative for salvation lies with God and not with humans (cf. 6:37). The Father enables people to come to Jesus, and Jesus gives them eternal life. Moreover, Jesus keeps the believer in relationship with himself and his Father; no one can snatch people out of Jesus' hand (which is not the case with the hired worker in 10:12).

All this is possible because of the unity between Jesus and the Father – they are one (v.30). We should not understand this last statement of Jesus – 'I and the Father are one' – in metaphysical terms (as if God and Jesus are the same person) but in relational terms. That is, the Father and the Son have an intimate relationship and are one in character, purpose, will, work, and so on.

The Response of 'the Jews' (10:31-42)

'The Jews' view Jesus' assertion that he is one with the Father as blasphemy and they try to kill him (vv.31, 33). Jesus' reply to his opponents in verses 34-36 is complicated. He essentially uses a rabbinic argument 'from the lesser to the greater'. Based on Psalm 82:6, Jesus reasons that if the children of Israel (the lesser) can be called 'gods', then how much more the one whom God has set apart and sent into the world (the greater).

In verses 37-38, Jesus explains the claim he made in verse 30, that he and the Father are 'one', in that the Father is 'in' Jesus and vice versa. We should interpret this language of mutual indwelling relationally. It denotes the intimate relationship between God and Jesus, which expresses itself, for example, in Jesus' doing the work of the Father and the Father's being at work in Jesus (cf. vv.32, 37-38; 5:17).

As with the other feasts, John uses the symbolism of the Feast of the Dedication to show that Jesus supersedes what Judaism has to offer. In verse 36, he describes Jesus as the one who is 'dedicated' by the Father (the Greek verb *hagiazō* means 'to sanctify', 'to set apart', 'to dedicate'). The careful reader will notice that John portrays Jesus as the dedicated temple (cf. 2:19-21). The temple was seen as the locus of God's presence, but from now on, God is present in Jesus.

After 'the Jews' make another attempt to arrest him (v.39), Jesus seeks refuge across the Jordan in a place where John used to baptize (v.40) – perhaps Aenon (3:23, 26). There Jesus finds a better reception, and many believe in him (vv.41-42). Jerusalem, the centre of Jewish socio-religious life, has proved to be a hostile and dangerous place. The world's response to Jesus in 1:10-11 seems to be played out on a micro scale when we see the reactions of those in Jerusalem, exemplifying the response of rejection.

Reflection

Looking back at the family debates Jesus had with 'the Jews' in John 7-10, it has become clear that 'the Jews' were greatly offended by Jesus and his teachings. Their responses, characterized by hostility and blindness, prove that they belong to their father the devil. They try to trap, accuse and kill Jesus, and clearly reject him.

Over two thousand years it has become evident that it is virtually impossible to ignore the person and message of Jesus. Jesus is (and always will be) a controversial figure to whom people will respond differently. Paul writes that the crucified Christ is a stumbling block to Jews and foolishness to Gentiles (1 Corinthians

1:23), and we see evidence of this in John's Gospel. Therefore, we should not be surprised by the negative reactions of people when we present Christ to them. We may not seek to cause offence, but as we proclaim the Gospel, especially the message of the cross, there will be people who will be offended either by the message or by the messenger. Our testimony may draw us into debates. Those who oppose the message may harass us, corner us with difficult questions, ostracize us, or, as is the case in some countries, imprison or even kill us. However, even in the face of various forms of persecution, we can take consolation in the fact that no one (not even the devil) can snatch us out of Jesus' hand.

The Resurrection of Lazarus (11:1-54)

We are coming closer to the end of Jesus' public ministry, and here we have an account of the last of Jesus' miraculous signs before the cross – the raising of Lazarus from the grave. Although Lazarus is at the centre in the story, he is almost entirely a passive character. He does not speak, and all the events – his illness, burial and resurrection – merely happen to him. The main responses come from his sisters Martha and Mary, and from 'the Jews'.

The episode consists of four parts: (i) the news of Lazarus' death (11:1-16); (ii) Jesus the resurrection and the life, and the responses of Martha, Mary and 'the Jews' (11:17-37); (iii) the resurrection of Lazarus (11:38-44); (iv) the final response of 'the Jews' (11:45-53).

The News of Lazarus' Death (11:1-16)

Lazarus, a man from Bethany, who was dear to Jesus, was ill, and his sisters Mary and Martha sent a message to Jesus about Lazarus' condition (vv.1-3). When Jesus heard the news about his friend Lazarus, he responded calmly, seeing the situation as an opportunity to glorify God (v.4), just as he had done with the man born blind (9:1-3). Jesus was so sure of the situation that instead of rushing to Bethany, he decided to stay where he was (vv.5-6).

Two days later, Jesus decides to return to Judea (v.7), taking his disciples by surprise. They are alarmed because that is where 'the Jews' were trying to kill him (v.8). Jesus, however, still looks for every opportunity to let his light shine. Verses 9-10 closely resemble 8:12; 9:4-5, informing us that as long as Jesus, the light of the world, is around, there is still opportunity to do God's work.

Jesus' speech in verse 11 is somewhat ambiguous. At one level, it speaks of Lazarus' having fallen asleep and of Jesus' waking him up, but, at another level, it is a figure of speech for someone having died and been made alive again. The disciples take Jesus' words literally (v.12) whereas he speaks figuratively (v.13). So, Jesus has to tell them plainly that Lazarus is dead (v.14). In fact, Jesus is glad not to have been there (to heal Lazarus) because Lazarus' death now provides an opportunity for the disciples to strengthen or increase their faith in him, the light of the world (v.15; cf. 9:3-5). When Jesus suggests that they go to Lazarus, Thomas misunderstands him, thinking that 'the Jews' may kill them all (vv.15b-16).

Jesus the Resurrection and the Life, and the Responses of Martha, Mary and 'the Jews' (11:17-37)

It has been a few days since Martha and Mary sent word to Jesus that their brother Lazarus was ill, but Jesus had deliberately deferred his visit to them. Now Jesus seems to have come too late. Lazarus is dead and has been buried for four days (v.17), and the mourning is well under way (vv.18-19). The disappointment of Martha and Mary about Jesus' late arrival is reflected in their implicit reproach, 'Lord, if you had been here, my brother would not have died' (v.21 and v.32). Each sister, in turn, expresses the same complaint. Besides, verses 18-19 state that many of 'the Jews' from Jerusalem had come to comfort the sisters in their grief. We shall examine the responses of each of the sisters and 'the Jews'.

Martha's response in verse 21 goes actually beyond reproach. She also expresses hope when she says that she is certain that God will give Jesus whatever he asks (v.22). Earlier, when the sisters heard that Jesus had come, it was Martha who went to Jesus while Mary remained at home (v.20). Jesus' assurance to Martha that Lazarus will rise again does not startle Martha, although she does not grasp the immediate significance of Jesus' statement (vv.23-

24). As usual, Jesus provides further revelation, indicating that he is the resurrection and the life (*zōē*) (v.25). This 'I am' saying and its development in verses 25-26 clearly echoes 5:29, where Jesus promises that, at the end of time, some people will experience the resurrection into eternal life. Apparently, Martha knows and believes this (v.24). Therefore, the immediate significance of Jesus' divine self-revelation here is that Lazarus' rising again need not wait until the last day but can happen *now* because of Jesus' presence; it 'simply' needs belief (v.26). Martha is able to respond in faith to Jesus and recognize him for who he is (v.27). After her confession, Martha hurries home to tell her sister Mary (v.28). It would probably not be too wide of the mark to see a parallel between Martha and the Samaritan woman, who also went back to her fellow-villagers to witness about Jesus. This would invite us to make a positive evaluation of Martha's response to Jesus.

After Martha's testimony, Mary hurries to Jesus (vv.29-30). Mary's falling at Jesus' feet and her implicit complaint (v.32), followed by her weeping (v.33), may indicate that she does not share the hope that Martha has, and is still in a state of despair. Besides, we do not read that Mary makes any progress in her understanding as her sister does. In fact, Jesus becomes emotionally distressed when he is confronted with the wailing Mary and 'the Jews' who accompany her (v.33). Nevertheless, we need not evaluate Mary too negatively. Though she may have been slower in understanding Jesus and what he could do than Martha, her reappearance in 12:3 reveals her devotion to Jesus.

As an aside, it is likely that the divine Spirit causes Jesus' agitation in verse 33 rather than that he is agitated 'in spirit' (as the NRSV and NIV have it). The Greek construction does not have the preposition 'in' but denotes the Spirit as the means or agent of Jesus' emotion. Therefore, a more probable translation of verse 33b may be that Jesus 'was indignant by the Spirit and greatly disturbed'. Without denying that Jesus empathizes with the mourners (v.35 mentions that he does weep), it appears that Jesus' primary reaction is one of great indignation and agitation. This is probably a reaction to the human response of Mary and 'the Jews' who are so preoccupied with death that they fail to grasp the life-giving potential of Jesus.

Besides the responses of the sisters, we have, in verses 31, 33-37, also the reaction of 'the Jews' who had come with Mary to the tomb. They show little or no understanding of Jesus' potential; their 'come and see' in verse 34 is an ironical and pale shadow of Jesus' invitation in 1:39 and that of the Samaritan woman in 4:29. Though some of them show some signs of understanding – the question in verse 37 expects the answer 'yes' – it does not go beyond a mere belief in Jesus' healing capacity. However, we must also examine their response to Jesus after he raises Lazarus, as narrated in verses 45-53.

The Resurrection of Lazarus (11:38-44)

Jesus finally comes to Lazarus' tomb, a cave sealed by a stone (v.38); similar to the tomb where Jesus would be buried – and raised (19:41-42; 20:1). Jesus' command to remove the stone sounds absurd to Martha (v.39), and Jesus has to remind her of what is possible for those who believe (v.40; cf. vv.25-26). Jesus' audible address to his Father in verses 41-42 confirms Martha's belief, stated in verse 22, but, more importantly, aims at awakening the belief of those present (cf. v.15). The miraculous sign Jesus is about to perform will reveal one more aspect of Jesus' identity – that he is the resurrection and the life – so that people may come to believe in him. Then, Jesus calls out in a loud voice, 'Lazarus, come out' (v.43), which reminds us of 5:28-29 where it says that the dead will also hear the voice of the Son of Man. Lazarus' resurrection in verse 44 is a powerful demonstration of Jesus' ability to give life and a foretaste of what awaits those who believe in Jesus. Verse 44 also shows that Lazarus, as a character, is not entirely passive: he hears Jesus' voice and obeys!

The raising of Lazarus is the last and greatest of Jesus' miracles that John records before the cross, and foreshadows Jesus' own resurrection. Therefore, Lazarus' resurrection is a sign of the greater resurrection to come (cf. for example, the taking away of the stone in 11:39, 41 and 20:1). Since Jesus is the resurrection and the life, death is no obstacle for him. In fact, as Jesus has said earlier, he can give life to whomever he chooses (5:21) and he can lay down and take up his life at his discretion (10:18).

As we mentioned, the resurrection of Lazarus not only prefigures the resurrection of Jesus but also of those who believe in him. John 11:43 echoes 5:28-29, where Jesus said, 'all who are in their graves will hear his voice and will come out.' Though 5:28-29 refers to the end of time, the resurrection of Lazarus is a foretaste of what is to come. Besides, in John 10, we read that Jesus' sheep hear his voice and follow him. Here, in Lazarus' case it becomes evident that even death is no hindrance for his sheep to hear the voice of the good shepherd. In essence, the hope of the believer is this: the good shepherd goes ahead of his sheep – even in death and resurrection – and the believer who dies in Christ will one day hear the shepherd's voice and rise from the dead to the abundant, eternal life.

The Final Response of 'the Jews' (11:45-54)

In John 7:45-52 we had a summit of the Jewish religious leaders discussing Jesus, and here, in 11:45-53, we have the final summit. Jesus' miracle had caused the usual division: many of 'the Jews' apparently believed in him (although perhaps only as a miracle worker), but others reported to their leaders what Jesus had done (vv.45-46). The Jewish leaders called a meeting of the council, which in all likelihood refers to the Sanhedrin, the Jewish Supreme Court in Jerusalem. This council had jurisdiction over civil and religious matters, but under Roman rule it had been stripped of its power over life and death (cf. 18:31).

This time, it was Jesus' miraculous signs that got him into trouble (v.47). The Jewish religious leaders, who largely collaborated with the Romans, were afraid that Jesus would gather such a following that the Romans might suspect him of having started a revolutionary movement. After the death of Herod in 4 B.C., there were widespread Jewish revolts, and some of these revolts took the form of messianic movements. The aim of these revolutionaries was to overthrow the Herodians and Romans and liberate Palestine. The Romans, however, suppressed these movements, though with difficulty. Therefore, the Jewish religious leaders were afraid that if the Romans suspected Jesus of leading an uprising, they would violently intervene and destroy the temple – the power base of the Jewish leaders (v.48). Therefore, at the final summit a resolution was passed that Jesus must die (v.53; cf. v.57).

The statement of Caiaphas the high priest in verse 50 is ironic. Without intending to, he prophesies that Jesus will die to save the Jewish nation – in fact, the entire world (vv.51-52). The gathering together of the dispersed people of God into one reminds us of John 10, where the good shepherd says he will call his sheep out of Judaism as well as from among the Gentiles in order to form one flock under one shepherd. The evil plan of 'the Jews' to sacrifice Jesus in order to safeguard their own position, ironically coincides with Jesus' own mission to give his life for the life of the world (cf. 3:16-17; 6:51; 10:11).

Learning of the plot to kill him, Jesus avoids any public appearances among 'the Jews'. Instead, he and his disciples withdraw to an isolated place (v.54; cf. Jesus' taking refuge across the Jordan in 10:40 after a previous attempt of 'the Jews' to kill him).

Reflection

Jesus' apparent tardiness in responding, and the consequent death of Lazarus, may appear to be shocking and even cruel, but within John's theological framework it would make sense. For John presents Jesus as one who is in control of things. Moreover, Jesus' delay will even precipitate a greater miracle – Lazarus has died, so a mere healing will not do, he must be resurrected. Thus, Lazarus' death creates the opportunity for Jesus to demonstrate that he is the resurrection and the life – something a mere illness would not have accomplished. In turn, this demonstration of his life-giving power, shown in practice in the resurrection of Lazarus, has as purpose to evoke belief (v.15). This may prompt us to wonder whether Jesus uses similar methods today. Does he sometimes delay and let the situation worsen in order to perform a 'greater' miracle? Does he perhaps allow or even cause delays to test our reactions and faith? Do these delays lead to a 'greater' belief-response or to implicit complaints, such as, 'Lord, if you had acted earlier, this or that would not have happened'?

Since the Enlightenment, especially in the West, we have developed a worldview based on reason and objectivity (although postmodernity has provided an important corrective). Consequently, miracles, of which the resurrection of a dead person may be the pinnacle, have caused problems or raised questions. Do miracles have a place within our worldview or do we try to explain them away? Do we say that Lazarus was in a comatose state, perhaps deadly ill but not clinically dead? For John, it is clear that Lazarus had died in every sense of the word – he had been buried for four days and there was a noticeable decay of his body (v.39). Jesus' action, then, was not a resuscitation of a deadly ill Lazarus but the resurrection of a dead person whose body was already rotting!

The murderous and evil intentions of 'the Jews', and Caiaphas' ironical prophecy, actually coincide with Jesus' salvific mission for the world. Or, to put it differently, the destructive plans of 'the Jews' were used by God to accomplish his beneficial purposes for humankind. In Romans 8:28, Paul draws a similar conclusion, 'We know that all things work together for good for those who love God'. God is so creative that he can even use evil purposes for his own end, and produce good out of any situation. God is in control of history and no one can thwart his plans, as Job also concluded at the end of his trial: 'I know that you can do all things, and that no purpose of yours can be thwarted' (Job 42:2). This should encourage us to a greater trust in God for the situations that we are and will be facing.

The Last Phase of Jesus' Public Ministry (11:55-12:50)

The final response of 'the Jews' has been firmly fixed in 11:45-53: Jesus must die. Hence, John 12, which describes the last phase of Jesus' public ministry, does not discuss Jesus' murderous opponents much further. Instead, the chapter gives special attention to a group (which we treat as a single character) that had manifested itself primarily in John 6-7 but had remained somewhat ambiguous: the crowd. At the end of this section, we shall evaluate the way the crowd (which does not appear any more in John's Gospel beyond chapter 12) responded to Jesus.

This passage has been divided into seven sections: (i) the approach of the last Passover (11:55-57); (ii) Mary's devotion and Judas' defection (12:1-8); (iii) the 'devotion' of the crowd (12:9-19); (iv) life through death (12:20-26); (v) cosmic judgement and reconciliation (12:27-36a); (vi) the closed minds and fearful hearts of the crowd (12:36b-43); (vii) Jesus' public farewell (12:44-50).

The Approach of the Last Passover (11:55-57)

The third (and final) Passover festival that John records is approaching (v.55) – two previous Passover feasts were mentioned in 2:13, 23 and 6:4. There must have been quite a commotion about Jesus because people, as they came to the temple, were discussing whether or not he would come to the feast (v.56). Apparently, the Jewish leaders had made a public announcement that there was a warrant for Jesus' arrest and anyone who knew his whereabouts were to inform them (v.57). On many previous occasions, the authorities had attempted to arrest Jesus (7:30, 32, 44; 8:20; 10:39) but they had not succeeded because Jesus' time had not yet come.

Mary's Devotion and Judas' Defection (12:1-8)

Not long after the raising of Lazarus, Jesus was back in Lazarus' home for a special thanksgiving dinner (vv.1-2). During this dinner, we encounter two characters and two attitudes: the devotion of Mary and the beginning of Judas' defection.

While Mary's attitude was not entirely positive in 11:28-33a, 12:3 shows her in a different light altogether. Mary is depicted as one who is totally devoted to Jesus. The pound of costly perfume made of pure nard was worth a year's wages according to Judas' estimation, since a labourer earned about one denarius per day (vv.4-5). Besides, the normal practice was to anoint one's head and wash one's feet, but Mary anoints Jesus' feet. Her act of wiping Jesus' feet with her hair would certainly have raised a few eyebrows since a respectable woman was not supposed to have her hair loose in public. For Mary, however, devotion was more important than convention. Scholars contend that Mary's act of anointing Jesus prefigures his death and anticipates Nicodemus' act of embalming Jesus' body for his burial in 19:39-40. Mary had apparently understood that Jesus would die soon because she had intended the perfume for his burial (v.7). Nevertheless, we cannot assume that she had grasped the theological significance of Jesus' death; she may simply have heard of the decision of the Jewish council (11:45-53), and understood the seriousness of the threat to Jesus' life.

In contrast to Mary's devotion, this episode also records the early stages of Judas' defection. Although we have known since 6:70-71 that Judas is going to betray Jesus, it is only in John 12-13 that the character, role and status of Judas emerge. John first reminds his readers that Judas will betray Jesus (v.4) and then tells us that Judas is a thief (v.6). As such, Judas was not really concerned about the 'waste' of expensive perfume or about the poor. As the treasurer, he would rather have received the large sum of money that the perfume would have fetched, so that he could keep a part for himself (v.6). The word for 'thief' in John's Gospel occurs only here and in chapter 10 (10:1, 8, 10), and perhaps John intends a deliberate echo since the mention of Judas as a thief is not recorded in the Synoptics or elsewhere. In this case, Judas is portrayed as a false shepherd and put on the same side as 'the Jews', whose intention is to destroy and kill (cf. 10:10).

Jesus' statement in verse 8 should not lead us to think that he did not care about the poor (notice they kept a common purse for the welfare of the poor [vv.5-6; cf. 13:29]). Instead, it indicates that Jesus should be given priority over others. He would be with them just a little longer and therefore, Mary's gesture was entirely appropriate. For they would always have opportunity to show their concern for the poor.

The 'Devotion' of the Crowd (12:9-19)

In this episode, John narrates Jesus' so-called 'triumphal entry into Jerusalem', and brings back on the stage the crowd, to which John 6-7 introduced us. In John 6, the crowd showed initial signs of 'following' Jesus, but it turned out that they were in pursuit of a free lunch rather than on a true spiritual quest. In John 7, the crowd was divided and unable to make up its mind about Jesus. Here, in John 12, the true attitude of the crowd will become clear. John's introduction of the crowd as 'the great crowd of the Jews' (v.9), however, is not promising. Is he indicating that the crowd will eventually side with 'the Jews'?

It is immediately apparent that the crowd remains focused on the spectacular: they have come primarily to see the controversial Jesus but also hoping to get a glimpse of the resurrected Lazarus (v.9). The authorities are afraid that if the crowd sees Lazarus it will lead to belief in Jesus – since many of their own are believing in Jesus for this reason (cf. 11:45) – therefore they plan to kill Lazarus as well (vv.10-11). When the crowd hears that Jesus is approaching Jerusalem, they meet him with palm branches and hail him as the long-awaited messianic king: 'Hosanna! Blessed is the one who comes in the name of the Lord – the king of Israel' (vv.12-13). Apparently, the crowd gives Jesus such a rousing welcome Jesus because of the raising of Lazarus (vv.9, 17-18).

The chant with which the crowd greets Jesus in verse 13 partially comes from Psalm 118:25-26 with the added phrase 'the king of Israel', which is a reference to the Davidic Messiah. This makes clear that the crowd expects Jesus to be a kind of nationalistic messianic leader who will liberate them from Roman oppression. Jesus' action in verses 14-15, however, serves to correct the crowd's misunderstanding. By riding on a young donkey, Jesus acts out the promise of Zechariah 9:9, which depicts the coming king to be gentle and riding on an ass. More importantly, Zechariah 9:10 depicts this king as one who will destroy Israel's war tools (including the war horse) and establish peace. Hence, the devotion and expectations of the crowd seem rather misplaced: Jesus' action reveals that he is a gentle shepherd-messiah rather than a warrior-messiah. On another occasion, the crowd had misunderstood Jesus similarly, and unsuccessfully attempted to make him king (6:14-15).

John mentions in an aside (v.16) that the disciples did not understand Jesus' action at that time; this understanding only came when they were reminded of it after his glorification. The Greek has the passive form 'to be reminded' rather than the active 'to remember', which implies that an agent was involved in the reminding. In the light of the coming Spirit-Paraclete who will be engaged in teaching and reminding the disciples (14:26; 16:7, 13), I suggest that the disciples were reminded of Jesus' action and were able to understand its significance precisely because of the Spirit-Paraclete (cf. our interpretation of 2:17, 22).

Life through Death (12:20-26)

The statement of the Pharisees in verse 19 that the world is following Jesus, ironically, finds its realization in verses 20-21. John tells us that some Greeks, or Gentiles, who had come for the Passover festival, came in search of Jesus (vv.20-21), probably because they had heard stories about him. When this is reported to Jesus, he understands it as the arrival of the hour of his glorification, i.e., the hour of his coming death and departure from this world (v.23). Jesus may well have had in mind the previous conversation with 'the Jews' in 7:32-36 – the only other passage where the word 'Greeks' or 'Gentiles' occurs. There Jesus had announced to 'the Jews' that his departure from this world was imminent (7:33-34), to which 'the Jews' replied sarcastically that surely he was not going into the Diaspora to teach the Gentiles (7:35). Ironically, the mockery of 'the Jews' now appears to be fulfilled; but, instead of Jesus going into the Diaspora to teach the Gentiles, they come to him.

Verses 24-25 encapsulate one of Jesus' most important lessons: *the principle of life through death*. Drawing from a natural principle, Jesus derives a spiritual one. A farmer plants a kernel or seed with the intention that it bears fruit, but it can only do so if it 'dies', i.e., if it bursts open and allows the life that it potentially has, to sprout. At a spiritual level, a similar principle is in operation. This is explained to us in verse 25 through the use of two different Greek words for life: *psuchē* and *zōē*, which refer to the physical, temporal life and the divine, eternal life respectively. A more literal translation of verse 25 would go as follows: 'those who love their *psuchē* lose it, but those who "hate" their *psuchē* in this world will keep it for (eternal) *zōē*.' To phrase it differently, if people treasure their life in the here and now above all else, they will eventually lose it, but if they are prepared to deny this life and let it be used by God they will gain eternal life. This denial calls for people to sow their earthly life and allow it to die: if they live for Jesus/God during their earthly existence rather than for their own pleasure, then their life will bear much fruit, everlasting fruit (v.24; 4:36; 15:16).

Obviously, Jesus was also speaking about his own life. He had come to this world to give his own life (*psuchē*) in order to give eternal life (*zōē*) to the world (6:51; 10:11, 15). Jesus did not hold on to his own life; it was meant to be 'sown' into the soil called 'the world' so that through his death, life might come to this world – the everlasting, divine, abundant life that satisfies all thirst and hunger. The allusion to Jesus' imminent death on the cross is clear: the Seed is sown, dies and releases life ultimately on the cross.

In verse 26, Jesus clarifies that whoever serves him must follow him, and that wherever he is, his servant will also be found. This implies that the 'sowing' of one's life and the way of the cross is also the believer's way.

Cosmic Judgement and Reconciliation (12:27-36a)

Verse 27 testifies to Jesus' acute mental or spiritual agitation, where he battles the temptation to avoid this hour of impending death, for he knows that this hour is the very reason for his coming. The hour of Jesus' death is, at the same time, the hour of Jesus' glorification (v.23), and is closely tied to the glorification of the Father (v.28a). In fact, when the Son is glorified, so is the Father, and vice versa (cf. 13:31-32; 17:1, 4-5). To glorify someone means to enhance someone's status or reputation by giving praise, honour, power, and so on. In verse 30, Jesus explains that the (Father's) voice which the crowd had heard (vv.28-29), had come not for his sake (as if his self-esteem needed boosting), but for the sake of the crowd (cf. 11:41-42).

Now that his hour is close at hand, Jesus announces the impending judgement and conquest of the world and its ruler (v.31; cf. 16:11, 32-33). The emphatic repetition of 'now' indicates the imminence of this event: '*Now* is the judgement of this world; *now* the ruler of this world will be thrown out.' Although John's Gospel, unlike the Synoptics, does not record any exorcisms, John evidences one major exorcism, namely, the 'exorcism' of the devil from his domain, i.e., the world.

The imminent cosmic defeat in verse 31 is immediately followed by the picture of cosmic restoration in verse 32: 'when I am lifted up from the earth, I will draw all people to myself.' The lifting up of Jesus refers to his crucifixion (v.33; cf. 3:14; 8:28), but the Greek word for 'to lift up' can also mean 'to exalt'. Using the literary technique of double entendre, John extends the meaning of the cross: the cross is not merely the place where Jesus dies but also where Jesus is glorified. The proximity of verses 31 and 32 indicates that both aspects – the judgement of the devil and the liberation of humankind – happen at the cross. For on the cross Jesus ultimately gives his life for the life of the world and deals with sin and the devil (cf. 3:14-15; 6:51; 12:24; 19:30).

It would be incorrect to take verse 32 as a picture of universal salvation, as if Jesus' death will automatically save everyone. From a wider reading of John's Gospel, it becomes clear that an individual response is needed in order to appropriate the divine benefits flowing from Jesus' death. That is, God's initiative of reconciling or 'drawing' the world to himself in Christ needs a human response if that cosmic reconciliation is to be appropriated at a personal level. Simply put, Jesus died for all so that all *who respond* may have life. Salvation is available to all – not automatically but to all *who believe*.

When Jesus announces his impending, necessary death, the crowd is scandalized (v.34). Perhaps having texts such as Psalms 89:3-4, 35-36; 110:4; Isaiah 9:6-7 and Daniel 7:13-14 in mind, they have no concept of a crucified messiah (although a later Jewish writing speaks of a dying messiah [4 *Ezra* 7:29]) and voice their doubts. In reply, Jesus urges the crowd in verses 35-36 to try to understand him and his mission. Jesus knows that the time is short because he will be around for just a little longer. So, while he – the light – is still around, he implores people to believe in him lest the darkness overtake them. Jesus' exhortation reminds us of the Prologue, where John asserts that the life-giving light shines in the darkness and the darkness could not grasp it (1:5). The flip side, it appears, is that those who do not walk, i.e., believe, in this light, will be grasped by the darkness (cf. 8:12; 11:9-10).

The Closed Minds and Fearful Hearts of the Crowd (12:36b-43)

Jesus finally withdraws and keeps himself hidden from the crowd (v.36b). Despite Jesus' admonitions and miraculous signs, the crowd as 'crowd' did not believe in him (v.37). Nevertheless, individual persons from the crowd may have believed in him (cf. 7:31; 10:42). The unbelief of the crowd fulfils an Old Testament prophecy in Isaiah 53:1, which speaks of the messianic Servant who is rejected (v.38). Moreover, in verses 39-40, John asserts that the reason for the crowd's unbelief can be found in the adapted quotation from Isaiah 6:10:

> And for this reason they were unable to believe, because Isaiah also said:
> 'He has blinded their eyes
> and
> he has hardened their heart
> so that they may not see with their eyes
> and may not understand with their heart
> and may not turn
> and (lest) I will heal them.'

The parallel expressions 'to blind the eyes' and 'to harden the heart' should be taken figuratively, denoting 'to cause to not understand' or 'to cause the mind to be closed'; and 'to turn' means 'to change', 'to repent'. Therefore, it would appear that the closed minds of people prevent understanding and repentance, and hinder God's 'healing', i.e., restoration or salvation.

The obvious difficulty is to explain who is responsible for the 'blinding of eyes' and 'hardening of hearts'. The answer, it would appear, is God. If God willingly or purposely closes people's minds and hence prevents belief, how can Jesus be so critical of people's attitude? A look at Isaiah 6:9-10 shows us what John might have in mind. God forewarned Isaiah that the people of Israel would reject his message, causing them to become dull in understanding. Likewise, Jesus' teaching will further close the minds of those who reject it and prevent understanding and possible belief. Verses 39-40, then, refer to the resultant condition or inevitable consequence of rejecting Jesus, rather than the result of divine predestination. By rejecting Jesus and his message a person remains blind, or, is plunged further into darkness (cf.

9:39-41). Thus, the main (and perhaps only) reason for people's unbelief appears to be found in people themselves (cf. 3:19-20).

In verse 42, John clarifies that despite the general unbelief, there are those who believe in Jesus. In fact, many, even of the Jewish leaders, 'believe' in Jesus, but a fear of being expelled from the synagogue prevents them from (publicly) confessing their belief (see also the excursus 'The Fear of the Jews' in 7:13). Moreover, as verse 43 explains, these 'secret believers' seem to be more concerned with winning human praise or recognition than God's. Such an attitude, as Jesus pointed out in 5:44, serves as an obstacle to faith. In John's final evaluation, then, this kind of belief is inadequate.

Jesus' Public Farewell (12:44-50)

Jesus, having reached the end of his public ministry, reiterates the essence of his mission and teaching. Based on the unity of the Father and the Son, Jesus says that if one sees and believes in him, one sees and believes in God himself (vv.44-45; cf. 1:18). Jesus is the means of access to God, the mediator between God and humankind (cf. 1:51). He has come into the world as the life-giving light so that people who believe in him can escape from the darkness they are in (v.46; cf. 1:4-5, 9; 8:12).

Concerning the purpose of his coming, Jesus reiterates that he has not come to judge the world but to save it (v.47; cf. 3:17). John sees judgement as something that is primarily self-inflicted: when one rejects Jesus and his teaching one precipitates judgement on oneself (cf. 3:18). On the last day, this very word/teaching that has been rejected will judge the person (v.48). This reminds us of 5:45-47, where Jesus said that if people reject the words of Moses, which witness to Jesus, Moses will in fact become their accuser.

Jesus stresses again that he does not act on his own but on behalf of his Father. Jesus has simply spoken God's words, which are words of eternal life (vv.49-50; cf. 3:34-36; 6:63). After Jesus has delivered his public 'farewell' speech, he will turn to his disciples for a private farewell, which is recorded in John 13-17.

Reflection

In this final episode of Jesus' public ministry, John draws our attention to four responses to Jesus: those of Mary, Judas, the crowd and the 'secret believers'. Mary's devotion to Jesus is striking: she humbly anoints Jesus' feet with a costly perfume, so that the fragrance of the perfume filled the house. Does our devotion to Jesus involve such affection, dedication and sacrifice? Does it spread a pleasing fragrance? In contrast to Mary's devotion, the signs of Judas' imminent defection are sad. One of Jesus' closest friends for over three years, who turns out to be a thief, has started on a road that will ultimately lead to the betrayal of Jesus and his own destruction. May we take heed and not presume that this will not happen to us or to our church (cf. 1 Corinthians 10:12; 16:13).

In the final evaluation, the crowd's attitude is disappointing. The crowd shows a misplaced devotion because it has misunderstood the nature of Jesus' mission. The crowd then continues in this misunderstanding, eventually leading to unbelief because its people are 'blind'. Although some people emerge from the crowd as believers, the crowd as a group, like 'the Jews', remains stuck in the darkness and chooses to respond with unbelief. John had already indicated that the crowd would side with 'the Jews' through the subtle introduction 'the great crowd of the Jews' (v.9).

John is also critical of those who remain 'secret believers', afraid to confess their belief publicly. For John, the fear of people and the threat of what they might do, no matter how real, should not keep believers from making a public confession of faith (cf. 15:18-16:4a). If we are primarily concerned with what people might say or think about our faith, we are at risk of putting people before God. Instead, let us be concerned with God's glory and how we can please him.

Jesus' comment, 'You always have the poor with you', sadly proves true. The World Bank estimates that 1.1 billion people live in extreme poverty today (i.e., people with an income of less than $1 a day), and more than 20,000 people die each day because of poverty. Although Asia leads in numbers, Africa has the largest proportion of poor people (almost 50% of its population). But even so-called 'moderate' poverty needs our attention. For example, in India, a country with over one billion people, 40% of the population survives on less than $1 a day, but another 40% lives on $1 to $2 a day. Despite India's recent economic growth, it remains one of the poorest countries in Asia.

Bureaucracy, corruption, lack of education, civil wars, natural disasters, and diseases like malaria and AIDS across Asia and Africa, seriously hamper efforts to overcome poverty. However, these factors should not be used as an excuse for the majority (or western) world, with all its wealth and resources, not to do their utmost to alleviate poverty in the non-western world. Nelson Mandela once said, 'Overcoming poverty is not a gesture of charity but an act of justice.' The United Nations Millennium Project (headed up by leading economist Jeffrey Sachs) is such an initiative, aiming to halve extreme poverty in the world by 2015. Another ongoing campaign is that of the Jubilee Movement International to cancel the debts of developing countries to the World Bank and IMF. Do we as Christians participate in such initiatives or perhaps start similar ones in order to eradicate poverty? In Hinduism, for instance, there is no incentive to reduce poverty in society. Elimination of structural oppression or disinterested benevolence are foreign concepts to Hinduism. For example, to give money to a beggar is considered a good deed – it improves the karma of the giver – but to help him out of the gutter is forbidden because either it makes the benefactor impure or it may ruin the beggar's chances of improving his karma.

The principle of life through death is not merely controversial but challenging. If we truly want to follow Jesus, we must take the path that he does, which is the way of servanthood and essentially the way of the cross. It follows that we must 'sow' our lives in the soil that is this world and die to self so that (to change the image) the living water in us may burst forth to quench the spiritual thirst of people. In 12:24-25, Jesus beautifully summarizes the teachings he set out during his ministry: the participation of believers in the harvest in John 4; the giving of his life for the life of the world in John 6; the believer as a secondary source of living water in John 7; and the shepherd who lays down his life for the sheep in John 10. In 12:24-25, what we have is essentially the Johannine version of the Synoptic principle 'to deny yourself and pick up your cross' (Mark 8:34; Matthew 16:24; Luke 9:23). Someone succinctly defined this *principle as the situation in which God's will and our will cross each other, and where we decide to give up our will in order to do God's will. This sowing of self and dying in order to bear fruit implies that we must be willing to let go of our dreams, desires, ambitions and plans, if these have the potential to become obstacles to God's purposes and the bringing forth of fruit.*

John's account of Jesus' public ministry in chapters 1-12 essentially seeks to convey the fact that in Jesus is life (1:4) and that people will be divided in their responses towards this Jesus (1:10-13). In John 5-12 especially, we saw the growing opposition towards Jesus, eventually leading to the call for his death. But, despite the evil schemes of Jesus' opponents, under the influence of the devil (8:44), Jesus is in control of things. He knows that his mission is to die, for ultimately life is found in or through death. Besides, it is not the devil and 'the Jews' who take Jesus' life, since no one can take it from him; he has the God-given authority to lay down his life and to pick it up again as he pleases (10:18). This perspective that John gives us, should encourage us. Jesus is in control of the world, even though, from a human perspective, things may seem bleak at times. The media, by and large, communicates negative rather than positive news. Endless reports of war, conflict, corruption, scandals, murder, rape, natural disasters, ungodliness, and so on, seem to be common to everyday life. Perhaps we recall another 'I am' saying of Jesus, borrowed from the last book of the bible but standing in the same tradition as John's Gospel: 'I am the Alpha and the Omega, the first and the last, the beginning and the end' (Revelation 22:13). It will work out all right, it really will because we know who holds everything together and safely guides us towards the end.

Jesus' Private Ministry (13:1-17:26)

John 1-12 or the so-called Book of Signs, describing Jesus' three-year public ministry, has ended, and we come to the Book of Glory or John 13-20. This section narrates Jesus' private teachings to his disciples, as well as Jesus' passion and resurrection. It is important to observe how John uses narrative time in his Gospel. While the first part of the Gospel (chapters 1-12) covers just over three years of Jesus' ministry, the second half (chapters 13-20) only accounts for a few days. In fact, the events of John 13-19 take place over twenty-four hours: from just before the Passover, possibly Thursday evening (13:1, 30), through the day of Preparation for the Passover, i.e., Friday (18:28 [morning]; 19:14 [noon]), to the start of the Sabbath on Friday evening (19:31, 42). The effect this has on the reader is one of heightened expectation; the slowing down in time indicates the approach of the climax.

As for the literary form of John 13-17, there are similarities to the symposium tradition in Graeco-Roman literature, where after a formal banquet, a symposium, i.e., a conference or discussion on a particular subject, took place (see Plato's *Symposium*). We could therefore refer to John 14-16 as Jesus' 'after-dinner speech'. However, the genre that best fits John 13-17 is the so-called 'farewell discourse' or 'testament', which is a common category in classical, biblical and extra-biblical literature. When facing imminent death, a leader or hero has a last meal with close friends or family, followed by a final address to his private audience.

The farewell discourse allows the departing person to hand over final teachings and instructions. Plato's *Phaedo*, for example, narrates the story of Socrates' death and his final discussion with his students. The Old Testament contains several examples of farewell discourses: in Genesis 48-49, Jacob addresses his sons; the entire book of Deuteronomy, but especially chapters 31-34, comprises Moses' farewell discourse to Israel; and king David speaks to an assembly in 1 Chronicles 28-29. In extra-biblical material, the *Testaments of the Twelve Patriarchs*, which allegedly narrates the last words of Jacob's twelve sons, is a good example.

The structure of John 13-17 also follows that of a classic farewell discourse: (i) Jesus' final meal with his twelve disciples (13:1-30); (ii) Jesus' farewell discourses (13:31-17:26), consisting of his final teachings (13:31-16:33) and a final prayer (17:1-26).

The Final Meal (13:1-30)

The final meal that Jesus has with his twelve disciples can be divided into three parts: (i) the footwashing (13:1-11); (ii) the explanation of the footwashing (13:12-20); (iii) the foretelling of the betrayal of Jesus (13:21-30). Some scholars prefer that verses 31-38 are part of this passage, but I think this is inappropriate. The short phrase 'And it was night' in verse 30 denotes a sharp and abrupt demarcation; Judas has left the intimate circle of Jesus' disciples, and from 13:31 on Jesus starts to instruct his remaining, eleven disciples. It would have been unfitting for Jesus to teach further on discipleship while a defector was around; Judas had to leave the scene before Jesus could continue.

The Footwashing (13:1-11)

The 'hour' in verse 1 is the hour of Jesus' glorification (cf. 12:23), referring to the process of Jesus' death-resurrection-ascension, which has been set in motion. Verse 1 informs us of Jesus' imminent return to his Father, which would mark the last stage of Jesus' V-journey (see the Prologue for Jesus' so-called 'V-journey').

The object of Jesus' love, referred to as 'his own who were in the world', is unclear (v.1). 'His own' may refer to Jesus' sheep, i.e., those who believe in him (10:3-4), with a specific reference to his twelve disciples. The difficulty with this, however, is that Judas is still present, while, it later turns out, he is not one of Jesus' sheep. More likely, it is a general reference to people in the world, as John has already mentioned in 1:11, 'He came to what was his own [the world] but his own people did not accept him'. In this case, Judas' presence can be readily explained, in that Jesus also loves Judas to the end (cf. Jesus' gesture to Judas in v.26). 'To the end' may denote both duration and completeness/perfection. Hence, Jesus loves the people in the world continually and completely – a love to which the cross testifies (cf. 3:16).

The narrator's aside in verse 2 serves to remind the reader that Judas is under the control of the devil, who has set him up to betray Jesus (cf. 6:70-71; 12:4). However, there is an immediate assurance in verse 3 that Jesus is in control, knowing that the Father has given everything into his hands (cf. 3:35). Secure in this knowledge, Jesus stands up during supper, takes off his robe, and ties a towel around his waist (v.4). The verb 'to take off' is the same one that is used in John 10 to indicate the laying down of the good shepherd's life. In the laying down of Jesus' robe, John probably intends a deliberate allusion to the cross as the place where Jesus will lay down his life (see also v.12 below).

The Greek expression *podas niptō*, used six times in verses 5-14, is another example of Johannine ambiguity or double entendre (see the section 'Characteristics' in the Introduction). Taken literally, it means 'to wash the feet' with the intention of showing hospitality, but figuratively it could mean 'to perform humble duties on behalf of someone'. This element of servanthood in Jesus' action will be elucidated in 13:12-20.

When it is Peter's turn to have his feet washed by Jesus, he questions the propriety of his master's action (v.6). But, again we see that it is a lack of knowledge/insight which prevents proper understanding of what Jesus is doing (v.7). Verse 7b, 'but you will know/understand later', may hint at the Spirit's reminding the disciples, after Easter, of the significance of Jesus' words (cf. 14:26 and the commentary on 2:17, 22; 12:16). It appears, therefore, that the disciples continue to misunderstand Jesus, and only with the coming of the Spirit-Paraclete their understanding will progress.

In verse 8b, Jesus asserts to Peter that unless he has washed his feet, he will have no part with Jesus. Peter then over-reacts, almost asking Jesus for an entire bath (v.9), and confirming that he has misunderstood Jesus. While Peter reasons at an earthly/material level, Jesus is speaking of a spiritual washing (cf. v.10). The point Jesus is trying to make is that unless he cleanses people spiritually they cannot be in a relationship with him.

The footwashing most likely points to or foreshadows Jesus' death, and signifies the disciples' spiritual cleansing, but this cleansing is not entirely in the future. In verse 10, Jesus assures Peter that he is already completely clean except for his feet (cf. 15:3). This implies that Peter has been cleansed and is in a saving relationship with Jesus, but the cleansing needs completion, this salvific relationship still needs securing – Jesus still has to die for Peter (and the others) on the cross. Thus, the completion of the disciples' cleansing and the securing of their salvation is only possible after the cross – with the giving of the Spirit (see 20:22).

However, not every one of the twelve disciples is clean, says Jesus, for he knows who will betray him (vv.10b-11). This shows, once again, Jesus' knowledge of people (cf. 2:24-25). In John, Jesus' knowledge/insight stands in sharp contrast to the lack of knowledge of the disciples and other people.

The Footwashing Explained (13:12-20)

In the 'laying down' of his robe in verse 4, and the 'taking up' of his robe here in verse 12 there are unmistakeable allusions to the laying down and taking up of his life in 10:17-18. Thus, the whole footwashing scene is acting out Jesus' ability to lay down and pick up his life at will. At the same time, it foreshadows the cross and the resurrection where Jesus will ultimately lay down and pick up his life.

There is more to Jesus' act than symbolism, as verses 13-16 clarify. The footwashing scene is also a demonstration of Jesus' humility and servanthood, and serves as an example for his disciples to follow. Jesus is teaching his disciples that if he as a person of higher status can show humility and serve them, then they must do likewise, for each other. Footwashing, as an act of hospitality, was normally done by servants and not by the host himself. But here, the master, Jesus, becomes the disciples' servant, demonstrating that servanthood is a necessary expression of discipleship. Jesus regards acts of service to others as honourable, whereas the society of that time considered them a sign of weakness. Even Jesus' laying down his life at the cross is an act of humility and servanthood, for through that act he provides eternal life, forgiveness of sins and reconciliation with God for humankind. The cross was a symbol of shame and derision, but Jesus subverts this symbolism, turning the cross into a symbol of glory and service.

Verse 17 reiterates that people need to know/understand what Jesus/God demands from them, before they can carry it out (cf. v.12). In verse 18a, Jesus exhibits *his* knowledge: he knows whom he has chosen/selected. Comparable to the idea of Jesus' and the Father's 'drawing' people (6:44; 12:32), and Jesus' 'choosing' people (6:70; 13:18; 15:16, 19), this remark has overtones of divine election (see also the commentary on 12:32). But rather than seeing this as a case for predestination, I suggest that John seeks to emphasize the priority of divine initiative over human response.

For it is God who sent his son into the world to save it; it is Jesus who came to provide eternal life and introduce people to the Father; it is the Spirit who assists people to gain insight into Jesus' teaching so that they can respond adequately to Jesus.

Jesus, in verse 18b, refers again to Judas' imminent betrayal. His words literally translate, 'The one who eats my bread has lifted his heel against me', but a freer translation that perhaps captures the meaning better would be, 'The one with whom I shared a close relationship has turned against me'. Jesus speaks of this event as a fulfilment of Psalm 41:9, where David speaks of the betrayal of an intimate friend whom he trusted and had table-fellowship with. In 13:21-30, a similar scene will be acted out between Jesus and Judas. Jesus, it appears, does not expect his disciples to grasp it now, but when they do understand the significance, in retrospect, it should cause them to believe that he is the manifestation of God on earth – 'so that you may believe that "I Am"' (v.19). The relationship of Jesus and his Father is in fact so intimate that to receive Jesus is to receive the Father himself (v.20).

Jesus Foretells His Betrayal (13:21-30)

Virtually every translation renders verse 21 as 'Jesus was troubled in spirit', indicating that Jesus was in acute mental and emotional distress at the thought of his betrayal. However, for two reasons I contend that we have a reference here to Jesus' being stirred up by the divine Spirit. First, the Greek syntax demands such a translation: there is no preposition 'in', only a passive verb, followed by a so-called 'instrumental dative' which refers to the agent of the action; hence, Jesus was stirred up by the Spirit (cf. 11:33). Second, we know that the Spirit upon Jesus provided him with revelatory wisdom, understanding and liberating power (see the commentary on 1:32 and 3:34). Hence, it is the Spirit who reveals to Jesus the identity of the betrayer. This understanding of the text actually enhances the translations, in that *the Spirit* stirs Jesus up emotionally by revealing to him the identity of the betrayer.

In verse 23, we have the first reference to 'the disciple whom Jesus loved', often referred to as the Beloved Disciple. His intimate relationship with Jesus becomes apparent when we read that the Beloved Disciple was reclining 'in the bosom of Jesus'. There is a clear echo of 1:18 where it says that Jesus is 'in the bosom of the Father'. The identity of the Beloved Disciple is much debated. Many have suggested it is John, the son of Zebedee and possibly the author; others argue that the Beloved Disciple is an idealized character who exemplifies the model disciple. I contend that the Beloved Disciple is a real historical character, one of the Twelve, but not the author. It is possible that the author has 'idealized' this person to function as an example of an ideal witness/disciple (cf. the section 'Author' in the Introduction).

Peter prompts the Beloved Disciple to ask Jesus about the identity of the betrayer (vv.24-25). Besides serving to identify Judas as the betrayer, Jesus' gesture of sharing bread in verse 26 may also symbolize a last effort to restore fellowship. Despite knowing that Judas would betray him, Jesus still reaches out to give him a last chance to be reconciled. Verse 1 mentioned that Jesus loves people to the end, and indeed, we see that Jesus loves Judas until the very 'end', when Satan enters into Judas after he takes the piece of bread (v.27). Judas' 'end' is now secured: not only does the devil prompt Judas (v.2) but also indwells him (v.27), thus Judas has become a devil (6:70-71; cf. 8:44). Judas, indwelled by the devil, stands in sharp contrast to the disciples, who are indwelled by the Father and Son (as we shall see in 14:23). Judas has become a defector, a non-disciple; in fact, he has become a disciple of Satan.

Verses 28-29 stress the disciples' lack of understanding; they neither grasp the symbolism of Jesus' gesture to Judas nor his words to him. Judas, however, does and leaves – literally, but also symbolically (he leaves the fellowship with Jesus) (v.30). The dramatic, abrupt sentence, 'And it was night', in verse 30 is an example of double entendre. Besides a literal reference to late evening, it also refers to a spiritual reality, namely, the darkness caused by Satan in driving Judas to his act of betrayal. Judas' being indwelled by the devil and leaving the presence of Jesus, heralds the approaching darkness that the devil has precipitated.

This passage records the tragic defection of Judas in a context that promotes aspects of discipleship. While Jesus exhorts his disciples to participate in him and to exemplify humility and service, the devil prompts Judas to defect, i.e., to demonstrate 'non-discipleship'. Many of Jesus' disciples have left him along the way (6:60-66) and now one of his closest disciples leaves, to betray Jesus. The character of Judas embodies the most negative response of all towards Jesus: defection and betrayal. Since John makes several allusions to chapter 10 in this chapter, we can rightly call Judas the black sheep of the family.

Reflection

Looking back at the entire passage, we see that the purpose of the footwashing is twofold. First, it suggests the need for some sort of spiritual cleansing – effected by Jesus' death at the cross – in order to partake in a saving relationship with Jesus (vv.1-11). Second, it exhorts the practice of humility and servanthood as an expression of discipleship in order to remain in a relationship with Jesus (vv.12-20).

John has spun a complex web of ideas to explain the concept of servanthood. First, through the unusual word choice of 'laying down' and 'taking up' his robe, John draws a parallel with Jesus' laying down and taking up his life in 10:18. Second, Jesus' teaching on servanthood, acted out in the footwashing, takes us back to 12:24-26, where Jesus spoke of the necessity for those who wish to serve him to go the way of the cross. If we combine all these thoughts we see that, for John, the way of the cross is the continual laying down or 'sowing' of one's life in servanthood. John exhorts us to develop a mindset or attitude of a servant. This has many implications for everyday life. Perhaps some of us are in positions of authority or power, for instance as pastors, teachers, managers and directors, where it is easy to think that we are exempt from servanthood. 'Far from it!', John would cry out. Positions of authority and power are not for lording it over people but are to be used as opportunities to serve those who are entrusted to us. In fact, no matter what position we are in, we should try to turn it into a position of service to others. If God himself, in Jesus, could stoop down and serve us, how much more we should serve others. Moreover, Jesus was impartial in his service – he served Peter and Judas alike.

I once heard someone preach from Philippians 2:5-11 about the concept of 'downward mobility'. Today, most of our societies are largely focused on upward mobility. People want to climb higher on the socio-economic ladder. There may be nothing wrong with such ambitions per se, but Jesus seems to set another challenge before us. John's Gospel presents the concept of downward mobility. The pre-existent Logos, who was God, left the realm above and came into this world as a human being. Then, instead of lording it over his disciples, he became their servant, kneeling before them and washing their feet. Finally, he became a servant of the entire human race when he laid down his life on a cross to provide life for the world (6:51) and to reconcile people to God (12:32). If we are serious about following Jesus, we must also take this concept of downward mobility seriously. The way of the cross is a downward path, the path of servanthood and rejection.

Judas, as a character, is a tragic example of defection and betrayal, and serves as a warning to us. Let us not become overconfident as we follow Jesus, thinking that discipleship is easy, or that Judas-like betrayal cannot happen today. The disciples are frequently shown struggling to understand Jesus' actions and teachings, for Jesus' words can be offensive and difficult or hard to take in. This can eventually become an obstacle for following Jesus, as 6:60-66 tragically narrates. The text does not clarify what went wrong with Judas and when (except for the single indication that he was a thief in 12:6), but he seems to have gradually come under the influence of Satan, until he reached the point of no return. Defection, betrayal, turning one's back on Jesus is something that happens even today – perhaps we know a person who once followed Jesus but who, for various reasons, gave up following him. Will we be able to stick to Jesus in fellowship and discipleship? Those in need of encouragement, remember 10:27-29: the good shepherd knows his sheep and if they listen to him and follow him, no one can snatch them out of his hand.

148 John 13:31-38 The New Commandment

Jesus' Farewell Discourses (13:31-17:26)

With the departure of Judas, we arrive at the farewell discourses where Jesus informs his disciples of his impending departure and teaches them about his ongoing mission that will involve them too. The farewell discourses can be divided into four speeches: (i) interactive teaching (13:31-14:31); (ii) teaching on discipleship (15:1-16:4a); (iii) final teaching (16:4b-33); (iv) Jesus' prayer (17:1-26). Speeches (i) and (iii) are interspersed with questions from the disciples, whereas speeches (ii) and (iv) are Jesus' monologues.

Interactive Teaching (13:31-14:31)

This section contains one of the interactive teaching sessions that Jesus has with his disciples, and we can structure it as follows:
    13:31-35   Jesus' teaching on the new commandment
        13:36-38   Jesus' dialogue with Peter
    14:1-4   Jesus' teaching on the way to the Father
        14:5-7   Jesus' dialogue with Thomas
        14:8-14   Jesus' dialogue with Philip
    14:15-21   Jesus' teaching on the Paraclete
        14:22-24   Jesus' dialogue with Judas (not Iscariot)
    14:25-31   Jesus concludes the session
Hence, this section contains three parts, each of which starts with a teaching from Jesus followed by an inquiry from a disciple, and a final part that presents some concluding teachings.

The New Commandment (13:31-38)

The descending darkness and Judas' exit (v.30) are also indicative of the arrival of Jesus' hour of glorification: 'Now the Son of Man has been glorified' (v.31; cf. 12:23). When John refers to Jesus' glorification, he refers to Jesus' death, resurrection and ascension. Hence, it includes Jesus' departure from this world to return to his Father. Jesus knows he must prepare his disciples for his departure, and his address to them in verse 33 reveals his pastoral attitude towards them. Verse 33 literally begins, '(little) children' but it is probably meant figuratively to express affection, so a better translation may be, 'dear friends' (cf. John's frequent use of the same address to his audience in 1 John).

After this affectionate address, Jesus reveals to his disciples the bad news that he will only be with them for a little longer, and where he goes they cannot come (v.33; cf. 7:33-34; 8:21 where Jesus said the same to 'the Jews'). Jesus then gives them a new commandment: they should love one another (v.34). The rationale for this commandment is twofold. First, the disciples should love one another because Jesus loved them (v.34). The 'just as Jesus did...so they should do' shows that the disciples should imitate Jesus (cf. 13:14-15; 17:18; 20:21). Second, the evidence of love among believers proves their status as true disciples, and has the effect of a testimony to others (v.35). This commandment is obviously important because Jesus repeats it in 15:12, 17; and John frequently stresses it in his Epistles (1 John 3:11, 23; 4:7, 11-12; 2 John 5). Thus, besides humility and servanthood (see 13:1-20), Jesus emphasizes another important aspect or characteristic of discipleship, namely, a concrete love for one another.

The disciples fail to understand Jesus' statement in verse 33 about his departure, and Peter represents their incomprehension here (v.36a). Earlier, 'the Jews' had also misunderstood Jesus when he said he is leaving (7:35-36; 8:22), because they were 'from below', i.e., they belonged to the world and its ruler the devil (8:23, 44). Though the disciples belonged to Jesus, they often think 'from below'. That Peter only reacts to what Jesus said in verse 33 and not to what he said in verses 34-35 probably indicates his shock at the news of Jesus' departure – it is quite likely that he has totally missed the giving of the new commandment.

Jesus' reply to Peter that where he is going Peter can only follow later (v.36b) must have seemed very enigmatic. The careful reader, however, may observe that Jesus refers to the way of the cross, where Peter cannot yet follow. That is, Peter is not yet ready to follow Jesus on that path. However, Jesus foretells that 'later', i.e., after the resurrection and after Peter's reinstatement, Peter will follow him on that same road (cf. 21:18-19). Peter, however, claims to be ready to demonstrate the highest principle of loyalty and discipleship, namely, to lay down his life for Jesus (v.37; cf. 10:11-18; 15:13). Jesus then painfully points out that Peter is not yet the disciple he thinks he is: Peter will deny/disown Jesus three times (v.38).

In the light of the principle stated in 12:24-25, Peter must learn, through painful experience, that he is not yet prepared to let go of his own life (*psuchē*) in order to keep/gain eternal life (*zōē*). Rather than affirming his discipleship by giving up his life, Peter will deny his discipleship by disowning his master. Peter will face a time of becoming a non-disciple, a defector, although, unlike Judas, Peter's defection will be temporary. Peter's threefold denial of Jesus will be matched by Jesus' threefold affirmation of Peter in 21:15-17. Then, and only then, Peter will understand and be ready to truly follow Jesus.

Reflection

The method of teaching through interaction, seen in 13:31-38 but also in 14:1-31 and elsewhere in Jesus' ministry, has proved to be valuable across time and cultures. Often, students' questions give a teacher the necessary feedback to check whether his teaching has been correctly understood, and, if not, to provide further explanation. Modern theories of communication all confirm that communication is a two-way street, i.e., communication is only successful when the receiver has given feedback to the sender and the sender has confirmed that the message has been correctly understood by the receiver. This means that a teacher has not succeeded until the student has understood the teaching.

Like some other passages, this one also reiterates the concept of discipleship as imitation. As we follow Jesus and imitate him, we show that we truly are his disciples. To mention a few examples: as he washed the feet of his disciples, so we must wash one another's feet (13:14-15); as he loved his disciples, so we are to love one another (13:34); as he obeyed his Father's commandments, so we ought to obey his commandments (15:10); as he and the Father are one, so we should be one (17:11, 22); as he was sent into the world, so we will be sent into the world (17:18; 20:21). Discipleship calls for imitation of and identification with the master; doing what he does and becoming who he is. It is encouraging to know that Jesus does not ask from his followers what he has not demonstrated first.

As for Peter's overconfidence, it was caused by a lack of understanding. He had not truly understood where Jesus was going, and hence made a bold statement that he was ready to follow Jesus wherever he went. Sometimes we too can make promises without grasping their full implication, and then we may also have to go through painful experiences that will eventually prepare us to follow through on our previous claims.

Jesus the Way to the Father (14:1-14)

Jesus continues to comfort his disciples who are troubled over his imminent departure, exhorting them not to be upset (v.1). He assures them that his departure will actually be to their advantage (vv.2-3). For in the Father's house or residence, which most probably refers to heaven, there are many dwelling places or homes (v.2). Here we may have an allusion to 8:35, where Jesus says that the son, contra to the slave, has a permanent place in the house(hold). In other words, those who belong to God's household or family – his children – have acquired a permanent residence in heaven, the realm where God dwells eternally. It is important to notice the family language that is used in John's Gospel – household/family, house/home, father, son, children – creating an atmosphere of intimacy, belonging/identity and security. Those who belong to God are insiders with special privileges and benefits; they have a share in the divine life, love, knowledge and glory that characterize the relationship between the Father and Son.

When Jesus goes to his Father, he will prepare a place for his disciples, and when it is ready, he will come back for them so that they will be where he is (v.3; cf. 12:26). It is likely that Jesus' promise of coming back to collect his disciples refers to the Parousia or Second Coming at the end of time. Ironically, Jesus was not given a home in this world (1:10-11), but he promises his followers a home in another world. In fact, since Jesus and the believers are from above, their home is not in this world (cf. 18:36).

When Jesus asserts that his disciples know the way to the place he is going (v.4), Thomas objects, saying that he does not even know where Jesus is going, let alone the way to it (v.5). Jesus then provides further revelation in order to resolve Thomas' incomprehension, stating, 'I am the way and the truth and the life. No one comes to the Father except through me.' (v.6).

This penultimate 'I am' saying reveals three further things about Jesus' identity and mission. First, Jesus himself is the way (to the Father). In Jewish wisdom literature, 'way' often refers to a way of life or conduct. For example, Psalm 1 speaks of the way of the righteous and the way of the wicked, and in Proverbs, the Hebrew word for 'way' occurs seventy-six times. The apocryphal books Sirach and Wisdom of Solomon also have many references to 'way'. Besides, there are many references to the way(s) of Wisdom (e.g., Proverbs 3:17; 4:11; 8:32; Sirach 6:26) and the invitation to journey through life with Wisdom (Proverbs 1:20-33; 4:5-13; 8:1-36; Wisdom of Solomon 6:12-9:18; Sirach 4:11-18; 6:18-31; 39:1-11). In these passages, Wisdom is presented as a divine travel companion on one's life-journey to God, providing guidance, assistance, advice and life. Similarly, Jesus, as Wisdom incarnate, is the believers' travel companion leading them on their life-journey to the Father.

The second aspect of the 'I am' saying is that Jesus is the truth. We already know that Jesus himself is full of truth (1:14, 17) and that his teaching contains liberating and cleansing truth (8:31-32; 17:17-19), but here Jesus claims that he is the very embodiment of truth. In the wisdom literature, we also find the phrase 'the way of truth' (Psalm 119:30; Wisdom of Solomon 5:6; cf. Psalms 25:10; 86:11; Sirach 37:15). Thus, Jesus as the way and the truth may mean that he is the way of truth.

The third dimension of Jesus' 'I am' saying is that he is the eternal life ($z\bar{o}\bar{e}$). Again, there is a parallel in the wisdom literature, which employs phrases such as 'the way of life' (Psalm 16:11; Proverbs 5:6; 6:23; 10:17; 15:24). Hence, Jesus, as Wisdom incarnate, is the way of/to life or even the way that is life itself.

Since these three aspects of Jesus' nature and mission are interrelated, verse 6a can then be paraphrased as 'I am the way that is truth and leads to eternal life'. The implicit invitation is to walk in that way – to stick to Jesus and his way of life. Perhaps John wants us to recognize that Jesus, as Wisdom incarnate, is the way to the Father, and if we follow him, travelling with him through life, we will reach the Father and hence home.

In the light of 1:18 (only the Son has seen the Father and can reveal him), it comes as no surprise when Jesus asserts in verse 6b that only through him people can come to the Father. So, when taken as a whole, the claim in verse 6 is that Jesus is the only way to God the Father; for through Jesus God has made himself known as Father. Jesus is the only way people can find liberating truth and eternal life because it is solely through an adequate belief-response to Jesus that one enters into a personal and saving relationship with the Father and Son.

Following on from verse 6b, Jesus states in verse 7 that if his disciples know him, then they know the Father also. Since the 'if' clause is true, Jesus' conclusion is that the disciples do, in fact, know the Father and have seen him. This time Philip reveals his incomprehension by asking Jesus to show them the Father (v.8). Jesus reiterates that anyone who has seen him has seen the Father, and appears to be amazed by Philip's request (v.9). Thus, verses 7-9 emphasize that in Jesus the disciples encounter God the Father himself. In 1:18, we learned that no one had seen God, but now we learn that those who have seen (and understood) Jesus have seen God himself. The disciples' misunderstanding, represented by Thomas and Philip, benefits the reader since Jesus provides more revelation.

In verse 10, Jesus elaborates on the close identification between him and the Father: (i) the language of mutual indwelling of the Father and Son denotes their intimate relationship; (ii) Jesus' teaching is an outflow of the Father's working in him. Consequently, Jesus exhorts his disciples to believe in him – whether on the basis of his words or his works (v.11). Jesus goes on to promise that the one who believes in him will do greater works than he because he is going to the Father (v.12), and that he will do whatever is asked of him so that his Father may be glorified (vv.13-14).

In John, 'works' frequently refers to Jesus' miracles (7:3, 21; 9:3-4; 10:25, 32, 37-38; 15:24), and so, the promise is that the disciples will also perform miracles, 'greater' than Jesus did. But how will the disciples do greater miracles than Jesus? I suggest the phrase 'because I am going to the Father' provides the clue. During his earthly ministry, it is the Spirit who provides Jesus with liberating power and functions as the channel between him and the Father (see the commentary on 1:32 and 3:34). So, it is likely that Jesus performs his miracles by means of the Spirit. After Jesus goes to the Father, he will send the Spirit-Paraclete to his disciples (15:26), implying that then the Spirit is not confined any more to himself but is released to all believers. As a result, the Spirit can perform miracles (through the believers) on a larger scale than was possible before the cross.

Finally, Jesus promises to do whatever his followers ask in his name (vv.13-14). The automatic question that follows is whether Jesus issues believers with a wild card for limitless requests which he is bound to grant or whether there are some implicit qualifications to Jesus' promise. I contend that the latter is nearer the truth. An examination of the phrase '(in) my/his name' throughout John will reveal that 'name' represents the entire person bearing that name – his authority, character, identity and conduct (1:12; 3:18; 5:43; 10:25; 12:13, 28; 14:26; 17:6, 11-12, 26; 20:31). The implication is that the believer can ask Jesus for anything (and now comes the qualification) *that is in accordance with his character and mission*. To put it differently, believers shall receive when they ask in accordance with a correct understanding of who Jesus is and what he does.

Reflection

When Jesus announces his impending departure to the Father, the disciples find it difficult to accept, but it turns out that his going will be advantageous because he is going to prepare their homes. The final destination of every believer is the heavenly home, and the only secure way to it is Jesus. God's desire is that we will be where we belong: in the Father's house forever, enjoying all the privileges and benefits that come with being part of God's family. To know the Father, through Jesus, is the ultimate goal, and our heavenly home in the Father's house is our ultimate destination. This gives us a sense of purpose, belonging and security. Our identity is bound up with Jesus, and not in our degrees, careers, achievements or in what other people think of us. Following from this, we should also behave and become like the one to whom we belong, which means that we should think 'from above' and imitate Jesus in all aspects. Belonging, behaviour and becoming are all inextricably linked.

How does Jesus' claim 'No one comes to the Father except through me' (14:6) stand in the face of religious pluralism that says that all religions lead to salvation or that there are many ways to the same God? Many people today find this kind of claim offensive, exclusive and intolerant. However, people's basic reactions are no different today than they were in Jesus' time. For, as we have seen, many were offended by Jesus' claims and hence rejected him. In dialogue with people who have a pluralistic worldview, we could perhaps suggest that although Jesus is the only way to salvation there are many ways that lead to Jesus. The sheer variety of people's stories of how they found Jesus testifies to this.

Jesus' claim that he is the truth also has important implications. It suggests that truth cannot be relative, where each person is entitled to his or her own truth (as postmodernity would have it). Ultimately, truth (and salvation) is not to be found in human doctrines or philosophies but in a person – Jesus of Nazareth. Although other religions, philosophies, science, and so on, have truth to offer (according to the maxim 'all truth is God's truth'), this truth is not saving truth. It does not give the information about the identity and mission of Jesus and God as Father that is needed to enter into a saving relationship with them. For John, the truth that is found in Jesus is primarily the truth about God, the truth that liberates from sin, the truth that cleanses and leads to salvation.

I have argued that 'to ask in his name' does not give us a carte blanche to ask for anything we wish but only that which is in line with what Jesus is and represents. Our requests must, therefore, be based on and motivated by a correct understanding of who Jesus is and what he does in this world. This reiterates the need for a sound understanding of Jesus and God in terms of their character, conduct and mission. So, what does this imply for us when we close our prayers with, '...and we ask this in Jesus' name. Amen'? Do we think that 'in Jesus' name' is a formula for making our prayer work? Or is it an empty phrase that we use because we are accustomed to it? *For John, the 'in Jesus' name' is not a tag or a formula that we put at the end of our prayers to make them work. Rather, it is the content of our prayers that should be 'in Jesus' name'.* Consequently, it is not a prerequisite that we close our prayers with the literal phrase 'in Jesus' name'. Conversely, the phrase can probably do no harm, especially if we use it as a reminder for ourselves that our prayer should be in agreement with who Jesus is and what he stands for. [As an interesting aside, Acts 19:11-20 narrates an incident where some Jewish exorcists unsuccessfully used 'the name' of Jesus as a magic formula to cast out evil spirits. They failed because they did not belong to Jesus and hence did not represent him.]

The Promise of the Paraclete (14:15-24)

Jesus' comforting promises to his disciples in verses 16-20 are bracketed by exhortations to keep his commandments in verses 15 and 21. If a disciple claims to love Jesus, then s/he should obey his commandments (v.15); conversely, obedience to Jesus' commandments reveals that the disciple loves Jesus (v.21). Thus, there seems to be a reciprocal relationship between love and obedience. One's love for Jesus, then, is measured by one's obedience. Moreover, if we recall 13:34 where Jesus explicitly gave the new commandment 'to love one another', the love believers have for one another also becomes a measure of their love for Jesus, just as their love for Jesus should result in loving each other.

In verse 16, Jesus continues to comfort his disciples by promising them a divine companion who will be with them forever. The Greek word used for this divine assistant is *paraklētos*, which has been translated in various ways: 'Advocate' (NRSV), 'Counselor' (NIV, RSV), 'Comforter' (KJV) or 'Helper' (NKJV, NASB). I suggest that 'Advocate' is the most secure translation for three reasons. First, grammatically, the word *paraklētos* means 'one called alongside', especially to offer legal assistance in a court, i.e., an advocate or attorney (but not necessarily as we define this function today). Second, it fits in with the forensic context of John's Gospel, where John presents his Gospel as a cosmic trial, in which Jesus stands accused for his divine claims and needs witnesses (see the commentary on 5:31-40). Third, 15:26-27 and 16:7-11 emphasize the forensic role of this *paraklētos*, and we shall argue that the teaching function of the *paraklētos* in 14:26 and 16:12-15 can (and should) also be interpreted in the context of a trial. Hence, I contend that *paraklētos* is best translated by 'Advocate'.

Other translations such as 'Counselor', 'Comforter' and 'Helper' do not do sufficient justice to the forensic dimension of the role of the *paraklētos*. The translation 'Advocate', however, does not rule out a counselling, comforting and helping role of the *paraklētos*, neither for the disciples nor for later generations of believers. We shall in this commentary use the transliteration 'Paraclete' as a way of rising above the various translations, but we must keep in mind that the term 'Paraclete' has strong forensic connotations.

When verse 16 says that the disciples will be given 'another Paraclete', it implies that Jesus was the first Paraclete (cf. 1 John 2:1 where John explicitly refers to Jesus as *paraklētos*). A brief investigation reveals that there are significant parallels between Jesus and the Paraclete: (i) both are characterized by truth (1:14, 17; 14:6; 14:17; 16:13); (ii) both are sent by the Father (3:17; 14:16, 26); (iii) both have a revelatory teaching role (3:2; 6:59; 14:26; 16:13-15). It would seem that the Paraclete is modelled on Jesus and will take over Jesus' role as 'Paraclete' in this world after he has departed. Besides, 14:26 makes clear that the Paraclete and the Holy Spirit are not two different entities; rather, the Paraclete is the Spirit in a special role.

In verse 17, Jesus clarifies that this Paraclete is the Spirit of truth, i.e., the Spirit who communicates truth (cf. 16:13; 1 John 5:6). The world is unable to receive the Paraclete because it neither sees nor knows him. However, Jesus stresses that the Paraclete will be no stranger to the disciples who already know him.

The obvious question that arises is how the disciples can already know the Paraclete when he is expected to come *after* Jesus' departure. Perhaps it is like this. During Jesus' earthly ministry, Jesus was endowed with the Spirit, and the Spirit provided Jesus with the necessary revelatory wisdom for his life-giving teaching. People who heard, understood and accepted

Jesus' teaching were able to experience and partake in the divine life that was available in Jesus and his words. More specifically, the Spirit actively worked through Jesus teaching, assisting people to grasp the meaning and significance of Jesus' words and so come to believe. Jesus succinctly summarized this notion as 'my words are Spirit and life' (6:63). In that sense, the disciples have already experienced the Spirit during Jesus' ministry. Nevertheless, the Spirit was still bound to the person of Jesus, and could only be released and come as the Paraclete to replace Jesus, after the cross and the ascension (cf. the commentary on 7:39).

Jesus assures his disciples that he will not leave them as orphans but will come to them (v.18). An orphan is one who has no parents, and consequently, is without help or protection. In the Old Testament there are numerous references to the vulnerability of orphans, and the duty to provide them food and protection, but especially justice. If the people did not provide these, then God would act on behalf of the orphans (Deuteronomy 10:18; 14:29; 24:17-21; 27:19; Psalms 10:14; 68:5; 82:3; 146:9; Isaiah 1:17; Jeremiah 7:6; 22:3; Zechariah 7:10; Malachi 3:5). Similarly, Jesus promises his disciples that he will not leave them unprotected or defenceless.

In the farewell discourses, it becomes clear that Jesus' departure from this world will not put an end to the cosmic trial. On the contrary, the trial will continue and it will be up to the disciples to defend the case through their continued testimony. If the witnesses fall silent, the case will be lost. Without a replacement for Jesus, the disciples would be like orphans, without defence against the attacks of the world and unable to continue the cosmic trial. For this reason, Jesus will send them an Advocate. In the section 15:18-16:4a, where Jesus forewarns his disciples that the world will hate and persecute them, it comes as no surprise that Jesus also mentions the Paraclete (15:26).

Jesus' statements 'I am coming to you' (v.18) and 'you will see me' (v.19) cannot possibly refer to Jesus' resurrection appearances (otherwise the disciples would be orphaned again after the ascension) or to the Parousia (otherwise the disciples would be orphans until then). So they must refer to Jesus' coming back to the disciples through the Paraclete. This does not mean that the Paraclete is Jesus in disguise because the Paraclete will replace

Jesus and *represent* him rather than being Jesus' *alter ego*. The Paraclete will mediate Jesus' presence to the believer. In other words, *the Paraclete is not another Jesus, but the Spirit is another Paraclete*. Therefore, after his departure from this world, Jesus will continue to be with his disciples in, or by means of, the person of the Spirit-Paraclete.

Let us now examine the use of 'in' in the phrases 'he...will be *in* you' (v.17) and 'I am *in* my Father, and you *in* me, and I *in* you' (v.20). I suggest that we should interpret this so-called 'indwelling' language primarily in *relational* terms. The Father 'in' the Son and vice versa denotes the intimacy of their relationship (cf. 10:38; 14:10); hence, Jesus 'in' the believer and the Paraclete 'in' the believer also indicate the closeness of the relationship (cf. 6:56). As a result, the indwelling language need not be taken literally, demanding a material or physical indwelling of Jesus or the Spirit (although we do not deny this possibility). Instead, the emphasis is on the intimate relationship between the believer, Jesus and the Paraclete. Thus, Jesus or the Paraclete being 'in' the believer means that they are present to the believer in some real but mystical way that we cannot entirely comprehend.

Judas (not Iscariot) interrupts and, probably referring to Jesus' statements in verses 19 and 21, asks about the mechanics of Jesus' revealing himself to them but not to the world (v.22). In the first part of his reply, Jesus simply reiterates that the disciples must obey his words if they claim to love him (v.23a; cf. vv.15 and 21). The latter part of verse 23, however, is more enigmatic. How is it that Jesus and the Father will come to the obedient believer and make their home (literally, 'a dwelling place') with him/her? In the light of the promised coming of the Paraclete, the indwelling of the believer by the Father and Jesus will probably be achieved by means of the Spirit-Paraclete. That is, the Paraclete will mediate to the believer the intimate presence of Jesus and the Father (1 John 3:24 and 4:13 confirm this concept more explicitly).

Jesus Concludes the Session (14:25-31)

Jesus now wraps up his first teaching session. He tells his disciples that the coming Spirit-Paraclete will teach them everything and will remind them of everything that he has said (v.26). Thus, it appears that one of the main functions of the Paraclete is that of a teacher, just as Jesus was a teacher. However, we must find out *how*, i.e., in what way, the Paraclete teaches.

The phrases 'he will teach them everything' and 'he will remind them of everything' are both governed by the single phrase 'that I said to you', which implies that the twofold 'everything' refers to 'everything *that Jesus taught*'. In other words, the Paraclete's teaching is based on what Jesus taught while he was on earth. Moreover, the Paraclete's task probably includes jogging the believer's memory to remember the words of Jesus, as well as explaining the significance of these words. We had suggested that the remembrance of the disciples in 2:17, 22 and 12:16 are examples of this activity of the Paraclete because (i) the remembering takes place after Jesus' resurrection/glorification, and (ii) the passive form of the verb used indicates that the disciples were reminded by someone – the Paraclete.

In verse 27a, the 'peace' that Jesus promises to give to his disciples is more than freedom from anxiety (although that is certainly included as v.27b indicates). It is almost equivalent to the Hebrew *shalom*, meaning 'wholeness' or 'salvation'. Jesus' peace is radically different from what the world has to give. At that time, the only peace on offer was the *pax Romana*, which was no peace at all. We know from various sources that Roman rule in first-century Palestine caused oppression, turmoil, conflict, injustice and resistance.

Jesus' imperative, 'do not be upset' (v.27b), is a repetition of 14:1, but is now coupled with another imperative: 'do not be afraid' or 'do not be cowards'. He may have added this command because 'the fear of the Jews' was affecting many people, including the disciples (20:19; see the excursus on 7:13) or perhaps because the disciples would have to face the hate and persecution of the world (15:18-16:4a).

Jesus reprimands his disciples, though mildly, for being upset at the news of his departure (v.28). If they loved him, they would rejoice that he is going to the Father because the Father is 'greater', i.e., more important, than he. Nevertheless, Jesus promises that their sorrow will be turned into joy (16:22) – and it will (20:20)!

Jesus realizes that his time is running out and the 'ruler of the world', i.e., the devil, is coming. Nevertheless, Jesus makes it clear that the devil has 'nothing' on him – no power, no authority, no control, nothing (v.30). The only reason Jesus displays a sense of urgency is his wilful obedience to the Father, demonstrating Jesus' love for him (v.31; cf. vv.15, 21).

The first farewell speech ends abruptly, 'Get up, let us go from here' (v.31), and it seems that the narrative only resumes in 18:1. As a result, many view chapters 15-17 as later material, inserted into the story by another author/editor. This view is strengthened by the fact that John 14:31 and 18:3 have strong parallels with Mark 14:42-43. This theory is certainly plausible – nothing demands that the Gospel was written or composed in one sitting or by one author (7:53-8:11, for example, was almost certainly inserted at a later stage) – but it seems rather clumsy that a later editor would choose to leave in the three Greek words that translate 'Get up, let us go from here.' We would expect the editor to have created a smooth transition to 15:1. This leads us to an alternative explanation, namely, that Jesus and his disciples left the house after 14:31, and *on the way* Jesus taught his disciples the material that is recorded in chapters 15-16 and prayed the prayer that is recorded in chapter 17, before his arrest in chapter 18.

It is tempting to think that Jesus' prayer in John 17 is the prayer in Gethsemane as recorded in the Synoptics, but there are two arguments against this view. First, whereas the prayer in Gethsemane reveals Jesus' agonizing struggle to submit to his Father's will (Mark 14:32-42), Jesus' prayer in John 17 has a distinct victorious tone, affirming that he has accomplished the work that the Father gave him. Second, John 18:1 says that Jesus and the disciples left a certain place, crossed the Kidron valley, and only then entered the garden (of Gethsemane). It is virtually certain that the garden in John 18:1 is the same location as the 'field' called Gethsemane near the Mount of Olives in Mark 14:26, 32, since both authors identify it as the location of Jesus' arrest. In that case, Jesus' prayer in chapter 17 must have happened before he entered the garden of Gethsemane.

Reflection

In 14:1-14, we learned that Jesus' departure is advantageous for the disciples because Jesus is going to prepare their homes and will return to collect them when the homes are ready. Then, in 14:15-24, we discovered another advantage, namely, the sending of the Spirit-Paraclete to the disciples. Rather than being a sad or disastrous event, Jesus' departure from this world proves to be a win-win situation: the disciples will gain the help of the Spirit-Paraclete, while remaining assured of Jesus' presence! 'Paraclete' is a functional label for the Spirit who will continue Jesus' functions in this world and will mediate the presence of Jesus (and the Father) to the obedient believer. This would mean that the believer can only know and experience Jesus and the Father through the Spirit. The Spirit, then, is the mode or channel of communication between the believer, Jesus, and the Father, just as the Spirit was the means of communication between Jesus and his Father while he was on earth. It also implies that just as Jesus was able to do on earth what he heard and saw from the Father by means of the Spirit, so should the believer because s/he has received the same Spirit.

These important concepts, as we reflect on them, may significantly influence our understanding of God and how he works in this world. In many churches, bible colleges and seminaries, the doctrine of the Spirit is given little attention with the result that the Spirit often is only at the periphery of people's theology. Pentecostal and charismatic traditions have brought a much-needed awareness of the Spirit, although sometimes their theology of the Spirit needs fine-tuning or correction. The issue is not whether we believe in the Spirit – we all probably affirm the belief in the one God: Father, Son and Holy Spirit – but rather how much we know about the Spirit and his functions. Who is he (I trust we have gone beyond referring to the Spirit as an impersonal 'it')? What is his role? How does he operate? These are questions we may not usually ask, but John certainly wants to inform us thoroughly about the person and work of the Spirit.

Teaching on Discipleship – Privileges, Obligations and Consequences (15:1-16:4a)

This section is essentially a didactic monologue of Jesus, and we can divide it into two parts: (i) obedience, abiding and bearing fruit (15:1-17); (ii) witness and persecution (15:18-16:4a). Here, Jesus portrays two contrasting groups and attitudes: the disciples who are to exemplify love, and the world which is characterized by hate. Moreover, in this didactic pericope, Jesus informs the disciples of their privileges and obligations, while also cautioning them of the consequences of being his disciples.

Obedience, Abiding and Bearing Fruit (15:1-17)

In this passage, Jesus speaks to his disciples about the attitude and conduct he expects them to display towards one another, whereas, in the next passage (15:18-16:4a) he informs them of their task in this world and what they can expect from the world.

In verse 1, we find Jesus' seventh and final 'I am' saying: 'I am the true vine'. In the Old Testament, the vine was a symbol for Israel, but sadly, she failed to bear the fruit that was expected of her (Psalm 80:8-16; Isaiah 5:1-10; Jeremiah 2:21; Ezekiel 19:10-14; Hosea 10:1; 14:7). The next excerpts vividly portray the situation:

> For the vineyard of the LORD of hosts is the house of Israel, and the people of Judah are his pleasant planting; he expected justice, but saw bloodshed; righteousness, but heard a cry! (Isaiah 5:7)

> Yet I [God] planted you [Israel] as a choice vine, from the purest stock. How then did you turn degenerate and become a wild vine? Though you wash yourself with lye and use much soap, the stain of your guilt is still before me, says the Lord GOD. (Jeremiah 2:21-22)

> Your mother [Israel] was like a vine in a vineyard transplanted by the water, fruitful and full of branches from abundant water. Its strongest stem became a ruler's scepter; it towered aloft among the thick boughs; it stood out in its height with its mass of branches. But it was plucked up in fury, cast down to the ground; the east wind dried it up; its fruit was stripped off, its strong stem was withered; the fire consumed it. Now it is transplanted into the wilderness, into a dry and thirsty land. And fire has gone out from its stem, has consumed its branches and fruit, so that there remains in it no strong stem, no scepter for ruling. This is a lamentation, and it is used as a lamentation. (Ezekiel 19:10-14)

In contrast to Israel in the Old Testament, as the vine which failed to produce the fruit that God had intended, Jesus, as the new and true Israel, will fulfil her divine purpose.

The Father is the vinedresser or gardener (v.1b). He removes every branch that does not bear fruit, and prunes every branch that does bear fruit so that it may bear more fruit (v.2). Both verbs 'to remove' and 'to prune' are related in the Greek (*airō* and *kathairō* respectively), and in both instances there is an element of taking away. However, while pruning is a partial taking away to increase the branch's fruitfulness, the removal of the fruitless branch is a permanent taking away implying destruction (cf. v.6). In verse 5a, Jesus tells his disciples that they are the branches. The following picture then emerges. Disciples who do not bear fruit, i.e., who do not demonstrate their discipleship, are useless and will be removed, but disciples who do bear fruit will be 'pruned' so that their fruit may increase. Perhaps Judas was a branch that did not bear fruit and had to be removed (cf. 13:27-30). In the final analysis, the aim of the branches is to bear fruit, and the bearing of fruit is a necessary aspect and demonstration of discipleship.

Almost before the disciples can wonder whether they are fruitless branches, Jesus assures them that they are already clean because of his word (v.3). Interestingly, the Greek verb for 'to prune' (v.2) can also mean 'to cleanse', and the associated adjective is intentionally used in verse 3 to translate 'clean'. Hence, as the gardener, God is 'pruning', i.e., cleansing or purifying, the disciples so that they can bear much fruit. Jesus' assertion that the disciples are already clean echoes his words in 13:10, but he now clarifies *how* they have become clean: by his word or teaching (cf. 4:10, 14; 6:63; 17:17). The picture that emerges, then, is that God continuously cleanses believers through his word (mediated through Jesus' teaching) in order to increase their fruitfulness, and make them better disciples.

Jesus stresses that there must be mutual indwelling between him and his disciples; they should remain or abide in him and he will abide in them (v.4). This requirement is simple to understand when we bear in mind the metaphor of the vine and the branches: just as a branch cannot bear fruit by itself unless it remains in the vine, so a disciple cannot bear fruit unless s/he abides in Jesus (v.4). A branch must be attached to the vine, in order to have access to the essential nutrients that come through the stem, if it is to produce fruit. Similarly, a believer must remain in Jesus in order to have access to whatever is necessary to produce fruit. To remain in Jesus means to remain in fellowship with him, so only when believers are in a relationship with Jesus they will be able to bear fruit (v.5). To remain in Jesus, then, is not an option but an absolute necessity, and the bearing of fruit is the inevitable outcome or demonstration of our fellowship with Jesus. The opposite is also true: without Jesus, the disciple can do nothing.

The consequence of not abiding in Jesus is vividly described in verse 6, creating a sombre and scary picture. The one who does not remain in Jesus will be thrown away like the branch and wither (v.6a). The comparative use of 'like' may be a reference to verse 2: the disciple who does not remain in Jesus will not bear fruit and will therefore be taken away, and dry up spiritually, just as a fruitless branch is removed from the vine and withers. Such branches are gathered, thrown into the fire and burned (v.6b).

This is how most English translations, such as the NRSV and NIV, render verse 6b, but the literal translation goes: 'They gather them [the withered branches] together, throw them into the fire and they are burned.' This raises some questions. Who gathers those 'disciples' who fail to abide in Jesus, are fruitless and therefore be burned? Further, when does this gathering together and throwing into the fire take place? The KJV says that 'men' gather these fruitless people, but there is nothing in the text to warrant such a translation. I suggest that we may have an allusion to the events described in Mark 13:27 and Matthew 24:31, speaking of the gathering of the elect by the angels at the Parousia, the Second Coming of Christ. John may be referring to the same event but only describing the fate of the unfaithful (cf. Matthew 24:51; 25:30-32, 41; Revelation 20:15). In this case, *angels* will gather the 'withered branches' at the day of judgement. Verse 6, then, may be speaking of the apostasy or defection of disciples, which causes them to dry up spiritually (v.6a), and eventually be thrown into the eternal fire on the day of the final judgement (v.6b).

Verse 7 echoes 14:13-14 and confirms our interpretation of these verses. We argued there that the 'ask whatever you want and I will do it' must be understood with the qualification, 'ask whatever you want *that is in accordance with Jesus' will, character and mission*'. A similar qualification is explicitly mentioned here in verse 7, namely that disciples must remain in Jesus and his words. Therefore, if believers adhere to Jesus and live in accordance with his teaching, then they should also ask in keeping with his teaching, and will receive accordingly.

Verse 8 presents us with a grammatical difficulty. The Father is glorified when the believers bear much fruit and 'be' (NIV) or 'become' (NRSV) Jesus' disciples. I prefer the NIV translation which says, 'This is to my Father's glory, that you bear much fruit, showing yourselves to be my disciples.' In the light of verses 4-5, I would argue that bearing fruit *demonstrates* rather than constitutes discipleship. The one who is engrafted into the vine is called to bear fruit rather than that bearing fruit causes engrafting. The bearing of fruit is evidence that someone *is* a disciple.

Jesus' command to bear fruit is not new. In 4:31-38, Jesus invited his disciples to participate in the harvest and gather fruit, although it was actually the Samaritan woman who gathered fruit, when she brought her whole village to Jesus. Furthermore, in 12:24 Jesus spoke of the need to die in order to bear much fruit, implying that one needs to be willing to let go of one's dreams, desires, ambitions and plans if these cause conflict with God's purposes, or if they have become obstacles to bearing fruit. Finally, glancing forward, the disciples' miraculous catch of fish in John 21 probably foreshadows the abundance of fruit their lives shall bear.

The imperative to remain in Jesus' love (v.9) is explained in verse 10: obedience to Jesus' commandments results in and guarantees one's abiding in Jesus' love. The call to remain in Jesus, his words and his love, as well as to obey his commandments, all amount to one requirement: to adhere to Jesus and his teachings (cf. 14:15, 21, 23, 31). This adherence to Jesus is not simply an intellectual assent to his teachings but is demonstrated in and as discipleship. To abide in Jesus, his teachings and love calls for a life of discipleship by imitation. As Jesus adhered to his Father's commandments and remained in his love, so we must adhere to Jesus and remain in his love.

Jesus' teachings apparently bring joy. In 3:29, we learn that John the Baptist's joy is made complete/perfect when he hears Jesus' voice. Again, in 17:13, Jesus speaks of the joy caused by his words. Here, in verse 11, Jesus says that through his teaching, his joy is transferred to the disciples, to make their joy complete/perfect. Perhaps we should understand this puzzling statement of Jesus in the light of the previous verse. In verse 10, Jesus asserts that he has obeyed his Father's commandments and remained in his love. This obedience to and resulting fellowship with his Father may have caused Jesus' joy. Similarly, if the disciples adhere to Jesus and his teachings, they will share in the fellowship with the Father and Son and experience the same divine joy. This principle seems to have been working in the Johannine church(es) (1 John 1:4; 2 John 12; 3 John 4). Hence, the faithful passing on of Jesus' teachings brings joy which is complete/perfect – both in the transmitter and the receiver.

In verse 12, Jesus repeats the new commandment he gave in 13:34, but elaborates on it in verse 13, saying that the greatest expression or demonstration of love is when one lays down one's life for one's friends. The laying down of one's life may be taken literally (as Jesus demonstrates on the cross) or figuratively, as servanthood (as Jesus did in the footwashing). If we synthesize these concepts, then love for one another is essentially an expression of servanthood.

Jesus then moves on to the theme of friendship (vv.14-15). Great people from the past were called friends of God, including Abraham (2 Chronicles 20:7), Moses (Exodus 33:11) and Job (Job 29:4). The Jewish wisdom literature also speaks of the friendship of Wisdom (Wisdom of Solomon 7:14, 27; 8:18), and a relationship with Wisdom that is characterized by love (Proverbs 8:17; Wisdom of Solomon 6:12; 7:10; 8:2). In John's Gospel, John the Baptist and Lazarus are called Jesus' friends (3:29; 11:11), and now his own disciples. The disciples are Jesus' friends, not his slaves because unlike a slave who does not know his master's business, his disciples are informed, for Jesus has revealed everything to them that he has heard from his Father (v.15). This reminds us of the son who, contra the slave, has a permanent place in the household (8:35). Hence, the disciples, as Jesus' friends and part of God's family, have inside knowledge of the Father and his business/work.

In essence, friendship with Jesus entails an inside knowledge of God revealed by Jesus; obedience guarantees the continuation of this friendship with Jesus; and love is *the* hallmark of the friendship; a love that finds its ultimate expression in the laying down of one's life for one's friends.

Reflection

This passage on discipleship presents a complex nexus of ideas, which can be summarized like this: through obedience, disciples ensure that they remain in Jesus, which in turn leads them to bear fruit. This implies that the focus of our efforts as disciples, should not be on bearing fruit but on obedience and abiding – and fruit will follow! Can you picture a branch concentrating extremely hard on producing fruit and worrying about how it can produce more fruit? Probably not. By simply remaining in the tree and absorbing vital fluids from the stem, the branch will naturally produce fruit. Likewise, if we are obedient to and continually abide in Jesus, the fruit will automatically follow. This does not mean that we never have to evaluate our fruit; for it is good to take stock of our walk with the Lord periodically, to see whether there are things that need change. However, the primary focus should be on our fellowship with Jesus rather than on our fruitfulness. This may be an encouragement for those who have a tendency to be over-anxious about results, and live in fear of being removed and thrown into the fire. Sobering as the picture of 15:2, 6 is, it is not meant to keep us in fear. It probably refers to those who have become apostates or defectors, and have given up following Jesus, rather than to those who earnestly seek to follow Jesus but occasionally fail.

Discipleship is a dynamic process, not a static existence. Branches that do not bear fruit are removed, whereas branches that do bear fruit will be pruned so that they can produce more fruit. One way or the other, the branches are affected. This means that we cannot rest on our laurels, nor can we ever assume that we have completed the task of a disciple. We are to remain in constant fellowship with Jesus, keep on following, and keep on manifesting our discipleship. Discipleship is also dynamic because it is essentially by imitation. As Jesus obeyed the Father and remained in him, so we should follow Jesus, obey his teachings and abide in him. Discipleship is an essential expression of our relationship with Jesus. Salvation, then, is not just coming to Jesus but also sticking to him, as a disciple. Salvation is not simply the one-time 'giving our heart to Jesus' but a life-long commitment to him in discipleship.

Notice the removal of the fruitless branch and the pruning of the fruitful branch. From both branches there is a taking away, but while there is a complete removal of the fruitless branch, from the fruitful branch what is taken away is that which is necessary to ensure the production of more fruit. Furthermore, the pruning need not always be the taking away of 'bad' things; healthy branches are also pruned of healthy bits; sometimes 'good' things are taken away in order to produce better things. Anything that does not glorify God, though not bad in itself, may be 'pruned'. There may be times, when our desires, ambitions and plans need pruning. This process of pruning often hurts, but let us trust the skilful Vinedresser, realizing that pruning is necessary to produce more fruit.

The idea of friendship with Jesus is unique. In which other religion are people invited to be friends with God? The status of a believer/disciple is that of a friend of Jesus and a child of God the Father. The image of friendship and family evokes ideas of relationship, fellowship, intimacy, trust and belonging. In addition, our friendship with Jesus is characterized by eternal life, love, peace, joy and an inside knowledge of the Father's business. How privileged are those who know they are friends of Jesus.

Witness and Persecution (15:18-16:4a)

Whereas the previous section spoke of the love and friendship between Jesus and his disciples, the present section describes the hate and persecution they will face from the world. The two sections present two contrasting groups – the disciples and the world – with two different attitudes – love and hate. The section

15:18-16:4a can be divided into three smaller segments: (i) the reason for persecution (15:18-25); (ii) the response to persecution (15:26-27); (iii) the nature of persecution (16:1-4a).

The Reason for Persecution (15:18-25). We know from previous passages that the world proved to be a hostile environment for Jesus, but apparently it will be the same for the disciples (v.18). The world or realm 'from below' is under the control of the devil (cf. the expression 'the ruler of the world' in 12:31; 14:30; 16:11), and is characterized by darkness, evil, lies, hate, lack of knowledge, and death. However, the basic attitude of the world seems to be that of hate: the world hated Jesus first and will also hate the disciples. The reason the world hates Jesus is that it does not want its evil deeds exposed, which is exactly what Jesus came to do (3:19-20; 7:7). The reason the world hates the disciples is that they do not belong to the world but to Jesus (v.19).

In verse 20, Jesus continues to explain to his disciples that the attitude of the world towards them is the outcome of their loyalty to him. He reminds them of what he said earlier, 'A servant is not greater than his master' (13:16), and therefore, if they persecuted Jesus, they will also persecute his disciples. Thus, the hate of the world is/will be expressed in persecution – both of Jesus (5:16) and his disciples (v.20).

Jesus explains in verse 21 that this persecution, fuelled by hate, will be directed at them on his account because the world does not know God, who sent him (cf. 7:28; 8:55). In fact, if Jesus had not come to the world, taught the people, and performed miracles, they would have no sin (vv.22, 24). However, as it is, they have no valid excuse for Jesus has brought revelatory teaching and done miraculous signs. Both his words and works reveal aspects of his identity, mission and relationship with God, which should evoke a belief-response. People see Jesus but instead of belief they express hate (cf. 6:36); in fact, their 'seeing' is not sight at all and hence their sin remains (9:41). Their sin is essentially the sin of unbelief, i.e., the sin of rejecting Jesus – both his revelatory words and his miraculous works (cf. 16:9). This rejection, blindness and unbelief cause their attitude of hate: they hate both Jesus and his Father (vv.23-24).

The world's unfounded hate of Jesus proves to be a fulfilment of Scripture. In verse 25, Jesus quotes from Psalms 35:19 and 69:4: 'They hated me without cause.' In both Psalms, David cries out to God for deliverance of his numerous enemies, who hate him for no reason, speak deceitful words and accuse him falsely (Psalms 35:19-20; 69:4).

The Response to Persecution (15:26-27). These two verses mention the Paraclete again, and some scholars contend that this material was inserted at a later stage in the composition of the Gospel. We will not go into the details of the debate, but we must point out that verses 26-27 dovetail seamlessly with verse 25, when we recognize the context of Psalms 35 and 69 to which verse 25 alludes.

In Psalm 35, David describes his distress over his evil enemies, who hate him without cause (vv.4, 19), and who turn out to be false witnesses (v.11), and in his agony, he cries out to God for deliverance, in particular to provide legal defence (vv.22-23). Similarly, in Psalm 69, David agonizes over his numerous enemies who hate him without cause, persecute him unjustly (v.4), and insult him (vv.10, 19-20), and he implores God to speak to him and act on his behalf (vv.16-18, 24, 27). Both Psalms employ forensic language to describe David's persecution (false accusations and insults, false witnesses). Moreover, David's request to God not to be silent but to speak on his behalf so that his persecutors may be judged, is essentially a request for God to be his witness and to provide legal defence. Similarly, in the light of the hate and persecution of the world, the disciples will be in need of a witness to come to their defence, which is precisely what we find in verses 26-27.

Verses 26-27 most probably speak of one *combined* witness of the Paraclete and the disciples, rather than two kinds of witnesses. The world is not able to receive the Paraclete's witness directly (14:17), and hence it is channelled through the disciples. That is, the Paraclete testifies to the world *through* the disciples' witness. Besides, when we take into account the Paraclete's role as the disciples' teacher (14:26), then it is probably not too wide of the mark to suggest that it is the Paraclete who informs the disciples' witness. As the Paraclete teaches the disciples the meaning and significance of Jesus' teachings, he prepares them as witnesses. To put it differently, the Paraclete empowers the disciples' testimony by communicating to them the truth that is in Jesus' teaching (cf. 8:32; 14:17; 16:13). In effect, Jesus exhorts his disciples to counter the false accusations of the world with their Paraclete-empowered witness of truth (cf. Jesus' witness to the truth in 18:37).

The Nature of Persecution (16:1-4a). Verse 1 can be translated as, 'I tell you this so that you may not stumble/be offended' (NRSV, KJV), but another possible translation is 'I tell you this so that you may not give up believing'. The latter translation is preferable since it is more likely that the impending persecution will cause the disciples to give up their faith than that it will offend them. Nevertheless, those who take offence at Jesus' words may also give up their faith, as we saw in 6:60-66 (6:61 is the only other occasion in John where this verb *skandalizō* occurs).

In verse 2, Jesus spells out the nature of the persecution that awaits the disciples: they will be expelled from the synagogue and perhaps even be killed. Expulsion from the local synagogue meant becoming a socio-religious outcast (cf. 9:22; 12:42), but it would not end there; they may be killed by their persecutors who would mistakenly think of it as an act of worship to God (cf. the prediction of Peter's death in 21:18-19, and Paul's persecution of the Church narrated in Acts 7:54-8:3). Verse 3 repeats the reason for the persecution: the world does neither know God nor Jesus (cf. 15:21).

Verse 4a parallels verse 1 in the repetition of 'I tell you this so that...' and reveals a related though not identical concept, namely that *remembrance enhances belief*. Remembrance occurs seven times in John (2:17, 22; 12:16; 14:26; 15:20; 16:4, 21), and, except for the last occurrence, all the referents are the disciples. On a few occasions, we read that the disciples' remembrance resulted in understanding and belief (2:22; 12:16; cf. 13:19, although there is no explicit mention of remembrance). Moreover, one of the functions of the Paraclete will be to cause the disciples to remember Jesus' teaching so that they may grow in understanding and belief (see the commentary on 14:26).

Thus, Jesus provides a twofold exhortation to his followers in the face of the future persecution: (i) do not give up believing; (ii) remember Jesus' words, in which the Paraclete will probably aid them. If we tie this in with 15:26-27, then the following picture emerges. When the believers face hate, accusations and persecution at the hands of the world, the Paraclete will prepare and inform the disciples' testimony by reminding them of Jesus' words and explaining their significance. In this way, the twofold role of the Paraclete as Teacher and Advocate is combined, something that the next section will confirm.

Reflection

John 15:1-16:4a, Jesus' second farewell discourse, spelled out the various privileges, obligations and consequences that come with discipleship. Amongst the privileges are friendship with Jesus, perfect joy, inside knowledge/revelation and the assistance of the Paraclete. The obligations of a disciple include obeying Jesus' commandments, abiding in him and his teaching, bearing fruit and bearing witness. However, discipleship also has a cost; the consequence of following Jesus is that the world is likely to hate, persecute, and perhaps even kill the believer. It may be worthwhile to read Dietrich Bonhoeffer's classic The Cost of Discipleship *on the subject.*

The two sub-sections, 15:1-17 and 15:18-16:4a, depict two mutually exclusive groups with different attitudes and conduct: (i) the disciples, who must exemplify mutual love and servanthood; and (ii) the world, which hates the disciples and will persecute them. Another contrast is in the lack of knowledge of the world versus the inside knowledge the disciples enjoy. This knowledge is provided by Jesus and, after Jesus' departure, the Paraclete will continue to do so by reminding the believer of Jesus' words and explaining them.

Francis Bacon, a philosopher and statesman, once said, 'Prosperity is the blessing of the Old Testament; adversity is the blessing of the New.' John's Gospel certainly seems to affirm this statement. As the world hated Jesus, persecuted him and eventually killed him, so it will treat those who belong to him. The concept of religious persecution, described in section 15:18-16:4a, sadly, is very relevant today. In many countries, Christians are persecuted to a greater or lesser extent because of their faith and their allegiance to Jesus. For this reality one only needs to glance at the Persecution List of Open Doors International, an organization serving persecuted Christians worldwide (http://www.opendoors.org) or the information provided by Christian Solidarity Worldwide, a human rights charity working on behalf of those persecuted for their Christian beliefs (http://www.csw.org.uk). Persecution is most rampant in the following countries: North Korea, Saudi Arabia, Laos, Vietnam, Iran, Turkmenistan, Maldives, Bhutan, Myanmar (former Burma) and Somalia.

Religious persecution is not limited to the persecution of Christians. In India, for example, besides Christians, other religious minorities, such as Muslims, Sikhs and Buddhists have been under threat of persecution from fundamentalist Hindus. About five states in India have a so-called 'anti-conversion law', which in practice prohibits people from changing from one religion to another.

What should our response be in the face of persecution? John would reply, 'Be a witness! Do not be silent; remember that Jesus' trial is ongoing and witnesses are still needed today.' Jesus never said that it would be easy; on the contrary, his exhortation not to give up believing reveals that the opposite is true. Becoming a believer has consequences in many countries, which may prevent people from openly confessing their faith in Christ. Without playing down the severity of religious persecution, John seems to say that persecution should not result in the silence or concealment of Christian witness. John's Gospel implicitly criticizes the 'secret Christian' who does not confess belief in Jesus because of the threat of becoming a social outcast. In John 9, for example, the fearful parents of the man born blind failed to give a proper testimony in contrast to their son who boldly testified despite the persecution at the hands of the religious leaders.

In response to persecution, John calls for witness, remembrance and belief. As believers, we should not give up our faith in the face of persecution, but remember Jesus' teachings and use them in/as our testimony to our persecutors. In this situation we are not alone but can expect the divine assistance from the Paraclete: he will remind us of Jesus' words, explain them to us and prepare our testimony so that we may remain steadfast in our faith (cf. Mark 13:11; Matthew 10:19-20; Luke 12:11-12).

Final Teaching (16:4b-33)

Jesus' third farewell discourse can be divided into three sections: (i) the work of the Paraclete (16:4b-15); (ii) sorrow turned into joy (16:16-24); (iii) parables and plain speech (16:25-33).

The Work of the Paraclete (16:4b-15)

This section contains two of the five Paraclete-sayings (the others are in 14:16-17; 14:26; 15:26), describing the Paraclete's forensic and didactic functions. Jesus begins by saying that only now, because he is about to depart, this kind of teaching has become necessary (v.4b). The disciples seem to have become resigned to the fact that Jesus will leave them and to have stopped asking him where he is going (v.5; cf. 14:5 where that question was still on Thomas' lips). Nevertheless, the disciples have not grasped the significance of Jesus' departure nor the benefits that it will bring to them, because it has only made them sad (v.6). Jesus reiterates that his going away will be to their advantage because it will pave the way for the Paraclete's coming (v.7).

Only when Jesus departs from this world (at the ascension), the Spirit-Paraclete, who until that time is only given to Jesus (1:32; 3:34), will become available to the disciples (v.7). This is the second prerequisite for the coming of the Spirit (the first was mentioned in 7:39), and we shall further interpret these prerequisites when we deal with the giving of the Spirit in 20:22.

The Paraclete as Advocate (vv.8-11). In Judaism, the role of an advocate or legal aid was not merely to defend the accused but also to prosecute the accusing party if necessary. This prosecuting function of the Paraclete is in view in verses 8-11. The Paraclete will prosecute the world in that he will convict it regarding sin, righteousness and judgement (v.8). The word for 'to convict' can also mean 'to expose' (as in 3:20), but that would be too weak here. Instead, the Paraclete will prove the wrong of the world about sin, righteousness and judgement, which verses 9-11 spell out further.

The difficulty with verses 9-11 is that they can be translated as causal (e.g., 'about sin *because* they do not believe in me') or explanatory (e.g., 'about sin *in that* they do not believe in me'). A causal interpretation answers the question of *why* the Paraclete will convict the world of its sin; giving the reason for the world's sin. An explanatory interpretation answers the question of *how* the Paraclete will convict the world of its sin; giving the content of the world's sin. We prefer the latter interpretation where verses 9-11 spell out the content of the world's sin, righteousness and judgement. In this case, the Paraclete will convict the world about sin in that its people do not believe in Jesus; about righteousness in that Jesus is going to the Father; about judgement in that the ruler of the world (the devil) has been judged. This needs further explanation.

The principal sin for John is that of unbelief: people do not accept and believe in Jesus and hence their sin remains (cf. 8:24, 46; 15:22-24). Jesus' departure to the Father at the ascension, after his death and resurrection, is the vindication of Jesus' righteousness, the proof that Jesus had done what God required of him. In his Epistle, John also shows the expected trajectory for the Church: believers are exhorted to do what is right with God (literally 'to do righteousness') (1 John 2:29; 3:7). This is virtually synonymous with John's earlier observation of those who 'do the truth' (3:21) – in contrast to those who do what is evil (3:20). Finally, the judgement of the world starts with the judgement of the ruler of the world, i.e., the 'exorcism' of the devil from his dominion (12:31), which, according to the context of 12:32-33, happens at the cross.

An important issue is to consider the *aim* of the Paraclete's prosecuting the world, and I suggest, for two reasons, that the intention of the Paraclete in convicting the world is soteriological. First, as Jesus' aim was to save and not to condemn (3:17), and as Jesus was the first paraclete (14:16), it is natural to assume that the mission of the Paraclete, as a continuation of Jesus' mission, is salvific. Second, the Paraclete cannot directly convict the world (14:17) but channels this conviction through the disciples' witness (15:26-27) – a witness which is aimed at evoking belief (17:20). Therefore, the Paraclete brings a case against the world, with the intention that people will repent and come to believe in Jesus.

The Paraclete as Teacher (vv.12-15). As Teacher, the Paraclete will guide the believer into all truth – truth being the content of Jesus' teaching (v.13a; cf. 8:31-32). Thus, when Jesus says that the Paraclete will guide the disciples into all truth, he means that the Paraclete will explain the meaning and significance of Jesus' teaching. This is clear from Jesus' qualification in verses 13-15: the Paraclete will not speak on his own but merely speak whatever he hears from Jesus (just as Jesus only spoke what he heard from his Father) and take what belongs to Jesus and announce it to the believer. In addition, the Paraclete will announce the things that are to come (v.13), which probably refers to the continual significance of Jesus' teaching in any time and context. This means that the Paraclete will reinterpret and contextualize Jesus' teachings in any given situation. Therefore, without denying a possible 'prophetic' or foretelling role for the Paraclete, I suggest that the announcement of things to come refers primarily to forth telling or proclamation.

We should not dichotomize the forensic and didactic functions of the Paraclete to the extent that the Paraclete appears to have two sides – sometimes being an Advocate and at other times a Teacher. As we suggested in the commentary on 15:18-16:4a, the roles of Advocate and Teacher are in fact combined. Moreover, the Paraclete as 'Spirit of truth' is employed both in a forensic context (15:26-27) and a didactic one (16:13-15). In sum, *as a Teacher*, the Paraclete will continually explain the significance of Jesus' teaching to the believer and hence prepare the believer's testimony to the world, so that, *as an Advocate*, the Paraclete will convict the world through the believer's testimony.

Reflection

While teaching about the Holy Spirit, preachers tend to refer to Luke-Acts, but it is John, more than any other Gospel, which expounds the person and work of the Spirit. We may know a lot about God the Father and about Jesus, but sometimes our theology shows a serious lacuna when it comes to the Spirit. Perhaps this is not surprising because the Spirit does not draw attention to himself; his aim is to glorify Jesus, to take whatever he hears from Jesus, and transmit it to us (16:13-14). However, if the Spirit functions as the channel of communication between Jesus and the believer; if the Spirit mediates the presence of the Father and Jesus to the believer; if Jesus dwells in the believer by means of the Spirit; if the Spirit continues Jesus' work in this world in and through the believer; if the Spirit is the believer's teacher and advocate; then it is vital to know this Spirit and to know about his role. Are we aware of the divine presence and assistance of the Spirit-Paraclete? Are our words and deeds informed and directed by the Spirit, aimed at convicting people so that they may come to belief in Jesus?

Sorrow Turned into Joy (16:16-24)

In verses 17-18, the disciples are greatly puzzled by Jesus' statement in verse 16, 'A little while and you will no longer see me, and again a little while and you will see me.' Jesus knows that his disciples want to resolve this riddle (v.19), but his reply in verses 20-22 seems equally mystifying.

A case can be made that 'you will no longer see me' refers to Jesus' impending death, and that 'you will see me again' refers to Jesus' resurrection appearances in John 20. The problem with this view is that after the resurrection Jesus will disappear again when he ascends to the Father. Therefore, I suggest that the first part of Jesus' statement in verse 16 refers to his ascension (or even to the entire process of glorification), and the latter part to the coming of the Paraclete who will mediate the presence of Jesus to the disciples. This ties in with Jesus' other statement that puzzles the disciples, namely, 'Because I am going to the Father' (v.17, referring back to v.10). Moreover, this interpretation also dovetails nicely with similar references in 13:33 and 14:18-19, 28.

In an attempt to explain this concept to his disciples, Jesus uses the analogy of childbirth (vv.20-22). A woman has pain when she is in labour, but when the child is born the joy her newborn brings, will erase the memory of the earlier pain. Similarly, Jesus explains, the disciples' sorrow/anguish will turn into joy (the same Greek word is used for the woman's pain and the disciples' sorrow). The disciples already experience sorrow at Jesus' leaving (cf. 14:1, 27; 16:6) but Jesus promises that when he sees them again they will experience joy (v.22).

Indeed, when Jesus appears to his disciples on resurrection Sunday, they rejoice (20:20). This may call for a revision of the interpretation of verse 16, where I suggested that 'you will see me' refers to Jesus' coming again by means of the Paraclete. It would mean that we must opt for the other explanation that 'you will no longer see me' refers to Jesus' death rather than his ascension. This would also explain the phrase 'the world will be joyful' in verse 20 since Jesus' death rather than his ascension will probably cause the world to rejoice. Nevertheless, passages such as 13:33; 14:18-19, 28; 16:10 all refer to Jesus' final departure and the coming of the Paraclete. So, making room for both explanations, perhaps John intends a double reference, in that Jesus' death and ascension are sorrowful events for the disciples but Jesus' resurrection and coming back by means of the Paraclete will be joyful occasions.

Jesus also promises his disciples that on that day (in which their sorrow will become joy) they will no longer have to ask him anything but can directly ask the Father (v.23). The 'ask and you will receive' is not meant to be a license for getting whatever one wants from God; rather, it is qualified by the phrase 'in my name' (vv.23-24). 'To ask in Jesus' name' means to ask in agreement with Jesus' character and mission (see 14:13-14; 15:16). Apparently, the disciples, until this point, have not asked anything of the Father, but the time will come (with the coming of the Paraclete) when they can, and this will make their joy complete.

Reflection

The concept of joy has not received much attention in most strands of Christianity, possibly a legacy of the Reformation. John, however, mentions on various occasions that people were joyful when they saw or heard Jesus: John the Baptist (3:29), Abraham (8:56) and the disciples (20:20). In his Epistles, John rejoices in the fact that he is able to pass on his testimony and experience of Jesus to other believers, and he is full of joy when he hears that people in his church are obedient to Christ (1 John 1:4; 2 John 4, 12; 3 John 3-4). This joy is Jesus' joy brought to completion in the believer (15:11;

17:13), which is the joy of participating in and fulfilling God's mission in this world (4:36; 11:15), and the joy of people accepting and obeying Jesus' teachings (15:11; 17:13-14).

Where God's work is resisted or rejected, however, Jesus expressed sorrow, agitation and distress. For example, in 11:33, 38, Jesus was probably more disturbed at the people's lack of faith than grieved by Lazarus' death. For we know that he had expressed joy earlier when he knew that Lazarus' resurrection would evoke belief (11:15; cf. 11:41-42). In 12:27, Jesus was troubled at the impending suffering. Finally, in 13:21, Jesus was distressed because he knew that Judas was going to betray him. Interestingly, except for 12:27, in all other instances, the text indicates that Jesus' emotions are most likely incited by the Spirit, which is not strange since this agitation is a divine one.

In sum, when John speaks of joy and sorrow, he primarily refers to divine emotions related to God's work in this world. Perhaps we have experienced this divine joy that results from pleasing God or from sharing Jesus with others, and divine sorrow/indignation when God's work is resisted. If so, it may well be that these godly emotions are brought about by the indwelling Spirit-Paraclete. There are of course other forms of sorrow and joy – we grieve when someone close to us dies and we experience joy when something good or pleasant happens – but this seems sorrow and joy at a different level from what John speaks about. When John speaks of mere human sorrow, as in the case of the disciples, it may, in time, be turned into divine joy.

Parables and Plain Speech (16:25-33)

Jesus opens the last section of the final farewell speech to his disciples with an enigmatic statement: 'I have said these things to you in "parables". An hour is coming when I will no longer speak to you in "parables", but will tell you "plainly" about the Father.' (v.25). The Greek word *paroimia*, translated 'parable', refers to 'veiled language' or 'figure of speech', and is synonymous with the word for parable in the Synoptics (*parabolē*). The word *paroimia* only occurs thrice in John: in 10:6, when Jesus speaks to the Pharisees or 'the Jews'; in 16:25, when Jesus addresses his disciples; and in 16:29, when the disciples reply to Jesus. The Greek word *parrēsia*, which is translated as 'plainly' in verse 25, can also mean 'openly/publicly' or 'boldly'. In 7:4, for instance, *parrēsia* should be translated 'openly/publicly' since it is contrasted with 'secretly', so that the sentence runs, 'for no one who seeks to be publicly known acts secretly' (cf. 18:20 for a similar contrast). However, here in verse 25, the contrast is between Jesus' past concealed speech and his future plain speech.

Jesus' statement raises certain questions which must be answered. When Jesus says that he spoke in parables, does he refer to his entire teaching ministry or only to the farewell discourses? Why would Jesus speak in parables? What does the plain speech in the future refer to?

Do 'these things' in 'I have said these things to you in parables' (v.25a) refer to all Jesus' teachings during his public ministry or just to the farewell discourses to his disciples? It can be argued that Jesus' parables refer to his farewell discourses since the phrase 'I have said these things to you' occurs in 14:25; 15:11; 16:1, 4, 6, 33. However, similar constructions are found in 8:28, 30 and 12:36. What is more, we have a perfect example of a parable during Jesus' ministry (10:1-6), which also provides a clue about Jesus' purpose for speaking in parables.

John 10:1-5 is labelled in 10:6 as a parable or figure of speech. This parable is told to the Pharisees, who have been characterized as blind (9:40-41). Their blindness is probably the reason that they are unable to understand the parable (10:6). This means that *parables require spiritual or cognitive 'sight' in order to be understood*. Hence, I suggest that throughout his public ministry and private ministry to his disciples, Jesus used parables to conceal his message (cf. Mark 4:1-34). Jesus' purpose for using parables is that he wants people to think 'from above' about his teachings, to develop spiritual insight into the things of God, and to overcome their blindness.

When Jesus promises to speak 'plainly' in the future (v.25b), what does he refer to? There are a couple of reasons to suggest that he refers to the time of the coming of the Spirit-Paraclete. First, as we had suggested in 16:4a, the Paraclete will cause the disciples to remember the things Jesus had said. Second, when

Jesus says, 'I still have many things to say to you, but you cannot bear them now' in 16:12, he refers explicitly to the future teaching of the Paraclete (explained in 16:13-15). Hence, from 14:26 and 16:12-15 we conclude that the Paraclete will teach everything that Jesus has said, interpreting Jesus' words in such a way that they become plain. Thus, the following picture emerges: (i) Jesus brings God's revelation in the form of 'parables', and (ii) the Spirit-Paraclete will reveal to people the meaning and significance of what Jesus teaches.

A few comments on the remainder of the passage. Verses 26-27 elaborate on verse 23, providing a rationale for why the disciples can directly ask the Father: the Father loves them and will give them what they ask because they love Jesus and believe that he came from the Father. Verse 28 describes in a nutshell the so-called 'V-journey' of Jesus as Wisdom, to which the Prologue had already hinted: (i) Jesus came from heaven, where the Father dwells, to this world; (ii) Jesus dwelled in this world for some time; (iii) Jesus will return to the Father, via the cross, resurrection and ascension. Verses 29-30 give us a preview of the revelation that is to come, for suddenly the disciples grasp the meaning of Jesus' words.

In some English translations of the bible (e.g., KJV, NRSV) verse 31 is phrased as a question, 'Do you now believe?', indicating that at last the disciples have come to believe. However, this is unlikely; the disciples have been firmly on Jesus' side right from the beginning, and there are several references to their faith, such as 2:11, and 6:69 where Peter confesses belief on behalf of the Twelve. Jesus' utterance in verse 31 is more likely to have been a statement, resulting in the alternative translation, 'Now you believe' (cf. NIV), although this remark still needs to be explained.

Verse 32 probably refers to the time when the disciples will leave Jesus alone after his arrest. Consequently, Jesus' prediction that they will be scattered to their own homes or to their own affairs may well foreshadow the situation of John 21 where the disciples had gone back to their old professions. If we now read verse 31 in the light of verse 32, it may well be that Jesus is saying that *now* they still believed, but a time of testing is coming when their belief and commitment to him will be found wanting.

Verse 33 succinctly sums up some of Jesus' earlier sayings, found in 14:27, 15:18-16:4a and 12:31. The reality of the persecution that the disciples will face in the world (and to which v.32 may allude) is sandwiched between a twofold encouragement from Jesus: (i) in their relationship with Jesus they will experience his peace; (ii) Jesus has conquered the world and its ruler. A glance at the Johannine Epistles shows that this has indeed become a reality for the believer: they have experienced this divine peace (2 John 3; 3 John 15) and they have also conquered the world (1 John 2:13-14; 4:4; 5:4-5).

Reflection

Have you ever considered that Jesus would deliberately couch his saving message in concealed language? This seems to be at odds with all modern theories about good and effective communication. Perhaps we can understand Jesus' communication technique as follows. Jesus came to reveal God, i.e., to make him known, because people are not from God and do not know him (8:47, 55). However, Jesus' life-giving revelation is not self-explanatory; it needs to be penetrated, it needs to be 'heard', i.e., understood, before it results in eternal life (cf. 5:24-25). His revelatory teaching is enigmatic; he frequently uses metaphors, double entendre and symbolism, which causes people to misunderstand him. In addition, people frequently find Jesus' teaching too difficult or too offensive to take it in, and hence they reject it (cf. 6:60-66).

Jesus' enigmatic teachings can be called 'parables', which need to be penetrated cognitively in order to extract their life-giving content (cf. 4:10, 14; 6:63). These 'parables' are communication in veiled language and hence need to be interpreted in order to be understood. The Spirit-Paraclete is the interpreter par excellence *who will explain the meaning and significance of Jesus' teaching. People need to be 'healed' from their spiritual blindness in order to understand Jesus' revelation and hence enter into eternal life (cf. 8:43-47). Some people do progress cognitively and spiritually, such as the Samaritan woman, the royal official and the man born blind; others, like Nicodemus and 'the Jews', make little or no progress.*

When the disciples are able to understand Jesus' words, and triumphantly exclaim that now they know and believe he is from God (vv.29-30), Jesus lovingly but almost ironically reprimands them, 'Yes, now you believe but soon that belief will crumble and you will leave me' (vv.31-32). We are probably sufficiently attuned to John's language to grasp that 'to leave Jesus' implies ceasing to follow him as a disciple – although with the Twelve this 'defection' was only temporary. The disciples' elation here almost parallels Peter's overconfidence in 13:36-38. At times, we may also fall into this trap, especially when we have finally grasped a spiritual truth, overcome a weakness or had a mountain-top experience. Let us be careful not to be too confident or underestimate the persecution we are likely to face in the world. May our confidence be in the peace that Jesus promises and in his victory of the world and the devil.

Jesus' Prayer (17:1-26)

Jesus' private teaching to his disciples is complete, and only a final prayer remains. This is the longest prayer of Jesus on record, and most likely said in the presence of his disciples. We can divide Jesus' prayer into three sections: (i) Jesus' request for his glorification (17:1-5); (ii) Jesus' prayer for his disciples (17:6-19); (iii) Jesus' prayer for others (17:20-26).

Jesus' Prayer for Glorification (17:1-5)

Realizing that the hour of his glorification has arrived, i.e., the inseparable events of his death, resurrection and ascension (cf. 13:1), Jesus dedicates his last 'farewell speech' to his Father (v.1). He requests his Father to glorify him so that, in turn, the Father may be glorified. Jesus had already announced his approaching glorification in public (12:23), but now he reiterates it in private (v.1). The concept of mutual glorification between the Father and Son was already introduced in 13:31-32.

Verse 1 runs into verse 2, indicating that Jesus requests for this mutual glorification inasmuch as the Father had given him authority over all people, especially the authority to dispense eternal life to all whom the Father has 'given' to Jesus.

The nature of eternal life is spelled out in verse 3: namely, that people may *know* the only true God and his son Jesus Christ. Throughout his Gospel, John has emphasized the importance of knowing God. In order to partake in the divine life, one needs to have a sufficient authentic understanding of God and Jesus in terms of their identity, mission and mutual relationship. The Spirit mediates this knowledge/understanding of the Godhead to people in his capacity as interpreter of Jesus' revelatory teaching. The Spirit opens up Jesus' revelation for understanding as it were. Although John does not spell out how much knowledge or understanding is 'sufficient', he has presented us with an array of characters who have varied responses to Jesus, and we have evaluated them along the way.

In verse 4, Jesus asserts that he has glorified the Father while he was in this world by finishing the work that the Father had assigned to him (cf. 4:34; 5:36). Indeed, that is why Jesus can triumphantly cry out on the cross, 'It is finished' (19:28, 30). The cross is the place where Jesus ultimately glorifies the Father, and where Jesus' glorification starts. As Jesus glorified the Father on earth, he now requests his Father to glorify him in heaven (v.5). Jesus literally asks to be glorified *beside* the Father with the pre-existent glory he enjoyed before his incarnation, harking back to 1:1-2, which spoke of the pre-existent Logos being with God. The place next to the Father is a unique place and denotes that the Father and Son are co-regents (cf. the shared throne between God and Jesus in Revelation 3:21; 22:1, 3).

Jesus' Prayer for His Disciples (17:6-19)

Jesus now moves on to petition the Father on behalf of his disciples. He asserts that he has revealed his Father's name, i.e., his Father's character and work, to those whom the Father has 'given' him from the world (v.6). Indeed, this was Jesus' mission: to reveal God as Father (cf. 1:18). Again, when we read that people from the world are 'given' to Jesus by the Father, it most likely refers to divine initiative rather than a doctrine of predestination (see the commentary on 6:37-40). What is especially in view here is the divine initiative Jesus showed in choosing the Twelve (6:70;

15:16, 19). This 'election' is probably the result of Jesus' doing what he heard from the Father. Subsequently, Jesus' disciples have kept, i.e., accepted and obeyed, God's word communicated by Jesus' teaching (vv.6-8). In other words, Jesus passed on God's words in his teaching to his disciples, and they have accepted, understood and believed these revelatory words (note the sequence of acceptance, knowing, belief in v.8).

Jesus reiterates that he is petitioning the Father on behalf of his disciples, who belong to him and to the Father (vv.9-10). In essence, Jesus' prayer on behalf of his disciples is a plea for protection and sanctification so that they may remain standing in this world (vv.11-19). While Jesus was with them, he was able to protect them and watch over them – except for Judas. Now that he is about to leave this world, his disciples will need protection. The disciples especially need protection against the hate of the world and the devil (I take the Greek phrase *ek tou ponērou* to mean 'from the evil one' rather than 'from evil') (vv.14-15).

The reason the disciples require protection is that they do not belong to the world – they belong to Jesus and are no longer part of the system of the world (v.16). Jesus does not request his Father to take the disciples out of this hostile environment but to protect them as long as they are in it. In fact, Jesus deliberately sends them into this hostile world, for they must continue his salvific mission. Just as Jesus was sent into the world (to save it), the disciples will be sent into the world to witness about Jesus, and convict the world of its guilt so that some may come to believe (cf. v.20). Since the Paraclete will assist the disciples in their witness and take the place and role of Jesus, it would not be too wide of the mark to suggest that God will protect the disciples *through the Paraclete*.

Besides the need for protection, the disciples also need sanctification (vv.17, 19). 'To sanctify' can mean 'to make holy' but also 'to dedicate for service'. The latter meaning is in view, for instance, in 10:36, where Jesus speaks of being dedicated or consecrated by the Father for his mission in this world. The only other occurrences of 'to sanctify' are here in verses 17 and 19, and on both occasions, the phrase 'in/by (the) truth' qualifies the sanctification.

'Your word is truth' most likely means that God's word contains truth, which coheres with 8:31-32, where truth is the content of Jesus' word. If we also remember that Jesus' word cleanses (15:3), then to ask that the disciples be sanctified in the truth is to ask that the disciples be made holy through God's word. The truth, as the content of God's word (which is Jesus' teaching), will cleanse the disciples and made them holy. This will most likely be a continual process rather than a one-off event. However, the other meaning of sanctification – to be dedicated for service – is probably also in view because wedged between verses 17 and 19 we have verse 18, which speaks of the disciples' mission in this world.

The Greek verb *hagiazō* ('to sanctify' [English does not know the verb 'to holify']) only occurs thrice in John (10:36; 17:17, 19). In addition, the adjective *hagios* ('holy') is only used to qualify the Father (17:11), Jesus (6:69), and the Spirit (1:33; 14:26; 20:22). Hence, we tentatively suggest that the primary means by which God sanctifies the disciples for their mission is *the Holy Spirit*.

In sum, although the text is not explicit, we have reason to believe that the protection and sanctification the disciples need in this world in order to continue and accomplish the salvific mission of Jesus is effected primarily by means of the Spirit-Paraclete. Moreover, the disciples' sanctification takes place at both a personal and global level. At a personal level, the Paraclete will continually cleanse the disciples through the truth of Jesus' word to help them grow in personal holiness and maturity. At a global level, the Paraclete will continually dedicate the disciples for missionary service in this world, both by preparing the disciples' witness and, through their witness, convicting the world of its guilt (cf. 15:26-27; 16:8-15).

Jesus' Prayer for Future Believers (17:20-26)

In the final part of his prayer, Jesus petitions the Father on behalf of those who will believe in the future (v.20). After his glorification, people will believe in Jesus through the disciples' word – most probably a reference to their ongoing testimony about Jesus to the world, prepared and empowered by the

Paraclete (see the commentary on 15:26-27; 16:8-15). The disciples' Spirit-imbued testimony will evoke belief because it is based on Jesus' historical teaching and because the same Spirit who actively reached out to people through Jesus' teaching will also reach out to the world through the disciples' testimony. When people are confronted with the combined witness of the Spirit-Paraclete and the disciples, they are essentially confronted with the life-giving teaching of Jesus' himself. To draw on 6:63, *the disciples' words are 'Paraclete' and 'life'*, in that their testimony is prepared and empowered by the Paraclete, and this testimony provides eternal life if it is accepted. Thus, the disciples' Spirit-informed witness is expected to have the same cleansing and liberating effect as Jesus' Spirit-imbued teaching. This should come as no surprise since Jesus' intention is to continue his mission in the world through his followers and to empower them just as he was empowered.

The purpose of people believing in Jesus is that they may all be one; a oneness that is explained as a (mutual) indwelling of the believer in the Father and Son (v.21 [and its elaboration in vv.22-23]; cf. 14:20). This reminds us of two earlier teachings of Jesus. First, in 10:16-17, Jesus speaks of the need to bring other sheep to his fold, so that there may be one flock under one shepherd. Jesus' aim is to constitute one community in which all who belong to him will be brought together. In this community, believers have an ongoing communion or fellowship with Jesus and the Father, participating in the eternal life (v.3), love (v.26), truth/knowledge (v.17) and glory (v.22) that the Father and Son share (cf. 1 John 1:3). This oneness will also function as a testimony to the world (vv.21, 23). The second teaching that we are reminded of when we read verses 21 and 23, is 14:23, which speaks of the Father and Son making their home with the believer – through the Paraclete. This implies that the oneness between the Father, Jesus and the believer is most likely created and sustained *by means of the Paraclete*.

In verses 25-26, Jesus wraps up his prayer. The world does not know God as Father (cf. 8:47, 55), but Jesus' followers do because he has revealed the Father to them, and Jesus will continue to do so (note the future tense in v.26).

Reflection

In verse 15, it is important to notice that Jesus does not ask for his disciples to be taken out of the world but for adequate protection as long as they are in this hostile environment. The reason for this request is twofold. First, if the disciples are withdrawn from the world, there would be no witnesses left to testify on behalf of Jesus, and the ongoing cosmic trial would be lost. Second, the world needs to be convinced of its guilt through the Paraclete-imbued testimony of the disciples so that some may come to believe on the basis of that testimony (v.20; 16:8-15). This implies that, as believers, we should not withdraw from this world or turn our backs on it. We have the task of testifying on behalf of Jesus and so to convince the world of its guilt so that some may respond in faith to him. John's Gospel urges us to reach out to the people of the world with the life-giving message of Jesus, no matter how the world reacts. In fact, we know that the world is and always will be a hostile environment for those who confess to belong to Jesus. But take courage, Jesus promised us his peace; he has conquered the world and we share in his victory (16:33); and we have the divine assistance of the Spirit-Paraclete.

Speaking of the Spirit-Paraclete, we tentatively suggested that 17:6-19 spells out two further functions of the Paraclete. First, to protect believers against the hate of the world and the kind of persecution described in 15:18-16:4a. Second, to sanctify the believers through the truth, which is the cleansing content of Jesus' teaching – both to keep the disciples holy so that they will remain in Jesus, and to prepare them for their mission in this world.

Even in 17:20-26, the Paraclete is present, though in the background: some people will come to believe through the believers' Paraclete-informed witness (v.20). Besides, the oneness of the Father, Jesus and the believer (vv.21-23) and the love between them (v.26) are probably the result of the Paraclete's activity. The presence of the Spirit may not always be obvious because the Spirit works behind the scenes in our lives, and directs, equips and sustains us more than we realize. If I am allowed to use the analogy of the wind, as John does in 3:8, often we do not know or understand how the Spirit works and where or when he is active but from the effects we can recognize that the Spirit is at work.

Sometimes the credibility and quality of our witness is limited to the extent that we have been able to grasp the liberating, sanctifying truth of Jesus' teaching that we read about in 8:31-32 and 17:17-19. Only to the extent that believers themselves live in the holistic, liberated state that Jesus intends are they able to influence (and probably justified in influencing) their society. In that respect, a significant part of the Indian Church, for example, must still rid herself of problems such as caste discrimination, dowry practice and denominational bigotry in order to improve her credibility as a witness. Similarly, many quarters of the western Church may still need to take a stronger or clearer stance on issues like homosexuality, same-sex marriage and wealth. In short, the challenge for the Church is whether she is different enough from the world in order to influence it. If we must believe Mahatma Gandhi's criticism of Christianity, especially Western Christianity, that its practical functioning does not correspond to Jesus' teachings, then perhaps the Church at large seems to have neglected to practise fully what her founder advocated!

Similarly, if Jesus commands his followers to continue his liberating mission in this world through their Spirit-imbued witness, Christians cannot simply stand on the sidelines but need to engage with various issues in today's societies. Jesus primarily targeted the religious core of the Jewish theocratic society of his day because the social, economic and political life was built around it. But in many of today's secular societies, we need a more multi-faceted approach. There must be Christian voices in every layer and area of society that speak up for justice, truth, liberation and equality. We need more Christians in 'secular' jobs to influence their society – Christian lawyers, judges, politicians, CEOs, business people, journalists, and so on. Every Christian is, in fact, in 'full-time ministry'. At present, secular humanitarian organizations, such as the United Nations, Amnesty International, Action Aid International, the World Bank and IMF, often lead the way on the issues mentioned above. These organizations may need a stronger Christian presence, or we may need more Christian organizations which have a clear biblical rather than a mere humanitarian basis.

Jesus' Passion and Resurrection (18:1-20:31)

Jesus has finished his farewell discourse to his disciples, and now stands at the threshold of the last hours of his life, leading to his passion and resurrection. Notice that even now, Jesus remains in control. From a human perspective, the betrayal of Jesus, his arrest, trial and death may cast him as the victim, humiliated and defeated. From a divine perspective, which John delineates for his readers, however, the same events are subverted and reinterpreted as glorious and victorious.

This section is structured as follows: (i) Jesus' betrayal and arrest (18:1-11); (ii) Jesus' trial (18:12-19:16a); (iii) Jesus' death (19:16b-42); (iv) Jesus' resurrection (20:1-31).

Jesus' Betrayal and Arrest (18:1-11)

We may need to go back to the commentary on 14:31 to recall the possible flow of historical events. There we had suggested that, on Thursday evening, Jesus had a meal and a discourse with his disciples (John 13-14), following which, Jesus and his disciples left the house (14:31). The events narrated in John 15-17 then happened along the way. After Jesus' had finished his prayer, he and his disciples left Jerusalem and crossed the Kidron valley to the garden of Gethsemane near the Mount of Olives (18:1).

Apparently, Jesus often met with his disciples in this garden, so his arrest was not difficult to plan (vv.2-3). As Judas' betrayal of Jesus was premeditated, he brought with him a detachment of Roman soldiers as well as temple guards or temple police sent by the chief priests and Pharisees. Earlier, the temple police had been unsuccessful in arresting Jesus (7:32, 44-45). In fact, up to this point, every attempt to capture or kill Jesus had failed because his hour had not yet come (7:30; 8:20, 59; 10:39). Perhaps these failed attempts were the reason that Judas had brought an unusually large number of soldiers and police to arrest a single man.

The careful reader will realize that we cannot attribute Jesus' arrest to the large number of soldiers and police. The real reason Jesus' arrest is successful, is because Jesus' hour has arrived and he allows these men to arrest him. In fact, the arrest almost makes a mockery of the authorities since verses 4-6 reveal that Jesus is still in full control. For example, Jesus' reply, 'I am', when they say that they are seeking Jesus of Nazareth, causes them to move back and fall to the ground (vv.5-6). At a human level, this response is amusing, but at a spiritual level, this incident is a demonstration of Jesus' power over the devil. For Jesus' divine self-revelation pushes back and overwhelms the powers of darkness, which Judas has come to embody (13:2, 27).

Jesus' powerful demonstration certainly gives him the bargaining power to keep his disciples from being arrested, so that he would not lose any of those whom the Father had entrusted to him (vv.8-9; cf. 6:39; 17:12). Peter, however, takes matters into his own hands: he draws his small sword or dagger and wounds Malchus, the servant of the high priest (v.10). Either Peter still clung to the idea of a messiah who would start a violent revolution, or perhaps Peter was quite serious about being willing to lay down his life for his master (13:37). Whatever Peter's reasons for carrying a weapon and for his violent action, it shows that he has still not understood the path Jesus had to go. Therefore, Jesus has to rebuke Peter (v.11). Jesus' kingdom cannot be established by means of human violence because his kingdom is not from this world; if it were, then Peter's action would have been justified (cf. 18:36). 'To drink the cup' that the Father has given Jesus is a metaphor for Jesus' extreme sufferings as described in John 18-19, which the Father has chosen for him.

Reflection

Although Jesus knew what was going to happen – that he was going to be arrested, suffer and die – he did not shrink back or flee. He was prepared to drink the cup of suffering because he knew that this was the way the Father had planned for him to save the world. Jesus demonstrated that he had the power to overcome his enemies (v.6), but he did not use it to resist or escape them. This cannot have been easy for Jesus, and we know from the Synoptic Gospels how Jesus struggled to escape this cup, but ultimately his desire to do the Father's will prevailed (Mark 14:36; Matthew 26:39; Luke 22:42).

May we learn from Jesus to have the same desire to obey God – no matter what the cost.

Peter's action, courageous as it may seem, showed that he was not aware of the divine plan. In contrast, Jesus knew his Father's plan and went along with it. Are we in touch with our heavenly Father to the extent that we know his plan and can act in step with it? Being unaware of God's strategies can lead to disastrous actions on our part, no matter how well we mean them. We need to think 'from above' – to know God's plans and mission – in order to be effective. Rather than launching our own plan and mission, we need to participate in his ongoing mission in this world.

Jesus' Trial (18:12-19:16a)

This section gives an account, first, of Jesus' trial before Caiaphas, the high priest (18:12-27), and later before Pilate, the Roman prefect or procurator (18:28-19:16a). Since Caiaphas, as high priest, presided over the Sanhedrin (the supreme Jewish religious and legal council), 18:12-27 represents Jesus' trial before the Jewish authorities; whereas 18:28-19:16a records Jesus' trial before the Roman authorities. During his trial, no one comes forward to speak in Jesus' defence – not even his disciples (cf. 16:32) – and Jesus' enemies seemingly have free rein.

Jesus before the High Priest and Peter's Denial of Jesus (18:12-27)

This passage has a parallel structure ABA'B', in which A (vv.12-14) and A' (vv.19-24) show Jesus before the high priest, and B (vv.15-18) and B' (vv.25-27) describe Peter's denial.

After his arrest, Jesus is taken to Annas, the father-in-law of Caiaphas, the high priest that year (vv.12-13). Although historical evidence shows that Caiaphas was high priest from A.D. 18-36, his father-in-law Annas, who held the office from A.D. 6-15, perhaps still enjoyed a great influence. Luke also seems to be ambiguous: he mentions 'the high priesthood of Annas and Caiaphas' in the beginning of his Gospel (Luke 3:2); but in his sequel, he refers to Annas rather than Caiaphas as the high priest (Acts 4:6).

In verse 14, John reminds his audience that Caiaphas was the one who had previously advised the Sanhedrin that it was better to have one person die for the people (11:47-53). The Sanhedrin was the highest authority on religious and legal matters concerning the Jews. It consisted of seventy-one members, including the chief priests and Pharisees like Nicodemus, with the high priest as the leader (cf. Mishnah *Sanhedrin* 1:6). However, the Romans had restricted the powers of the Sanhedrin in certain areas. For example, 18:31 records that the Council could not carry out the death penalty.

In verse 14, John's aim is not simply to remind the reader about who Caiaphas is, but, more specifically, to inform the careful reader that Jesus will not receive a fair trial. The outcome of the trial has been decided a long time ago: Jesus needed to die in order to 'save' the Jewish nation – as well as the position of the Jewish religious leaders (11:48-50). The Johannine irony is that the reader also knows that Jesus must die – in order to save *the entire world* from the oppression of the devil and sin (3:16; 6:51; 8:31-36; 12:31-32).

From Jesus, the camera swings to Peter. Peter and another disciple follow Jesus to Annas' house – they still follow as disciples (v.15a). Although Peter's companion is not identified, it most likely is the Beloved Disciple because (i) the Beloved Disciple is intimate with Jesus (13:23), and probably stays also now closest to him (v.15b; cf. 19:26); (ii) Peter and the Beloved Disciple are contrasted both here and in 21:15-25. Since the Beloved Disciple is known to the high priest, he is able to go with Jesus into the courtyard of the high priest. Peter has to remain standing outside at the gate; only when the Beloved Disciple arranges for it, can Peter come in (vv.15-16).

The Greek word for 'courtyard' in verse 15 also occurs in 10:1, 16, but there it refers to the sheepfold. In addition, just as there is a gate to the courtyard (v.16), so there is a gate for the sheepfold (10:1-2, 7, 9). The significance of John's allusion to chapter 10 is that the Beloved Disciple, contra Peter, is the true or ideal disciple; the former can freely go in and out and stay close to Jesus (cf. 10:9), whereas Peter has to remain at the gate and can only get in with the help of the Beloved Disciple. Unlike the Beloved Disciple,

John 18:12-27 Jesus before the High Priest and Peter's Denial

Peter is not able to follow Jesus closely, and it will get worse! In verse 17, we see Peter deny Jesus for the first time. He will do so twice more, as Jesus foretold in 13:38. The mention of the charcoal fire in verse 18 may seem unimportant, but it will gain significance when we reach 21:9 where Jesus is making breakfast on a charcoal fire. As an aside, the mention of a *female* gatekeeper in verses 16-17 (cf. 10:3), may indicate the prominence John gives to women throughout his Gospel!

John takes us back to Jesus before the high priest. The high priest (or Annas, as verse 24 clarifies) questions Jesus about his disciples and his teaching (v.19). Indeed, Jesus' teaching had caused contention on various occasions (e.g., 5:18; 6:41, 52, 60; 7:40-44; 8:39-59; 10:19, 33). Jesus replies that there is nothing secret about his teaching because he has always taught openly to the world; he has always taught in synagogues and the temple, the places where the Jews gather (v.20; cf. 2:16-22; 5:14; 6:59; 7:14, 28; 8:2, 20; 10:23-30). Jesus suggests, perhaps mockingly, that Annas should question the people who heard his teaching if he wants to know more about what he said (v.21). This answer infuriates one of the temple police who strikes Jesus, although the Greek text does not specify where he struck him and whether with an open hand, fist, club or rod (v.22). In turn, Jesus challenges his interrogators to justify the blow or testify to his wrongdoing (v.23). This apparently silences his opponents and they send him to Caiaphas the high priest (v.24). It is clear that there is no real case against Jesus.

The final scene takes us back to Peter. Peter is still standing near the fire, warming himself, when he is asked again whether he is one of Jesus' followers (v.25). As in verse 17, the question is formulated in such a way that the expected answer is 'no', and indeed this is the answer Peter gives, denying Jesus and his own discipleship for the second time (v.25). Finally, a relative of Malchus, whose ear Peter had chopped off, challenges Peter (in Greek, the question expects the answer 'yes' this time), Peter denies having any association with Jesus for the third time – at this point the cock crows (vv.26-27).

This would probably rate as the worst moment in Peter's life. First, he is unable to follow Jesus as closely as the Beloved

Disciple, and worse, when the heat is on, he becomes a defector, a non-disciple. Peter's bravado in 13:37, sadly, amounts to nothing, as Jesus has foretold (13:38). By denying his master, Peter also denies his own discipleship. Peter is not (yet) able to follow Jesus the whole way, but fortunately, the story does not end here, as we shall see in John 21.

Reflection

This part of Jesus' trial reveals that, for the Jewish religious authorities, the most controversial and therefore, central issue, was Jesus' teaching, including his discourses and disputes with people. Jesus claims to have the divine prerogatives to give life and to judge, and to have a unique, intimate relationship with God his Father. Besides, he asserts that being Jewish is no guarantee (any longer) that a person belongs to the true people of God. In his teaching, Jesus also unmasks the hypocrisy and ignorance of his opponents: they were no experts on the Mosaic Law as they thought; they neither knew God nor belonged to him; in fact, they were 'from below', belonging to the family of the devil. These kinds of claims and assertions must have upset the Jewish religious leaders and threatened both their beliefs and status to the extent that they decided to kill Jesus. As his followers, when we seek to pass on Jesus' teachings, we should not be surprised if we encounter similar reactions.

This story always evokes in us sympathy for Peter – perhaps because we recognize ourselves in him at times. Peter, the spokesman for the Twelve, the one who confesses his faith in Jesus (6:68-69), says he is willing to die for Jesus (13:37) and rushes to defend him (18:10), now fails tragically. Perhaps we remember similar incidents in our lives. Or, perhaps we remember a situation when Jesus was ridiculed and we did not speak up, afraid that we too would be mocked. Like Peter, we are all human, are we not? As we shall see, Peter will be restored, and Acts 2 will demonstrate that he picks up his leadership role again. So, we will learn that there is restoration for those who fail in their commitment and discipleship.

Jesus before Pilate (18:28-19:16a)

Jesus' trial before Pilate is a complicated one. Structurally, this episode consists of seven rounds as it were, in which Pilate alternately moves in and out of his palace or fortress. In rounds one, three, five and seven, Pilate comes *out of* his palace (18:29; 18:38b; 19:4; 19:13); in rounds two, four and six, he goes *into* his palace (18:33; 19:1; 19:9).

Pilate was the Roman governor of Judea from A.D. 26-36/37, and as such, stood for the rule of Rome. Therefore, this episode represents Jesus' trial before the Roman authorities, the ultimate power of the then-known 'civilized' world. Indeed, we shall see that the Romans, the human rulers of the world, and the devil, the spiritual ruler of the world, are on the same side. Moreover, we will be reminded of the Prologue, which told us that the world does not know or accept Jesus (1:10-11).

It is no coincidence that Jesus is taken from the Jewish authorities (with their limited authority) to the Roman authorities (with seemingly unlimited authority). Jesus' trial needs to be played out on a cosmic scale because he was sent into the world. His mission is directed to the world, and his saving act on the cross will have consequences for the entire world. The rejection and trial of Jesus at the hands of the world will ultimately lead to Jesus' giving his life for the life of the world and becoming the saviour of the world.

Round One (18:28-32)

John has not recorded the trial proceedings before Caiaphas; only that Jesus was taken to him (v.24) and then from Caiaphas to Pilate (v.28). It is now Friday morning, and Jesus appears before Pilate in his fortress or residential palace. Ironically, 'the Jews' do not enter the Roman palace since that would render them ritually unclean and keep them from participating in the Passover meal (v.28). Little do they realize that their action towards Jesus makes them spiritually 'unclean' and prevents them from partaking in the real Passover meal on the cross (cf. 1:29; 6:51-55).

So, Pilate is forced to come out to inquire about the accusation that 'the Jews' are bringing against Jesus (v.29). Rather than answering Pilate's question, 'the Jews' say somewhat aggressively that if this man had not done evil they would not have brought him to Pilate (v.30). Pilate, in turn, says that they should take him and judge him according to their own law (v.31a). The case would have ended there, had it not been for 'the Jews' who believed that Jesus deserved the death penalty, a sentence which they were not authorized to execute (v.31b).

The bell rings, announcing the end of round one, and it is time to check the score. The first round raises two fundamental questions. First, why is Jesus on trial, what are the charges against him? Second, who has the authority to judge?

Round Two (18:33-38a)

Pilate now enters his palace, summons Jesus, and asks him whether he is the king of the Jews (v.33). This is a loaded question since it is essentially a query whether Jesus is a sort of nationalistic leader who poses a threat to Rome. Jesus, in turn, asks whether this question comes from Pilate himself or if he has heard this from others (v.34). The latter is quite possible since John records at least two occasions where the crowd sought to promote Jesus as king (although merely in a worldly sense) (6:15; 12:13). Pilate replies rather sarcastically that he is not Jewish, so how would he know (v.35a). Jesus is handed over to Pilate by his fellow-Jews, so they should be the ones to come up with the allegation. Pilate simply wants to know what Jesus has done to be brought to him (v.35).

Jesus ignores this last question and instead addresses Pilate's earlier question enquiring whether he is the king of the Jews. Jesus asserts that his kingdom is not from this world; if it were, his followers would have defended him (v.36). This reply is in fact a political statement because Jesus acknowledges that he has a kingdom – and hence is a king – although his kingdom does not belong to this world. Moreover, Jesus demands an exclusive allegiance from his followers. This will automatically lead to confrontations with regimes or kingdoms that are of this world, like the Roman empire, which also demand the allegiance of their subjects. It would make it impossible to be loyal to both Jesus and his kingdom, and to the Roman emperor and his empire.

We can understand this distinction between Jesus' kingdom and kingdoms from this world as follows: Although Jesus' kingdom is not *from* this world – for it neither belongs to nor has its source in this world, and therefore, transcends any 'worldly' kingdom – it nevertheless exists and operates *in* this world. Jesus' kingdom can be equated with God's kingdom (cf. 3:3, 5), and is made up of people who are born from above – believers who no longer belong to the world but are active in it (cf. 17:15-16). This kingdom is a kingdom 'from above'; it belongs to the realm above but it has penetrated the realm below.

Although Pilate cannot have understood the significance of Jesus' statement, he does infer that Jesus is a king (v.37a; the question is phrased in such a way that it expects the answer 'yes'). Jesus affirms Pilate's inference, and adds that (i) the purpose for his coming to this world was to witness to the truth, and (ii) everyone who belongs to the truth hears his voice (v.37). Jesus' witness to the truth is shorthand for his entire ministry, during which he taught about the divine reality. In other words, he communicated God's words, which contain saving truth. 'To witness to the truth' was not just Jesus' task; John the Baptist also witnessed to the truth (5:33), and Jesus' followers are also expected to do the same (15:26-27; cf. 3 John 3). All who belong to the truth belong to Jesus and have heard his voice (cf. 5:25; 10:3-4, 16).

Pilate's question, 'What is truth?' (v.38a), shows that he has not understood who Jesus is and what he has to offer, although it may also be proof that Pilate has some interest in Jesus. Many philosophers since Pilate have asked the same question, but for John, truth is bound up to Jesus. Jesus is the embodiment and dispenser of divine truth – truth that cleanses and liberates (see the commentary on 14:6). And so, at the end of the second round, it seems that Jesus has scored a few points. He throws Pilate off balance by affirming that he is a king with a kingdom (although different from the way people understand it) and he speaks of his witness to the truth, a concept Pilate is unable to grasp.

Round Three (18:38b-40)

Pilate goes out of his residence again and tells 'the Jews' that he has not found a case against Jesus (v.38b). After all the questioning, there is still no case against Jesus. Pilate, perhaps sensing that 'the Jews' would be dissatisfied, suggests a way out of the impasse. There was a custom to release a prisoner at the Passover to please 'the Jews', and Pilate proposes that perhaps this someone could be Jesus, the king of the Jews (v.39).

Unable to establish a case against Jesus, Pilate tries to be diplomatic and even appears to favour releasing Jesus. However, when Pilate, in verse 39, refers to Jesus as the 'king of the Jews', he can hardly be serious, for if he was, he could never offer to release him. It is more likely that Pilate is mocking 'the Jews' and perhaps perceives Jesus as somewhat odd. Anyway, 'the Jews' reject Pilate's proposition and demand the release of Barabbas instead (v.40). John clarifies that Barabbas was a social bandit, i.e., someone who robbed the rural aristocracy and who was seen as a potential revolutionary (cf. 10:1, 8). Ironically, 'Barabbas' means 'son of the father', whereas, in reality, Jesus is the true son of the Father.

At the end of this round, it becomes clear that although Pilate seems sympathetic towards Jesus, he does not take him very seriously and perhaps uses him to ridicule 'the Jews'. 'The Jews', however, do not want Jesus to be released. They would rather have a criminal set free than the one who can truly liberate them.

Round Four (19:1-3)

After his second exchange with 'the Jews', Pilate takes Jesus into the palace and has him flogged (v.1). The soldiers continue to mock Jesus in the same vein as Pilate, dressing him up as a king and putting a crown of thorns on his head (v.2). In addition, they ridicule him with their salutations and physically assault him (v.3). No one takes Jesus' kingship seriously: it infuriates 'the Jews'; Pilate does not find it entirely credible; and the soldiers boldly attack him. End of round four.

Round Five (19:4-7)

Pilate comes out of his palace again and addresses 'the Jews', saying that he still finds no case against Jesus (v.4). He has Jesus brought out with his thorny crown and purple robe, and presents him to 'the Jews' saying, 'See, the man' (v.5). The significance of this phrase is not clear. Is it simply Pilate's way of mocking 'the Jews' and their so-called king; is John emphasizing the humanity of Jesus; or is it perhaps an allusion to Jesus as the Son of Man? Whatever the case, Pilate's non-committal attitude towards Jesus and his mockery of 'the Jews', forces them to put their cards on the table, demanding that Jesus be crucified (v.6a). Crucifixion was the Roman form of capital punishment for criminals and insurrectionists. Pilate authorizes 'the Jews' to carry out their demand but he does not pronounce this judgement himself, since he has found no case against Jesus (v.6b). 'The Jews' finally frame their charges: Jesus is guilty of blasphemy for he made himself equal to God. This is a crime for which the Mosaic Law prescribed death by stoning (v.7; cf. 5:18; 10:33; Leviticus 24:16).

Thus, round five, partially answers the questions of round one: (i) Why is Jesus on trial?; and (ii) Who has the authority to judge? The Jewish religious leaders accuse Jesus of blasphemy, for equating himself to God, and use their authority to judge him. However, the reader knows that these are false charges, for 'the Jews' have not understood Jesus and his teaching. Moreover, Jesus' opponents have already demonstrated that they are unable to judge rightly (7:24; 7:53-8:11; 8:15). In fact, 'the Jews' do not have the authority to judge him. First, the Romans have limited their jurisdiction (18:31), but, more importantly, to judge is a divine prerogative given to Jesus by the Father (5:22, 27). Interestingly, Pilate is unable to find any basis for punishing Jesus and avoids passing any judgement (although, of course, he condones the judgement that 'the Jews' have passed on to Jesus).

Round Six (19:8-12)

When Pilate hears what 'the Jews' have to say, he is rather afraid (v.8). ['Rather afraid' makes more sense than 'even more afraid' (NIV) or 'more afraid than ever' (NRSV) since Pilate has not shown fear previously.] The text does not clarify what makes Pilate afraid, but perhaps it is the fierceness of 'the Jews' demand for Jesus' death and the threat of a potential revolt. Pilate goes back into his palace and asks Jesus where he is from, but Jesus does not reply (v.9).

This seems to irritate Pilate for he says to Jesus, 'You know that I have authority to release you and authority to crucify you, don't you?' (v.10). Jesus now replies that Pilate has no authority over him except what God has given to him (literally 'given to him from above') (v.11a). Ironically, Pilate presumes to have authority, whereas in reality it is Jesus who has authority (1:12; 5:27; 10:18; 17:2). Any authority Pilate has, comes not from Rome but from God. In that sense, Judas' sin is greater than Pilate's because Judas has no divine authority; rather, his 'authority' to betray Jesus came from the devil (v.11b; cf. 13:2, 27 [in v.11b, 'the one who handed me over' is singular and therefore cannot refer to 'the Jews']).

Jesus' words seem to have a strong impact because from then on Pilate makes an effort to release him. However, 'the Jews' skillfully manipulate Pilate: they shout at him that if he releases Jesus, he is no friend of the emperor because Jesus, by virtue of his claim to be a king, opposes the emperor (v.12). This is obviously a clever move from 'the Jews'. Their logic: Jesus implicitly affirms that he is a king, which is an act of rebellion against Rome, and hence, if Pilate releases Jesus, he would place himself on the side of Jesus rather than of Rome. Although Jesus scores points with Pilate, this penultimate round seems to go to 'the Jews'. They shrewdly modify their earlier charges against Jesus from his claim to be equal to God (v.7) to his implicit claim to be a king (v.12). In this way, they force Pilate's hand because the option to release Jesus is no longer open to him. This brings us to the final round.

Round Seven (19:13-16a)

When Pilate hears what 'the Jews' have to say, he brings Jesus outside and sits on the judge's seat at a place called The Stone Pavement, or Gabbatha in Aramaic (v.13). It is also possible to translate part of verse 13 as, 'and he [Pilate] seated him [Jesus] on the judge's seat'. It depends on what Pilate makes of Jesus' words in verse 11. If he accepts that Jesus has more authority than he, then perhaps he seated Jesus on the judicial bench. However, this would amount to mocking Jesus, and would contradict the fact that Pilate took Jesus' words in verse 11 seriously and tried to release him (v.12). It is more likely that Pilate himself sat down on the judicial bench – perhaps a final attempt to exercise his authority to release Jesus, or perhaps to mock 'the Jews' further.

It is now about noon, so the trial before Pilate has been going on for approximately six hours (cf. 18:28). Pilate taunts 'the Jews' saying, 'See, your king!' (v.14), to which they respond with calls for Jesus' crucifixion (v.15). Once again he mockingly asks them whether he should crucify their king, but 'the Jews' corner Pilate for a second time saying, 'We have no king except the emperor' (v.15). This cunning statement leaves Pilate with no choice but to give in to their demand, so he hands Jesus over to be crucified (v.16). The final statement of 'the Jews' in verse 15 is saddening because they put themselves firmly on the side of the Romans. In their rejection of Jesus, they have chosen to align themselves with the Roman empire and its oppressive rule.

In the end, Pilate has been unable to use his position of authority. Much as he tried to release Jesus (18:39; 19:12), he was shrewdly manipulated by 'the Jews' to crucify him. From a human perspective, 'the Jews' would be declared 'winners', Pilate labelled as too weak and Jesus as the 'loser'. Besides, from the beginning it was clear that Jesus was not going to receive a fair trial. The reader will also know that from God's perspective it had gone according to plan and Jesus remained in control.

Reflection

From a human perspective, Jesus seems the loser and his opponents the clever winners, but, from a divine perspective, things are going according to plan and Jesus is in full control. Once again, we are invited to view the situation 'from above'. How often do we look at circumstances 'from above'? It may surprise us to find that certain situations from God's perspective look very different from the way we see them with the human eye. Faith, in fact, is the means by which we view things from a divine perspective.

What do we make of Pilate? He seems the most complex character in John. In dealing with Jesus, Pilate is diplomatic and sympathetic – he does not find a case against him, tries to release him and seems interested in the truth – but it appears that he does not take Jesus seriously and even uses him to ridicule 'the Jews'. As for 'the Jews', Pilate is cruel and condescending towards them; he mocks and probably despises them. At the same time, Pilate may have been afraid of the Jewish mob gathered before him. And, while assuming to be in authority, Pilate finds himself being manipulated by 'the Jews' and forced to take their side. Despite all his diplomatic skills, Pilate is shrewdly outmanoeuvred by the Jewish religious authorities. In sum, John portrays Pilate as a complex character who does not clearly take sides. The length of the trial and Pilate's frequent moves in and out of his palace perhaps reflect that he also goes back and forth in his mind. He is not decisive enough to use his authority to make the right judgement. In the final evaluation, Pilate's response to Jesus falters and fails.

Jesus' remark that Pilate's authority is 'from above', i.e., a God-given authority, may trigger questions about today's governments. Is the authority of every government a God-given authority? If so, is it aware of its responsibility and accountability towards God? To what extent do we need to respect and adhere to a government? What about oppressive regimes such as the former regime of Saddam Hussein in Iraq; the communist regime of Kim Jong Il in North Korea; or the military junta in Myanmar?

Jesus' assertion that his kingdom is not from this world (18:36), and the implication that the allegiance to Jesus and his kingdom will clash with an allegiance to other kingdoms, virtually announces a revolution: a revolution that will change lives and values of people, and eventually also social, religious, economic and political structures. Jesus' kingdom operates subversively in this world, liberating people from spiritual and other forms of oppression as well as confronting oppressive structures in society. Not surprisingly, almost three centuries later the Roman empire became a Christian empire under Constantine!

Jesus' Death (19:16b-42)

Jesus' trial is complete, a sentence has been passed, and only the execution of the sentence remains – death by crucifixion. We can divide the account of Jesus' death into four sections: (i) Jesus' crucifixion (19:16b-27); (ii) Jesus' death (19:28-30); (iii) Jesus' piercing (19:31-37); (iv) Jesus' burial (19:38-42). We shall see that even when he is nailed to the cross, Jesus remains in control and aware of his mission.

Jesus' Crucifixion (19:16b-27)

'The Jews' took Jesus, making him carry his own cross, to what is called The Place of the Skull, or Golgotha in Aramaic (vv.16b-17). There they crucified Jesus between two other people (v.18). While the Synoptics provide other details of the crucifixion, John focuses on three issues: (i) the inscription on the cross (vv.19-22); (ii) the division of Jesus' clothes (vv.23-25a); (iii) the people at the foot of the cross (vv.25b-27).

The Inscription on the Cross (vv.19-22). Pilate had the following inscription put on the cross: 'Jesus of Nazareth, the king of the Jews' (v.19). What is more, he had it written in Aramaic (the language of the Jews), Latin (the language of Rome) and Greek (v.20). He thus made sure that everyone would be able to read the inscription since it was in all the major languages of the then-known world. The significance of this is that Jesus' crucifixion gained universal meaning, which fits the cosmic dimension of Jesus' salvific mission. The entire world must know that Jesus died – as king – in order to provide life for the world. It was usual, at the time of Passover, for many people (Jews and non-Jews) to come into Jerusalem for the festival, and a large crowd would naturally assemble for a public spectacle like a crucifixion. Therefore, a multi-cultural crowd at the foot of the cross depicts on a micro level what Jesus meant at a macro level when he declared that he would draw all people to himself when he was lifted up on the cross (12:32). Jesus' opponents objected to Pilate's wording; they would have preferred that it said Jesus *pretended* to be the king of the Jews (v.21). However, this time, Pilate does not give in to the demand of 'the Jews' (v.22).

The Division of Jesus' Clothes (vv.23-25a). The four soldiers divide Jesus' outer clothes amongst themselves, but when it comes to Jesus' tunic (a loose, often sleeveless, undergarment reaching to the knees), they decide to cast lots for it rather than tear it up, because it was seamless, woven in one piece from the top (literally, 'woven in one piece *from above*') (vv.23-24). This decision of the soldiers to divide Jesus' tunic by casting lots fulfils Psalm 22:18. With this mention, John echoes the writers of the Synoptic Gospels since they also refer to this Psalm with Jesus' well-known cry, 'My God, my God, why have you forsaken me' (Psalm 22:1). Moreover, Jesus' exclamation, 'I am thirsty', in 19:28 is also an allusion to this psalm (Psalm 22:15). The significance of this is that Jesus probably has all of Psalm 22 in mind during his crucifixion. In which case, Jesus also expects or trusts God to deliver him, just as the Psalm writer did. If Psalm 22 is a psalm of hope for divine deliverance amidst suffering and hostility, and if this psalm is on Jesus' mind while he hangs on the cross, then Jesus' mindset is not one of despair or accusation but of hope – hope in his Father who is near, and quick to deliver him!

The People at the Foot of the Cross (vv.25b-27). Meanwhile, standing at the foot of the cross are, amongst others, four women – Jesus' mother, Jesus mother's sister, Mary the wife of Clopas, and Mary Magdalene – and the Beloved Disciple (vv.25-26). Any comparison with the women at the cross mentioned in the Synoptics will only complicate rather than solve the identity of these four women. However, all the four Gospels mention that Mary Magdalene was present both at the cross (except for Luke) and at the resurrection. John gives special prominence to women (see the section 'Characteristics' in the Introduction), and to Mary Magdalene in particular, as we shall see in 20:1-2, 11-18. It is unlikely, however, that Mary Magdalene is the same as Lazarus' sister Mary in John 11 since 'Mary' was a popular name.

When Jesus sees his mother and the Beloved Disciple standing next to each other, he says to her, 'Woman, see, your son', and to the Beloved Disciple, 'See, your mother' (vv.26-27). From that moment, the Beloved Disciple takes Jesus' mother into his own home (v.27). How shall we understand this incident? First, and perhaps most importantly, it shows Jesus' concern for his dear ones in a practical sense. Knowing that he would not be able to take care of his mother any longer, he provides a home for her with the disciple he was closest to. Some scholars have proposed that this event symbolizes the birth of the Church, but this seems somewhat farfetched. I suggest that we should interpret this incident as an example of how the community of believers that Jesus has constituted should function, namely, with practical care for one another's needs.

Jesus' Death (19:28-30)

When Jesus knows that 'everything' has been completed, he says, 'I am thirsty' (v.28). This was in order to fulfil Scripture. The reference is to Psalm 22:15, showing, once again, that this psalm of vindication-amidst-suffering is on Jesus' mind as he hangs on the cross (see the commentary on 19:24). The completion of 'everything' probably refers to the work that the Father had entrusted to him, i.e., his mission to save the world (cf. 3:16-17; 4:34; 5:36; 17:4). Mission impossible? No, mission accomplished – once and for all.

Once Jesus receives the sour wine from the soldiers, he says, 'It is finished', and dies (vv.29-30). In this, Jesus follows the sequence of Psalm 22:15, where David first expresses his thirst, and then, requests God 'to lay him in the dust of death'. Jesus' exclamation, 'It is finished', is a cry of victory because he knows that he has successfully completed his Father's work (cf. v.28). Thus, his death on the cross is the triumphant culmination of Jesus' mission, where he gives his life to provide eternal life for the world (cf. 6:51). Moreover, elsewhere, John uses the verb *hupsoō* to refer to Jesus' death on the cross (3:14; 8:28; 12:32), which means either 'to lift up' or 'to exalt', and both meanings are intended (an example of John's use of double entendre). This implies that, for John, the cross is Jesus' throne; on the cross, Jesus is exalted as king. Furthermore, the 'lifting up' or enthronement of Jesus has a salvific effect, in that belief in the crucified king brings eternal life (cf. 3:15). John, then, subverts the meaning of the cross from being a symbol of defeat, shame and death to becoming a symbol of victory, glorification and life.

John's description of Jesus' death in verse 30 is an unusual one. A literal translation would read, 'And bowing his head, he handed over the Spirit' (it does not say '*his* spirit'). Hence, I do not see a reference here to Jesus' handing over his human spirit, but to his handing over (to God) the Holy Spirit who was his life force.

John's somewhat peculiar expression may be reminiscent of the understanding of the Spirit in the Old Testament. In the Old Testament, the Spirit was understood to create and maintain the physical life, and a withdrawal of the Spirit meant death (Genesis 6:3, 17; 7:15; Job 27:3; 32:8; 33:4; 34:14-15). The apocryphal book Wisdom of Solomon expresses this concept of the Spirit as follows: God has breathed his life-giving Spirit into people, and they have received the Spirit on loan (15:11, 16). Hence, we can speak of 'my spirit' when we understand it as the life-giving Holy Spirit who has been 'given' to us on loan, as it were, until we die. Thus, John describes Jesus' death as his giving back to the Father the Spirit who had not only empowered him during his ministry but also sustained his physical life. There are perhaps two reasons for John's portrayal of Jesus' death in this way. First, it shows that Jesus is in control of his life; he has the authority to lay it down as he pleases (cf. 10:18). Second, Jesus' handing over the Spirit may foreshadow the future release of the Spirit (see 20:22).

Jesus' Piercing (19:31-37)

Since the crucifixion has taken place on the day of Preparation, i.e., the Friday preceding the Sabbath of the Passover, it poses a problem for two reasons. First, according to the Mosaic Law, bodies should not remain hanging on the cross overnight (Deuteronomy 21:23). Second, once the Sabbath begins (officially at sunset), no work is allowed (v.31). So 'the Jews' have to ensure that those who have been crucified have died and their bodies taken down before sunset. This is why they request Pilate to have the legs of the crucified men broken and to have the dead bodies removed (v.31). Once a crucified person's legs are broken, it causes the person to die quicker because he cannot use the crossbar on which his feet rest to support his upper body. His spread-out arms would then have to carry his entire weight, which would make it almost impossible to breathe. So the soldiers proceed to break the legs of the men hanging on either side of Jesus (v.32), but when they come to Jesus, they discover that he is already dead (v.33). Therefore, instead of breaking his legs, a soldier pierces Jesus' side (somewhere between his ribs) causing blood and water to gush out (v.34).

Some scholars have suggested that this reference to water coming out of Jesus' side signifies the release of the Spirit as foretold in 7:38-39, but we should reject this view for two reasons. First, 7:38-39 refers to the living water flowing out of the *believer* rather than Jesus. Second, the living water is expected to flow out of the believer's *inner being* (literally, 'belly') in 7:38, which is different from the water gushing out of Jesus' *side* in 19:34. Therefore, I contend that the significance of blood and water gushing out of Jesus' side merely confirms that Jesus is dead. Physiologically, this explanation would also be sustainable because verse 34 can refer to the piercing of the so-called pericardial sac, which encloses the heart and can contain fluid.

The narrative aside in verse 35 raises the question of the identity of the witness. A good case can be made that it is the Beloved Disciple because (i) this disciple was certainly at the scene (19:26) and (ii) 21:20, 24 makes a similar reference to the Beloved Disciple's witness. This does not necessarily mean that the Beloved Disciple is the author of the Gospel; the author may simply refer to the Beloved Disciple's testimony as the authentic source for his Gospel. Moreover, considering the anonymity with which this Gospel comes to us, it would be somewhat unusual for the author to put himself forward as the subject in verse 21:24 (cf. the section 'Author' in the Introduction). In any case, once again the author emphasizes the purpose of the testimony of witnesses, namely, that the reader may come or continue to believe (cf. 1:7; 20:31 and the section 'Purpose' in the Introduction).

John frequently quotes from or alludes to the Hebrew Scriptures (our Old Testament), to demonstrate how Jesus fulfils the Old Testament (see the section 'Characteristics' in the Introduction). Verses 36-37 contain two of such references. The phrase 'not one of his bones shall be broken' in verse 36 is probably not a reference to Psalm 34:20 (which mentions the plural 'bones'), but rather to Exodus 12:46 and Numbers 9:12, which prohibit the breaking of any of the bones of the Passover lamb. Since Jesus' trial and death occur at the time of the Jewish Passover festival (13:1; 18:28, 39; 19:14), this reference in verse 36 evokes and heightens the imagery of the Passover as the background to Jesus' death. Played out against this backdrop, Jesus' sacrificial death evokes the image of God's liberating act of the Exodus. God's consent in Jesus' death on the cross, then, is an act of liberation – from the slavery of sin and the oppression of the devil (cf. 8:32-34; 12:31-32).

This picture also fits in with the reference to Zechariah 12:10 in verse 37. In the context of a larger prophecy about Israel's future restoration, Zechariah 12:10 says that Judea will mourn for 'me/the one whom they have pierced' (possibly a reference to God himself). The subsequent verses describe the remorse of the house of David over their sins and God's promised cleansing from sin, impurity and idolatry (Zechariah 12:11-13:6). Thus, this quotation of Zechariah 12:10 in verse 37 signifies that people's cleansing from sin and impurity flows from Jesus' death on the cross. Moreover, according to Zechariah 12:10 and 13:1, the means by which God will cleanse his people is the Spirit of compassion and supplication poured out on the house of David. This would dovetail with the Johannine picture of Jesus' Spirit-imbued teaching that cleanses (4:10-14; 15:3; 17:17), and of Jesus' release of the Spirit in 19:30 and 20:22.

Jesus' Burial (19:38-42)

Jesus is buried according to the Jewish customs, wrapped in strips of linen cloths with aromatic oils/spices, in a nearby tomb, which has not yet been used (vv.40-42). John's emphasis is not on Jesus' burial itself but on those who bury him – Joseph of Arimathea and Nicodemus. So, what do we make of them?

Joseph from Arimathea, a place north-west of Jerusalem, is described as a 'secret' disciple due to his fear of 'the Jews' (v.38). He probably does not dare to profess openly that he is a follower of Jesus because of a fear of being excommunicated from the synagogue by the Jewish authorities (9:22; 12:42). For John, however, this kind of discipleship is not sufficient; he expects a public confession about one's exclusive allegiance to Jesus (cf. 15:18-16:4a, including its reflection, and the excursus 'The Fear of the Jews' in 7:13). Nevertheless, Joseph is bold enough to ask permission from Pilate to remove the body of an executed criminal. Perhaps this signals the hope that Joseph may also progress towards an open confession of his belief in Jesus.

Joseph's companion is Nicodemus, whom we have met in 2:23-3:15 and 7:50-52. John 3 introduces Nicodemus as a prominent religious leader, a member of the Sanhedrin, who is interested in Jesus but unable or unwilling to make a commitment of faith. At the end of John 7, Nicodemus shows the courage to defend Jesus before his colleagues, but they briskly brush him aside. Here, in verse 39, we learn more about Nicodemus. For Jesus' burial, he brings an extraordinary amount of spices (about 32.5 kilograms), which would have been worth a fortune. Why does he do this? Scholars do not agree. Some say that Nicodemus seems preoccupied with death and does not find life in/with Jesus. Others argue that such an extraordinary amount of spices was used only for a royal burial, so Nicodemus must have recognized something of Jesus' kingship. The text does not provide enough clues, so, we cannot be certain of Nicodemus' faith-stance. What is clear, however, is that John has skilfully retained Nicodemus' basic characteristic: his ambiguity. Nicodemus remains as ambiguous as he was in the beginning and we will never know whether he came to a saving belief in Jesus.

In John's evaluation, the attitudes of both Joseph and Nicodemus come up short. Joseph is portrayed as secretive and fearful (he does not have the courage to profess Jesus publicly) and Nicodemus is characterized by ambiguity (he cannot make up his mind about Jesus and take a clear position). Nevertheless, John ends on a hopeful note: Joseph shows the courage to ask openly for Jesus' body, and Nicodemus may have recognized something of Jesus' kingship. Moreover, their burial of Jesus would certainly not have remained a secret, so they display some willingness to risk being associated with Jesus.

Reflection

Since the cross is the symbol and focus of the Christian faith, we can never study its meaning and significance enough. John highlights various aspects of the cross. First, the cross acquires universal significance in that the charges against Jesus were written in the major languages of the then-known world. This fits the cosmic outlook of the Gospel, which presents Jesus as the saviour of the world, the one who will provide life for the world by giving up his life (1:29; 3:14-16; 4:10-14, 42; 6:35, 51; 12:32-33). Second, rather than the symbol of defeat and shame, John depicts the cross as Jesus' throne (Jesus is crucified as king); as the point of victory (Jesus' cry, 'It is finished', is a victorious cry); and as the place where Jesus is in control (he instructs his mother and the Beloved Disciple from the cross, and determines when he lays down his life). Third, theologically, the cross signifies God's act of liberation in Jesus on behalf of humankind, bringing life to the world; provides spiritual cleansing from sin and moral contagion; and effects the symbolic release of the Spirit, which foreshadows the giving of the Spirit in 20:22.

To remain secretive or ambiguous about our relationship with Jesus are, according to John, inadequate positions. John challenges us to make up our minds about Jesus and to confess him openly. I remember the time when I had just become a believer. I had just started a new job in a new company and I kept my relationship with Jesus a secret, afraid that my new colleagues would ridicule me. This secrecy lasted for more than two years, and I felt very unhappy, ashamed and guilty about it. When I knew I would be promoted to another department within the same company, I decided that this was the opportunity to change my attitude. Right from the beginning I made it clear that I was a Christian, I openly prayed before my meals in the company restaurant, had evangelistic tracts at my desk, and had occasional discussions with my colleagues. And yes, I was sometimes ridiculed about my faith, which was not always easy, but this was nothing in comparison to the uneasiness that came from not daring to confess my association with Jesus openly. John encourages us to take a public stand for Jesus, no matter what the consequences are.

Jesus' Resurrection (20:1-31)

John 20 narrates the resurrection of Jesus, and his appearances to various people. John 20:1-10 records the resurrection itself, but John goes on to emphasize the interaction between the resurrected Jesus and Mary Magdalene (20:11-18), the disciples (20:19-23) and Thomas (20:24-29). The common element in these three encounters is that these characters will make a greater commitment of faith in the resurrected Jesus. The chapter finishes with an explicit statement of the purpose of the Gospel (20:30-31).

The Resurrection (20:1-10)

Jesus had died and was buried on Friday before the Sabbath began. Now it is Sunday morning (v.1). Mary Magdalene goes to Jesus' tomb, sees that the stone has been removed, and runs to Peter and the Beloved Disciple to report that Jesus' body is missing (vv.1-2). In turn, Peter and the Beloved Disciple run to the tomb to investigate the matter for themselves (vv.3-7).

John makes an interesting remark about the Beloved Disciple in verse 8, namely that, when the Beloved Disciple went into the tomb, 'he saw and believed.' The issue at hand is to resolve what it is that the Beloved Disciple believed. We are so conditioned by John's use of belief that our immediate reaction may be to reply that the Beloved Disciple believes that Jesus is resurrected. However, this would contradict verse 9, where John explains that they still do not know/understand that, according to the Scriptures, Jesus must rise from the dead. Hence, what the Beloved Disciple must have believed is Mary Magdalene's report in verse 2 that Jesus' body has been removed! This is the first time that the Beloved Disciple, a model of discipleship, does not live up to expectations; he does not display the insight and belief we would expect from him. Subsequently, Peter and the Beloved Disciple go back to their homes, probably depressed.

The Appearance to Mary Magdalene (20:11-18)

Mary Magdalene remains at the tomb, giving vent to her grief (v.11a). When she looks into the tomb, she sees two radiant angels who ask her why she is weeping (vv.11b-13). We must make two observations. First, Peter and the Beloved Disciple have been denied the opportunity to see the angels, while a woman has been given the privilege of being the first witness to the resurrection (cf. the Synoptic accounts). This reveals the importance that John gives to women in his Gospel (see the section 'Characteristics' in the Introduction). Second, in the Synoptics, the angels reveal to the women (including Mary Magdalene) that Jesus is risen, whereas in John, Jesus himself reveals this to Mary Magdalene (vv.14-16). This should come as no surprise since, for John, Jesus is the Revealer *par excellence*.

Jesus' revelation of his resurrection to Mary unfolds gradually. At first, Mary sees Jesus but does not recognize him; she mistakenly assumes that he is the gardener (vv.14-15). The text does not indicate whether Jesus deliberately keeps her from recognizing him or if her tears blur the vision. Whatever the case, the reason for her not recognizing Jesus is not the most important issue. Interestingly, Jesus asks Mary the same question as the angels did ('Woman, why are you weeping?'), but it is Jesus as the Revealer who has the privilege to resolve Mary's problem. Jesus reveals himself by calling Mary by her name, to which she replies, 'My teacher', indicating that she has recognized his voice and identity (v.16). Jesus' calling her name must be placed against the background of the good shepherd calling his sheep by name so that they may find life (10:3-4, 9; cf. 5:25; 11:43). Thus, Jesus' calling Mary's name probably has salvific overtones in that her saving relationship with the risen Jesus is confirmed.

Apparently Mary holds on or clings tightly to Jesus but he explains that this is not necessary (v.17). Jesus is not leaving just yet to the Father in the ascension, and hence there will be further opportunities to see him again. More importantly, however, Jesus appoints Mary as a witness to announce to the disciples the good news of his resurrection and that his ascension to the Father is near (vv.17-18). Jesus' words for the disciples that he is about to ascend to his Father and their Father, to his God and their God, are surely also meant for Mary. From this, we may infer that she is firmly included within the family of God. As the first witness to the risen Lord, Mary tells the disciples about her encounter (v.18).

The Appearance to the Disciples (20:19-23)

The text does not indicate whether the disciples believe Mary's report, but it does mention that the disciples are gripped by fear of the religious authorities (v.19). Perhaps they remain out of sight, behind locked doors, because they are afraid that the authorities will accuse them of having removed Jesus' body (as one tradition records in Matthew 28:11-15). Alternatively, in the light of Mary's report, the disciples may fear harassment from the authorities for being associated with Jesus.

In this situation, Jesus appears supernaturally amongst his disciples, saying, 'Peace be with you' (v.19). Jesus' statement echoes his promise in 14:27 and 16:33 to provide peace to his followers in the midst of turmoil and persecution from the world. Jesus' pronouncement, 'Peace be with you', is more holistic than simply the freedom from anxiety or fear; it is virtually equal to the Hebrew *shalom*, which has the connotation of 'salvation'.

The disciples experienced sorrow when they heard that Jesus would be leaving (cf. 14:1, 27; 16:6), but he promised that their sorrow would turn into joy when they saw him again (16:22). Indeed, when the disciples see the risen Jesus for the first time, they rejoice (v.20). Perhaps the disciples get so carried away with this joyful experience that Jesus has to remind them of their future task. After repeating his greeting or benediction, he gives his disciples their mission mandate, 'Just as the Father has sent me, I also send you' (v.21; cf. 17:18). The disciples' mission is not different from Jesus' mission; rather, it is patterned on and a continuation of Jesus' mission in this world.

After Jesus commissions his disciples, he breathes on or into them and declares, 'Receive the Holy Spirit' (v.21). At first sight, this verse seems simple enough: Jesus, having commissioned his disciples for mission, now equips them for this task by giving them the promised Spirit-Paraclete. This is the so-called 'Johannine Pentecost', i.e., John's version of what Luke describes in Acts 2. However, this understanding creates a few problems. First, if the disciples have now been empowered for mission, why do we read in John 21 that they return to their old profession rather than going into the world to witness about Jesus? Second, according to 16:7, the Spirit-Paraclete can only come when Jesus has gone away, i.e., when Jesus has left this world permanently and ascended to his Father. Proponents of the Johannine Pentecost reply that, in John's timeframe, Easter, the ascension and Pentecost all come together. We dispute this. Although John, at times, is flexible with his chronology, he does retain the chronological separation between the various (theological) events. The ascension (and hence Pentecost) lies beyond the chronological horizons of John's Gospel.

The improbability of a Johannine Pentecost has led some scholars to view the event in verse 22 as a *symbolic* gesture for the later gift of the Spirit-Paraclete at Pentecost. Attractive as this view may be, it denies the immediate significance of the event for the disciples. The verb *emphusaō* ('to breathe into or on') is an unusual one in the bible, but, taken in conjunction with the imperative 'Receive the Holy Spirit', we find three texts that form a suitable background for 20:22. First, Genesis 2:7 (Septuagint) describes the creation of the first human being as follows: 'the LORD God formed man from the dust of the ground, and breathed into his nostrils the breath of life; and the man became a living being.' Similarly, the apocryphal book Wisdom of Solomon 15:11 reminds the reader of God's creative act: '[B]ecause they failed to know the one [God] who formed them and inspired them with active souls and breathed the life-giving Spirit into them.' Third, in Ezekiel 37:9 (Septuagint), God commands Ezekiel to prophesy regarding Israel's future restoration in terms of a re-creation: 'Then he [God] said to me [Ezekiel], "Prophesy to the Spirit, prophesy, mortal, and say to the Spirit: Thus says the Lord GOD: Come from the four winds, O Spirit, and breathe into these slain, that they may live."' (I contend that God commands Ezekiel to prophesy to the divine Spirit rather than to 'the breath/wind' [contra NRSV, NIV and KJV]). The common idea in these three texts is that *God (re-)creates people by means of an insufflation* (an act of breathing on or into) *with the Spirit*. The gift of the Spirit in 20:22, then, must be a real, tangible event rather than a symbolic gesture.

Having refuted the previous arguments for 20:22 being the 'Johannine Pentecost' or a symbolic gesture, I offer an alternative interpretation that fits the facts better. I suggest that John 20:22

describes Jesus' breathing the Spirit on or into the disciples as an act of their re-creation. This event may be understood as the disciples' birth of water-and-Spirit, described in John 3, which completes or secures their salvation. This does not mean that the disciples were not saved prior to 20:22. There is sufficient indication in the Gospel to suggest that the disciples were already in a saving or life-giving relationship with Jesus before the cross. However, 13:10, for example, indicated that although the disciples had already been cleansed, this cleansing still needed completion – Jesus still had to die on the cross. Similarly, the disciples had already experienced the Spirit through Jesus, but they had not yet 'received' the Spirit (7:39). They were in a unique situation where they could only receive from Jesus what was in step with what he had achieved and what was available.

Jesus' imminent departure from this world requires that the disciples' salvation be secured. With the reception of the Spirit, their saving relationship with Jesus can now be assured and sustained in a way that was not possible before. Prior to the cross, eternal life and the Spirit were limited to the earthly Jesus, and the Spirit upon Jesus communicated to the disciples the life that was available in him. After the cross, however, this life and Spirit become available in greater measure to Jesus' disciples. If the disciples had not received the Spirit, how would their salvation be sustained between Jesus' ascension and Pentecost?

John 7:39 and 16:7 each mention a condition for the giving of the Spirit and virtually all scholars assume that both texts express one and the same condition. I shall argue, however, that 7:39 and 16:7 refer to two distinct conditions, which are fulfilled at two different times.

John 7:39 states that 'the Spirit was *not yet* (given/available), because Jesus was *not yet* glorified', i.e., Jesus' glorification is the prerequisite for the giving of the Spirit. The 'not yet' of the Spirit is matched by the 'not yet' of Jesus' glorification. For John, however, Jesus' glorification is not a single event but consists of Jesus death, resurrection and ascension. Moreover, 7:39 does not say that the Spirit will only be given after Jesus' glorification is *complete*; perhaps the Spirit can already be given once the process of Jesus' glorification has *started*. Furthermore, if Jesus' glorification is a process made up of more than one event, then the giving of the Spirit may also be a process rather than a single event. From this we infer that if Jesus' death on the cross signals the beginning of his glorification, perhaps it also signals the beginning of the release of the Spirit. In other words, the crucifixion not only lifts the 'not yet' of Jesus' glorification but also the 'not yet' of the Spirit mentioned in 7:39. Thus, in 19:30, when Jesus hands over the Spirit on the cross, it symbolizes the release of the Spirit, marking the start of the process of the giving of the Spirit. Subsequently, 20:22 marks the real giving of the Spirit, when, on the evening of resurrection Sunday, Jesus imparts the Spirit to his disciples to secure their salvation. The condition of 7:39, then, is fulfilled in 19:30 (symbolically) and 20:22 (in reality).

The condition of 16:7, however, is not fulfilled by 20:22 because it is a different condition. John 16:7 states that 'unless I [Jesus] go away, the Paraclete will not come to you', i.e., the gift of the Spirit-Paraclete is dependent on Jesus' physical departure from this world to the Father. This condition is not fulfilled because Jesus' ascension has not yet happened, and hence the coming of the Paraclete still lies in the future. In fact, John describes neither the ascension nor the giving of the Spirit-Paraclete.

One could then raise the question whether the Spirit and the Paraclete are two different entities, but John would object to such a dichotomy. There is only one Spirit-Paraclete, but that does not mean that the giving of this Spirit cannot happen over time, or, that the Spirit cannot unfold his activities in stages. For John, the giving of the Spirit is one theological gift that happens in various chronological stages. The giving of the Spirit is a process that consists of, or occurs in, three events/stages. First, Jesus' handing over the Spirit on the cross in 19:30 symbolizes the subsequent release of the Spirit that begins in 20:22. Second, in 20:22, the Spirit is given to secure and sustain the disciples' salvation, fulfilling the condition of 7:39. Third, beyond the chronological horizon of John's Gospel, at Pentecost, the Spirit is given to the disciples in his role as Paraclete, fulfilling the condition of 16:7.

What holds these last two events theologically together rather than creating two distinct gifts is that in 20:22 the Spirit is given *as the Spirit of salvation* whereas at Pentecost the Spirit is given *as*

Paraclete. This experience was unique to Jesus' original disciples and we cannot use it as a paradigm for today. For later generations of believers there is only one reception of the Spirit: the reception of the Spirit-Paraclete at conversion. The Spirit-Paraclete that convicts people of sin is the same Spirit who communicates to them the life that is available in Jesus and who equips people for mission. In other words, the Spirit-Paraclete is both the Spirit of salvation and the Spirit of mission. We can visualize the gradual release of the Spirit and the unfolding of his activities as follows:

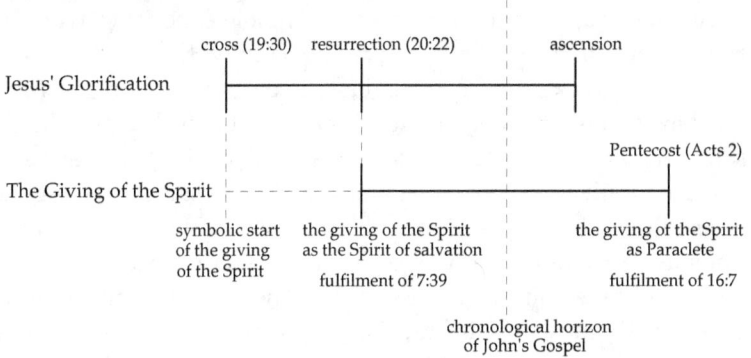

One last issue that needs to be resolved is how this understanding of verse 22 ties in with verses 21 and 23, which have strong missiological overtones. One simple explanation may be that there was a danger that with the release of the Spirit as the Spirit of salvation in 20:22, the disciples, carried away by the experience, would think that this is all there is. John 20:21, 23 reminds them that there is an unfinished task: to participate in the ongoing mission of Jesus in this world through the empowerment of the Spirit as Paraclete. For their future mission, the disciples still need to receive the Paraclete, i.e., they still need to experience the Spirit as Paraclete in order to be empowered for that mission.

The Appearance to Thomas (20:24-29)

For reasons unknown to us, Thomas was not present in the house on Sunday evening when Jesus appeared to the disciples (v.24).

When the others report to him that they have seen the risen Lord, Thomas replies that he would have to see Jesus for himself in order to believe (v.25). This reply has earned him the nickname 'doubting Thomas', but perhaps this is not entirely fair. First, we cannot be certain that the other disciples accepted a similar report from Mary when she said that she had seen the risen Lord (vv.18-19). Moreover, the literal translation of verse 27 is 'Do not be unbelieving but believing' rather than 'Do not doubt but believe', as most English translations have it. Finally, Jesus' 'rebuke' in verse 29 is certainly not harsh. Thus, it seems that all the characters in John 20 – Mary Magdalene, the disciples, Thomas – have one thing in common: it takes a tangible experience with the risen Lord to assure their saving relationship with him.

Thus, a week later, Thomas has his encounter with the risen Lord in a similar fashion and location as the other disciples. In the same house (with the doors still shut!), again Jesus appears supernaturally and greets Thomas with the same greeting he greeted the others ('Peace be with you') (v.26). Then, Jesus invites Thomas to examine the physical evidence as he had requested, and encourages him to believe (v.27). The text does not indicate whether Thomas actually touches Jesus (the sight of Jesus may have been sufficient), but his reply certainly expresses the highest confession of Jesus in the entire Gospel: 'My Lord and my God!' (v.28).

Nowhere in the Gospel is Jesus called 'God', except for the Prologue where John identifies the Logos as (being in nature) God (1:1). John's concept of 'God' certainly takes on a binitarian form, in which Jesus, as the Son, is included in the Godhead. Perhaps one could even make a case that John already leans in the direction of a trinitarian belief if we consider: (i) the 'personal' traits of the Spirit-Paraclete; (ii) the Spirit-Paraclete being co-sent by the Father and Son; (iii) the 'divine' functions of the Spirit-Paraclete as life-giver (6:63) and judge (16:8-11).

Jesus' response in verse 29 should perhaps be understood as a mild rebuke directed at Thomas and as an encouragement for later generations of believers to progress towards a belief that is less dependent on signs (cf. the commentary on 4:48). It cannot have been a sharp rebuke, condemning the request for a sign, for otherwise, John's assertion in verses 30-31 that he has recorded Jesus' signs in order to evoke belief does not make much sense. Nevertheless, a belief that is less dependent on the tangible (and more on Jesus' word) seems more secure.

The Purpose of the Gospel (20:30-31)

John spells out his purpose for writing this Gospel in 20:30-31 (see also the section 'Purpose' in the Introduction). One thing is clear: John has given a written account of a selection of Jesus' miraculous signs in order to evoke an adequate belief-response from his readers (cf. 1 John 5:13). What remains unclear is whether John had evangelistic or pastoral intentions. Did he write in order to bring unbelievers to a saving belief in Christ or to encourage believers to continue in their faith? This ambiguity is due to the existence of two equally valid Greek variant readings of the verb 'to believe' in verse 31a.

Verse 31 has two purpose clauses, and we can translate it as:

But these [signs] are written
    so that you may (*come to* or *continue to*) believe that Jesus is the Christ/Messiah, the Son of God,
and
    so that as/while you believe you may (continuously) have eternal life in his name.

If the reading 'to come to believe' is the original one, then John had an evangelistic purpose in mind; if 'to continue to believe' is the authentic reading, then John's purpose was pastoral. In the section 'Purpose' in the Introduction, I argued that we cannot solve this issue purely on the basis of syntax since a good case can be made for both readings. Hence, the entire discussion of whether John's purpose was evangelistic or pastoral leads into a *cul-de-sac*. I suggest that the way forward is to recognize that John had *one* purpose in mind: to evoke belief in Jesus as the Messiah, the Son of God. This single salvific purpose for John's Gospel serves both to bring people to an initial belief in Jesus (the evangelistic dimension) as well as to encourage believers to continue in their belief (the pastoral dimension).

Reflection

Just as it took a tangible experience with the risen Lord for Mary Magdalene, the disciples and Thomas to secure their saving relationship with him, many of us need or want a similar experience. Some of us may have such an experience, but let us not forget Jesus' challenge to move beyond the visible and physical. Blessed are those who believe without having seen and touched. Will we believe on the basis of the witness of John's Gospel itself? The bible is the testimony to God's dealings with humankind, God's communication to us. Can we accept it or do we need more?

John's purpose for writing the Gospel is unmistakable: to evoke a saving belief in Jesus. Every episode in his Gospel has been carefully selected and constructed in order to accomplish this purpose. As John the Baptist knew he had to decrease so that Jesus could increase, this Gospel comes to us with such anonymity that it is clear who is in the spotlight. The challenge for us, as believers, is that our lives may also be such a clear testimony to other people.

John's understanding of the gift of the Spirit as we presented it, has an important implication (cf. also our discussion on 1:33). In some Pentecostal, Charismatic and Evangelical traditions, there is a widespread belief in the gift of the Spirit as a 'second blessing', i.e., as an additional gift for missionary empowerment distinct from and subsequent to salvation (the classical Pentecostal position). Although this seems to be the case with the disciples, it was a unique situation in history that cannot be taken as a paradigm for later generations of believers. In the case of the disciples, the giving of the Spirit happened in two stages in order to be in step with the process of Jesus' glorification. However, after Jesus' glorification is completed, there is only one gift of the Spirit available for the believer, namely, the reception of the Spirit-Paraclete at conversion – both as the Spirit of salvation and as the Spirit of mission. This does not mean, however, that after the reception of the Spirit-Paraclete one cannot have further experiences of the Spirit, in which, for example, the Spirit starts new activities in or gives 'spiritual gifts' to the believer.

Epilogue (21:1-25)

John's Gospel began with a Prologue, so it seems fitting that it should end with an Epilogue. But is this really part of the original Gospel? John has narrated how Jesus was resurrected, imparted the Spirit to his disciples, and reminded them of their future mission. What more is there to tell? In fact, stating the purpose of the Gospel, in 20:30-31, seems a very appropriate way to finish.

My starting point is to accept the text as we have it without ignoring how this text came into existence. In other words, I allow for the possibility that the final form of the Gospel is the work of more than one author or editor, and that certain material may have been edited or added at a later stage. In my understanding, this does not deny the co-authorship of the Holy Spirit and the inspiration of the Gospel – could a later editor not have been divinely inspired and guided just as the original author was? The Prologue (1:1-18), for example, may well have been added (either by the original author or someone else) at a later stage; just as 7:53-8:11 was almost certainly not part of the original Gospel.

Similarly, John 21 may well have been an addition to an earlier version of the Gospel. I hope it is clear to the reader that even if this is the case there is no reason to reject it; rather, we accept the final form of the Gospel and try to make sense of why this Epilogue was added. One reason for the possible addition of chapter 21 might be to conclude the story of Peter. Peter's denial of Jesus in John 18 has probably left the reader wondering how this will be resolved (for the Synoptics do not settle it). Another reason may be to delineate the magnitude of the disciples' future mission, as indicated by the miraculous catch of fish.

Structurally, we divide the chapter into four sections: (i) the miraculous catch of fish (21:1-14); (ii) the restoration and commissioning of Peter (21:15-19); (iii) Peter and the Beloved Disciple (21:20-23); (iv) the closure of the Gospel (21:24-25).

The Miraculous Catch of Fish (21:1-14)

This story describes Jesus' fourth resurrection appearance (the third to his disciples [cf. v.14]), which takes place at the Sea of

Tiberias or Sea of Galilee (v.1). Why at the Sea of Galilee? First, this story may coincide with an early Christian tradition, found in Matthew 28:10, 16-20 (so, the ascension may have happened shortly after the events in John 21). Second, the only other mention of Jesus' being at the Sea of Galilee is in 6:1, therefore, the miraculous catch of fish in John 21 could be understood against the background of Jesus' having miraculously provided food for the multitude in 6:1-15.

Verses 2-3 tell us that seven of Jesus' disciples had gone to Galilee, and Peter resumes his old profession (which is only mentioned here in John), joined by the others (cf. 16:32). Why did they return to their old profession after having met the risen Jesus twice previously? Did they misunderstand Jesus' commission in 20:21? Have they become disillusioned for some reason? The text does not answer these questions but my guess is that Peter is devastated, ashamed and probably feels inadequate to carry out the task that Jesus has called them to in 20:21, and, as the leader, he drags the others with him. This would also make sense of the episode in verses 15-19, where Jesus deals with Peter. Another reason may be that the disciples are waiting to receive the Spirit as Paraclete in order to be empowered for their mission (see the commentary on 20:22).

Just after dawn, when the best time to catch fish has passed, Jesus stands on the shore, but the disciples do not recognize him (v.4; cf. 20:14). When Jesus addresses his disciples as 'Children', or better still, 'Dear friends' (v.5), he expresses affection (cf. 13:33; in 1 John, John frequently uses the same language to address his readers). Verse 6 describes the miracle that follows when the disciples obey Jesus' command. The miracle causes the Beloved Disciple to recognize Jesus, which in turn prompts Peter to rush towards Jesus (v.7). Subsequently, verses 9-13 describe Jesus' breakfast with his disciples. The charcoal fire in verse 9 is also mentioned in 18:18, and perhaps indicates that Peter's imminent restoration and commissioning is related to his denial.

Verse 11 speaks of the magnitude of the miracle: hundred and fifty-three fish are caught, without even causing the net to tear. What is important, is to understand the significance of this episode. Sometimes the miraculous catch of fish is counted as the eighth sign (or seven plus one) or as the seventh sign (instead of the miracle of Jesus' walking on the water in 6:19-21). However, I prefer to count the seven signs during Jesus' public ministry as recorded in John 1-12, and consider the sign in John 21 as the first sign to the disciples, to give them a foretaste of what is to come (cf. 14:12). This sign foreshadows the 'success' or achievement of the disciples' future mission.

Seen against the background of John 6, Jesus again, miraculously, provides food, but this time Jesus enables his disciples to participate in the miracle. Thus, the disciples' miraculous catch of fish symbolizes their newly-given ability to bring people into the kingdom. In the light of 6:44 and 12:32, where the verb 'to draw' is used in relation to people, its occurrence here in verses 6 and 11 then symbolizes the disciples' drawing of people provided to them by Jesus and the Father. Where the disciples previously failed to participate in Jesus' mission (4:31-38), Jesus now foretells that soon they will be bringing in the harvest. Soon the disciples will start to bear everlasting fruit (cf. 15:1-8, 16).

This story of the miraculous catch of fish may also have been John's reworking of Luke 5:1-11, where Jesus calls his disciples to become fishers of people at the beginning of his ministry. For theological reasons, however, John may have put this event at the end of his Gospel in order to indicate that the disciples' ministry of 'catching' people would start soon and would be of an unexpected magnitude.

The Restoration and Commissioning of Peter (21:15-19)

Only in John's Gospel do we learn that after his denial of Jesus, Peter's fellowship with Jesus is restored. When he disowned his master, it must have left Peter devastated and feeling inadequate to carry out the mission that Jesus had in store for his disciples. Peter knows that he has denied his relationship with Jesus and hence his discipleship. Jesus, however, does not leave him in this situation. He takes time to deal with Peter and restore him. The accounts of Peter's denial of Jesus in John 18 and his restoration here have many parallels: (i) the charcoal fire (18:18; 21:9); (ii) both the denial and the restoration happen in the presence of others (the 'they' in v.15 refers to all disciples present); (iii) Peter's threefold denial is matched by Jesus' threefold repetition of the same question in verses 15-17.

When Jesus and the disciples had finished eating, Jesus directs his attention to Peter, and in verses 15-17 we read of Peter's restoration and commissioning. The three verses follow the same pattern (Jesus asks Peter a question; Peter replies; Jesus gives Peter a commission), and are virtually identical in content. Some people make too much of the different uses of the verb 'to love'. A popular theory, not just based on this episode, is that John uses two different kinds of love: the divine or 'agape' love (based on the verb *agapaō*) and the human love (based on the verb *fileō*).

A quick examination of John's Gospel would reveal that such a theory does not stand under scrutiny. The love between the Father and Son is also expressed by the verb *fileō* (5:20), and the Father's love for the disciples is described in 16:27 using the verb *fileō*. On the other hand, the verb *agapaō* is used to denote people's love of the darkness (3:19) as well as the love of the Jewish authorities for human glory (12:43). Moreover, the term 'Beloved Disciple' comes from the more literal phrase 'the disciple whom Jesus loved', and although in almost every occurrence the verb *agapaō* is used, in 20:2 the verb *fileō* is used! In essence, John seems to use the verbs *agapaō* and *fileō* interchangeably, just as he uses two verbs for 'to know' and four verbs for 'to see' without any substantial variation in meaning. It simply appears that John varies his style.

With this insight, we return to verses 15-17. In the first two questions to Peter, Jesus uses the verb *agapaō*, but in the third question he employs *fileō*, whereas Peter uses the verb *fileō* in all his replies. We can no longer hold a position that Jesus asks Peter twice whether he loves him with a divine, sacrificial love, and only goes down to Peter's level in the third question because Peter replies that he merely loves Jesus with a human, friendly love. This view does not make sense of Peter's sadness at the third question.

In all likelihood, Peter's sadness is caused by the fact that he knows all too well that he has denied his love for Jesus thrice, and Jesus' threefold repetition of his question serves as a very painful reminder. Moreover, the text does not give any indication that Jesus is disappointed with Peter's replies; on the contrary, each time Jesus affirms Peter by giving him his commission. Furthermore, in the threefold repetition of Peter's commissioning ('Feed my lambs', 'Tend my sheep', 'Feed my sheep') there is very little or no difference in meaning. [As an aside, it becomes evident in his first Letter that Peter has understood and realized his mission, and that, in turn, he is able to exhort others to follow in his footsteps and humbly tend God's flock (1 Peter 5:1-4).]

After commissioning him, Jesus finds it necessary to prepare Peter for his future mission by warning him about what lies ahead (v.18). The 'Amen, amen' (often translated, 'Truly, truly') stresses the seriousness and certainty of what Jesus has to say (this phrase occurs twenty-five times in John's Gospel). Jesus explains that when Peter was younger, he was able to determine his own course in life, but when he grows old, it will be determined for him. In verse 19a, John explains that Jesus is foretelling that Peter will die – probably on a cross (v.18b; cf. 16:2). Next, Jesus encourages Peter to follow him (v.19b). Earlier, Peter pledged that he would follow Jesus and even lay down his life for him, but he was not able to stick to Jesus when it mattered (13:36-38; 18:15-27). But now Jesus ensures that he is ready to follow him all the way – even unto death!

Peter and the Beloved Disciple (21:20-23)

Jesus' affirmation, commissioning and foretelling the future martyrdom of Peter does not make him instantly perfect. Peter, true to his nature, immediately compares himself to the Beloved Disciple (vv.20-21).

In his Gospel, John seems to portray a 'rivalry' between Peter and the Beloved Disciple, where most often the Beloved Disciple outclasses Peter. The Beloved Disciple seems to be closer to Jesus (13:23-25), and is able to follow Jesus farther than Peter because he has access to the courtyard (18:15-16). Peter denies Jesus and stops following (18:17-27), whereas the Beloved Disciple remains with Jesus, even at the cross, where he is given a privileged position (19:26-27). The Beloved Disciple is also identified as the prime witness or source for John's Gospel (19:35; 21:24). He outruns Peter on the way to the tomb (20:4) and is the first one to recognize Jesus (21:7). In sum, the Beloved Disciple functions as a paradigm of discipleship: one who is intimate with Jesus, ready to follow and stick with him, and a loyal and credible witness.

In response to Peter's petulant question, Jesus says that Peter should mind his own business, focus on following him and not be distracted by how Jesus treats others (v.22). Verse 23 is John's aside, explaining that Jesus' reply to Peter caused a rumour among the believers that the Beloved Disciple would not die. At the same time, however, John provides a corrective to this notion. Whether verse 23 refers to the so-called 'Johannine community', in which the Beloved Disciple may have become a prominent leader, is not certain (cf. the section 'Audience' in the Introduction).

The Closure of the Gospel (21:24-25)

In two verses the Gospel rapidly draws to a close. Verse 24 parallels 19:35, reiterating that the Beloved Disciple is the eyewitness to the things written in this Gospel. As I mentioned earlier, the Beloved Disciple is not necessarily the author of the Gospel (it would also be strange to refer to oneself in that way) but functions as a reliable source. By clarifying that the Beloved Disciple is the source of his Gospel, the author adds to its reliability. There is a greater probability that his readers will accept his Gospel as a true and trustworthy story of Jesus and come to believe in him. We may also recall that the purpose of bearing witness is to evoke belief (1:7; 17:20; 20:31). Verse 25 parallels 20:30, clarifying that this Gospel is a selective (rather than an exhaustive) account of Jesus' life.

In sum, John cleverly connects verses 24-25 with 19:35 and 20:30 (and 20:31 is not far away): stressing the authenticity of the Beloved Disciple's witness on which his Gospel is based, John implicitly urges the reader to accept the truth claim of his Gospel, so that they may receive eternal life.

Reflection

The story of Peter demonstrates that reconciliation and restoration are possible with Jesus. The difference between Judas and Peter is that Judas defected permanently, having come under full control of the devil, whereas Peter's 'defection' is temporary. The shame of Peter's defection is only matched by the honour of being called to follow in Jesus' footsteps, even unto death. In following his master, he will ultimately glorify God. Peter's willingness to lay down his life for his master (13:37) will eventually be honoured! At the beach of the Sea of Galilee, he is being prepared to fulfil his own promise, to follow his master no matter the cost. His love for and devotion to his master will ultimately demonstrate itself in his laying down his life for his friend. In this sense, Peter, like the Beloved Disciple, is a paradigm of discipleship. While the Beloved Disciple is the epitome of a good witness for Jesus, who is intimate with him, Peter functions as an example of self-sacrifice in following Jesus.

Peter's compulsion to compare himself with others is natural to most of us. When we compare ourselves to others, we may find ourselves falling short and develop negative attitudes about ourselves. On the other hand, if we see ourselves as better than others, we might become proud, self-reliant or arrogant. Instead of focusing on others and their performance, Jesus encourages us to focus on him and our duty of following him. Jesus would say, 'Mind your own business and follow me.'

Having excavated John's Gospel, we find that the leitmotif or recurrent theme is the interaction of various characters with Jesus and their responses to him. At the end of a movie, we usually see the list of actors who have taken part. When we look at John's cast, we see an impressive list of players. We have been introduced, inter alios, *to John the Baptist, Nicodemus, the Samaritan woman and her kinsfolk, the royal official, the lame man at the pool, the man born blind, the crowd, 'the Jews', the disciples (especially Judas, Peter and the Beloved Disciple), various women (Jesus' mother, Martha and her sister Mary, Mary Magdalene) and Pilate.*

But what does characterization do for a story, in particular for John's story? First, the characters act as foils, enhancing the reader's understanding of Jesus' identity and mission. For example, the struggle of the Samaritan woman in John 4 to grasp Jesus' identity, leads to more revelation on Jesus' part, which eventually benefits us readers. Second, the use of characters creates a resemblance to reality. This may help the reader to identify with one or more characters and may persuade the reader to take a stand, preferably the one the author recommends.

John wants us to evaluate the responses of the various characters to Jesus. Some respond positively, others negatively; some hesitantly, others ambiguously, and still others remain undecided. In John's dualistic worldview, however, all responses fall into one of two categories – acceptance or rejection of Jesus and the life he offers – and each choice has its own consequences. Besides, it is not enough to enter into a life-giving relationship with Jesus; a person must also remain in that relationship. For John, what matters is whether people are able to stick with Jesus.

John still speaks to us today. He challenges us to discover who this Jesus is, and proves that an encounter with Jesus will force us to make a choice. Have you started on this spiritual journey? Do you know where you stand in relation to Jesus? If you have accepted Jesus, are you still following him? Do you present Jesus to others in such a way that they are able to make a choice?

Index of Subjects

Abiding *see* Remaining
Abortion 119
Abraham 54, 102-105, 167, 179
Acceptance of Jesus 12, 22, 25, 27-28, 49-52, 55-56, 70-71, 79, 83, 94, 102, 106, 112, 157, 186, 230
Adulteress 96, 101
Advocate *see* Spirit as Advocate
Agent 13, 15, 41, 46, 48, 84-85, 124, 131, 144
AIDS 60, 113-114, 138
Ambiguity 12, 49, 63, 78, 128, 142, 211-212, 221, 230
Andrew 33-34, 76
Annas 193-195
Anti-conversion law 174
Anti-semitism/Anti-Jewish 86, 103
Apartheid 60
Apostasy *see* Defection
Arrest, Jesus' 91-94, 121, 129, 161, 191-193
Ascension 39, 82, 141, 148, 158, 175-179, 182, 184, 214-218, 224
Ask in Jesus' name 154-156, 166, 179
Authority 29-30, 38, 41, 69-70, 92, 94, 97, 99, 117, 139, 146, 161, 184, 194, 197-198, 201-204, 208

Bandit, Social 115, 200
Banquet 39, 79, 84-85, 140
Baptism/Baptize 17, 30-32, 51, 121
Barabbas 200
Bearing fruit 139, 163-168, 173
Belief/Believe 9-10, 12, 22, 24-28, 31, 34, 36, 40-44, 48-49, 53, 55-59, 62-64, 70-72, 77-86, 91, 93, 95, 102-104, 111, 121, 125-127, 131, 134-136, 141, 144, 153, 158, 170, 172, 176, 178, 180, 182, 184, 186-189, 207, 209, 211, 220-222, 228
Beloved Disciple 5, 145, 194-195, 206, 209, 212-214, 224, 226-229
Betrayal 68, 74, 130, 137, 141-147, 191, 202
Betrothal 54, 60-61
Biography, ancient 6-9
Birth of the Spirit 15, 17, 22, 25, 44-50, 53, 57, 61, 83, 103-105, 117, 217
Blasphemy 105, 120, 201
Blind(ness) 12, 68-69, 107-113, 115, 118, 119, 121, 135, 137, 170, 181, 183
Blood 41, 81-82, 209
Bread 11-13, 56, 75-85, 144-145
Bride/Bridegroom 51, 54, 60-61
Buddhism 174
Building bridges 60, 113
Burial 122-123, 128, 130, 205, 210-211

Caiaphas 127-128, 193-195, 197
Cana 36-39, 42, 53, 61, 63-65, 88
Caste 60, 190
Characterization 12, 229
Church 5, 6,10, 33, 60, 61, 85, 107, 114, 119, 137, 162, 167, 172, 176, 179, 190, 207
Clean(sing) 30, 32, 36-40, 42, 45-46, 50, 55, 120, 142, 146, 152, 155, 164, 187-189, 197, 199, 210, 212, 217
Cloning 119
Cognition 36, 47, 83-84, 91, 115, 118, 181, 183
Commission 215, 223-227
Communion (*see also* Fellowship) 52, 188
Community 4-8, 30, 53, 82, 117, 188, 207, 228

Condemnation 60, 90, 94, 97-99, 101, 176, 220
Conflict (*see also* Opposition) 14, 29, 64-65, 86-87, 99, 103, 119, 139, 160, 166
Convict/Convince (of guilt) 8, 71, 109, 175-178, 186-189, 219
Corruption 99, 138-139
Create/Creation 22-27, 30, 119, 128, 208, 216
Cross 15, 23, 48-49, 61, 81-84, 93, 116, 122, 125, 133-134, 138, 141-143, 146-147, 149, 154, 158, 167, 176, 182, 185, 197, 205-212, 217-218, 227
Crowd 75-80, 83-84, 86, 88, 90-92, 94-95, 109-110, 128-137, 198, 229
Crucified/Crucifixion 48, 50, 64, 81, 105, 121, 134, 201-208, 212, 218

Dalit 60
Darkness 11-12, 22, 27, 48, 76, 86, 100, 102, 105, 109, 111-112, 119, 134-137, 145, 148, 170, 192, 226
Death 12, 17, 29, 35, 39, 41, 49, 61, 68, 74, 81-86, 97, 116, 122-127, 130, 132-134, 138-142, 146, 148, 170, 172, 176, 178-180, 184, 191, 198, 201-202, 205, 207-208, 210-211, 217-218, 227, 229
Defection 83-85, 129-130, 137, 141, 145-147, 150, 165, 168, 184, 196, 229
Demon-possessed 90, 99, 105, 117
Denial 89, 133, 150, 193, 195-196, 223-227
Departure, Jesus' 92, 100-101, 132, 148-149, 151, 154, 157-162, 173, 175-176, 179, 217-218
Devil 12, 14, 17, 40, 87, 99, 104-107, 116, 121-122, 134, 139, 141, 145-147, 149, 161, 170, 176, 184, 186, 192, 194, 196-197, 202, 210, 229
Devotion 116, 124, 129-131, 137, 229
Diaspora 4, 6-7, 92, 132
Discipleship 33-34, 59, 75, 83-84, 86, 89, 106, 141, 143, 146-150, 163-169, 173, 195-196, 211, 213, 225, 228-229

Divine life *see* Eternal life
Division 88, 94-95, 99, 109, 117, 126, 131, 139
Divorce 60, 113, 119
Double entendre 12, 23, 25, 78, 118, 134, 142, 145, 183, 207
Drawing of people 80, 134, 143, 205, 225
Drinking 55-56, 59, 79, 81-82, 93, 192
Dualism 12, 25, 28, 44, 46, 51, 87, 230

Eating 56, 79, 81, 144, 226
Election *see* Predestination
Eternal life 10-15, 23, 27, 38, 48-49, 52-53, 55, 69-71, 78-85, 93, 116, 118, 120, 124, 126, 132-133, 136, 143-144, 150-153, 169, 183-185, 188, 207, 217, 221, 228
Ethics (*see also* Moral[ity]) 74
Ethnocentric 60, 119
Eucharist 17, 82
Eunuch 60
Euthanasia 119
Evil 31, 48, 86, 127-128, 139, 170, 176, 186, 198
Exalt(ation) 134, 207
Exorcism 133-134, 176
Expulsion 5, 110-111, 136, 172

Faith *see* Belief
Family 25-27, 48-49, 53, 57, 62, 73, 86-87, 100, 103-106, 112, 115, 119, 121, 140, 146, 151, 154, 168-169, 196, 214
Farewell discourse 140, 148, 158, 173, 175, 181, 191
Father, God as 26-28, 53, 57, 87, 101, 104, 112, 155, 185, 188
Fear 13, 29, 48, 77, 88-89, 95-96, 110, 112, 126, 131, 135-137, 160, 168, 174, 196, 201-202, 204, 210-212, 215
Feast/Festival, Jewish 7, 15-16, 26, 40-41, 65-66, 87-92, 94, 100, 120-121, 129, 132, 205, 210
Fellowship (*see also* Communion) 145, 147, 165, 167-169, 188, 225

Index of Subjects

Fish 12, 166, 223-225
Flesh 12, 25, 45-46, 81-83, 101
Flock/Fold 115-117, 119, 127, 188, 227
Follow (as disciple) 10, 33-35, 50, 63, 75, 77-78, 80, 82, 84, 89, 115-116, 119-120, 126, 130, 132-133, 138, 147, 149-154, 168-169, 173, 184, 188, 190, 194-196, 198-199, 210, 215, 227-229
Footwashing 141-143, 146, 167
Forgive(ness) 143
Free(dom) (*see also* Liberation) 12, 32-33, 97, 102, 160, 194, 200, 215
Friend(ship) 51, 73, 122, 137, 140, 144, 149, 167-169, 173, 202, 224, 229
Fruit *see* Bearing fruit
Fulfilment (of Judaism/Scripture) 13, 16, 26, 38, 41-42, 65, 79, 135, 144, 171, 206-207, 209

Galilee 16, 28, 33, 36-37, 54, 61-62, 64, 75-77, 88, 224, 229
Gate/Gatekeeper 13, 15, 115-116, 118, 194-195
Genre 2, 6-7, 9, 140
Gentile 7, 30, 63, 92, 104, 117, 121, 127, 132
Geography 7, 16, 54
Gethsemane 161, 191
Glory/Glorification 38-39, 74, 94, 122, 131-134, 141, 148, 153, 160, 166, 169, 177-178, 184-187, 208, 217-218, 222, 229
Gnosticism 4, 22
Golgotha 88, 205
Government 113-114, 204
Grace 25-26, 97, 99
Guilt(y) 97-98, 163, 186-189, 201

Harvest 16, 37, 58, 66, 87, 138, 166, 225
Hate 99, 104, 158, 160, 163, 169-171, 173, 186, 189
Healing 12, 42, 62, 64, 66-69, 72, 90, 107-109, 113-114, 118, 123, 125, 135, 183

Hearing 51-52, 59, 69-71, 75, 80, 83, 90, 103, 105, 116, 118-120, 125-126, 132-133, 157, 162, 167, 177, 179, 183, 186, 195, 199
Heart 45, 85, 135, 169, 209
Herod(ian) 29, 62, 76, 126
High priest 127, 192-195
Hinduism 32, 60, 73, 106, 138, 174
HIV *see* AIDS
Holistic (Jesus' view of people) 72-73, 90, 108, 113-114, 190
Holy Spirit *see* Spirit
Homeless 60
Homosexual 60, 73, 113, 119, 190
Hostile/Hostility 13, 16, 27-29, 61, 64-65, 80, 84, 86-87, 91, 95, 112, 121, 170, 186, 189, 206
Hour, Jesus' 38-39, 57, 70, 91, 132-133, 141, 148, 180, 184, 191
House/Home 61, 87, 103, 137, 151, 153-154, 159, 161-163, 168, 182, 188, 191, 194, 207, 210, 219-220
Humility/Humble 27, 142-143, 146, 149
Hunger 56, 79, 85, 133

'I am' sayings 11, 13, 57, 77, 79, 100, 116, 124, 139, 152, 163
Illness 12, 61-62, 66-67, 113, 122-123, 127-128
Illumination 83, 102, 105, 112
India 32, 60, 74, 114, 137-138, 174, 190
Indwelling 46, 71, 81, 121, 145, 153, 159, 164, 180, 188
Irony 11, 24, 55, 58, 71, 72, 88, 89, 92, 94, 105, 110, 125, 127, 128, 132, 151, 184, 194, 197, 200, 202
Islam *see* Muslim
Israel 29-35, 41, 43, 45-47, 61, 63, 75, 78, 80, 87, 115, 117, 131, 135, 140, 163-164, 210, 216

Jacob 34, 48, 54-56, 140
Jerusalem 6, 13, 16, 29-30, 36-37, 40, 43, 61-66, 86-88, 103, 121, 123, 126, 130-131, 191, 205, 210

Jesus
- as/equal to God 68-69, 79, 105, 201-202
- as mediator 34, 36, 51, 136
- as Wisdom 22-23, 48, 55-56, 79, 84, 152, 167, 182
- as the Word *see* Logos
Jewish Supreme Court *see* Sanhedrin
Jews, the 12-14, 29-30, 64-74, 80-92, 95, 99-106, 109-110, 117-132, 137, 139, 149, 180, 183, 197-210, 229
Johannine community/church 5-8, 10, 17, 82, 167, 228
John the author 5, 22, 27, 51-52, 71, 98, 145, 161, 209, 223, 228-230
John the Baptist 9, 24, 27-35, 71, 86, 105, 167, 179, 199, 222, 229
Josephus 29-30
Journey 22-23, 37, 75, 141, 152, 182, 230
Joy 92, 160, 167, 169, 173, 178-180, 215
Judaism 7, 13-14, 16, 22, 26, 29-31, 37-42, 55, 65-66, 70, 103, 115, 117, 121, 127, 175
Judas 83, 129-130, 137, 141, 144-148, 159, 164, 180, 186, 191-192, 202, 229
Judea 16, 28, 36, 54, 61, 64, 65, 88, 122, 197, 210
Judge/Judgement 14, 24, 31, 49, 52, 69-70, 84, 90-91, 95, 97-99, 101-102, 106, 129, 133-134, 136, 165, 171, 175-176, 196, 198, 201-202, 204, 220
Justice/Injustice (*see also* Social justice) 29, 38, 94, 97, 99, 107, 138, 158, 160, 163, 190

King 29, 34, 62, 120, 131, 140, 198-203, 205-207, 211-212
Kingdom (of God/Jesus) 11, 14-15, 40, 44-48, 58, 63, 104, 106, 118, 192, 198-199, 204, 225
Knowledge/Knowing 4, 11, 22, 24-25, 27, 30-31, 35-36, 48, 52-53, 57, 67-70, 77, 80, 83, 85, 89, 91, 94, 98, 102, 104, 108, 110, 115-116, 118, 133-134, 139, 141-143, 147-148, 151, 153-154, 157, 162, 168-173, 178, 184-186, 193, 197, 207, 213

Lamb of God 31-32, 35, 41
Lame man at Bethesda 28, 65-69, 72, 74, 86, 90, 106-108, 111, 113-114, 229
Law, Mosaic/Jewish 7, 23, 25-26, 41-43, 56, 66, 70, 72, 90, 94-97, 101, 103, 196, 198, 201, 208
Lawsuit *see* Trial
Laying down one's life 38, 116-117, 125, 139, 141-143, 146, 149, 167-168, 192, 227, 229
Lazarus 12, 39, 122-129, 131, 167, 180
Liberate/Liberation 7, 31-32, 100, 102-103, 105-107, 126, 131, 134, 144, 152-155, 188, 190, 199-200, 204, 210, 212
Light 11-13, 22-24, 27, 36, 49, 51, 53, 71, 85-87, 100-102, 105, 107, 111-112, 123, 134, 136
Living water 37, 53-56, 59, 61, 78-79, 87, 92-93, 138, 209
Logos 22-25, 147, 185, 220
Love 48-50, 69, 71, 81, 84, 86, 89, 117, 128, 132, 141, 145, 149-151, 156, 159-161, 163, 166-169, 173, 182, 188-189, 226, 229

Malchus 192, 195
Man born blind 6, 12, 68, 86, 89, 106-113, 118, 122, 174, 183, 229
Manna 75, 78, 82
Marginalized 60, 63, 67, 107, 111, 113
Martha 15, 122-125, 229
Mary Magdalene 15, 73, 206, 213-215, 220, 222, 229
Mary (sister of Lazarus) 15, 122-125, 129-130, 137, 229
Meaning of a text 1-4, 11-12, 19, 26
Messiah/Messianic 7, 9-10, 13, 29-32, 34-35, 38-40, 57-58, 61, 89, 91, 94-95, 104, 110, 120, 126, 131, 134-135, 192, 221
Metaphor(ical) 11, 13, 20, 45-47, 55, 79, 81, 115, 118, 164, 183, 192

Index of Subjects

Mind(set) 41, 83, 85, 94-95, 99, 102, 129, 131, 135, 146, 204, 206, 211-212
Miracle/Miraculous (*see also* Sign) 11-13, 25, 27, 39-40, 42-45, 49, 62, 64, 68, 71, 74-78, 88, 91, 95, 109, 111, 122, 125-128, 135, 153-154, 166, 170, 221, 223-225
Mission 13, 15, 25, 31, 33, 36, 39-40, 50, 52, 58-59, 71, 76, 79, 84-88, 95, 102, 127, 136, 139, 148, 152, 154-155, 166, 176, 185-190, 197, 205, 207, 215, 219, 222-225, 227, 229
Misunderstanding 11, 23-24, 30, 41, 45, 49, 55, 77, 81, 91, 102, 118, 123, 131, 137, 142, 153, 183, 224
Moral(ity) 15, 32, 45-46, 57, 74, 105, 212
Moses 13, 25-26, 29, 54, 56-57, 66, 72, 75-76, 78-79, 89-90, 94, 110, 136, 140, 167
Mother of Jesus 15, 38, 42, 88, 206-207, 212, 229
Muslim 60, 73, 174

Nathanael 33-35
New Age movement 50, 105
Nicodemus 8, 17, 28, 36, 43-49, 53, 55-56, 59, 62-63, 78, 86, 89, 91, 94, 104, 109, 118, 130, 183, 194, 210-211, 229

Obedience 42, 156, 159, 161-163, 166-168, 179
Old Testament 7, 16, 25-26, 45, 52, 54, 69, 71, 79, 135, 140, 158, 163-164, 173, 208-209
Oneness (*see also* Unity) 101, 120, 150, 188-189
Opposition (*see also* Conflict) 7, 14, 64-65, 139
Orphan 113, 158
Outcast 14, 53-54, 60, 63, 66, 72, 89, 108, 172, 174

Parable 115, 117-118, 175, 180-183
Paraclete *see* Spirit
Parochialism 119
Parousia 151, 158, 165

Passion, Jesus' 16, 18, 91, 139, 191
Passover 15-16, 31, 37, 40-41, 65-66, 75-76, 84, 129, 132, 140, 197, 200, 205, 208, 210
Pastor 99, 118, 146
Path (*see also* Way) 138, 147, 149, 192
Peace 38, 89, 105, 131, 160, 169, 183-184, 189, 215, 220
Pentecost 31, 66, 162, 215-219, 222
Persecution 7, 13-14, 32, 65, 68, 73-74, 89-90, 95, 112-113, 122, 158, 160, 163, 169-174, 183-184, 189, 215
Peter 33-34, 82, 85, 89, 142, 145, 147-151, 172, 182, 184, 192-196, 213-214, 223-229
Pharisee(s) 43, 54, 67, 92, 94, 97, 103, 111-112, 115, 132, 180-181, 191, 194
Philip 33-34, 75-76, 85, 148, 153
Pilate 38, 89, 193, 197-206, 208, 211, 229
Plain speech 180-182
Pluralism 60, 155
Politics/Political 32, 65, 107, 190, 198, 204
Poor/Poverty 107, 130, 137-138
Postmodernism 128, 155
Power 31-32, 66, 70, 73, 117, 125-127, 133, 144-146, 154, 161, 192, 194, 197
Praise 74, 89, 92, 133, 136
Prayer 32, 74, 140, 155-156, 161, 184-188, 191, 212
Predestination 80, 120, 135, 143, 185
Prologue 18, 22-23, 25, 27-28, 36, 41, 48-49, 51, 59, 64, 84, 101, 134, 141, 182, 197, 220, 223
Prophet 29-30, 40-42, 52, 57-58, 61, 73, 76, 94, 109, 111, 177
Prosecute 14, 175-176
Prostitute 60
Protection 115-116, 118, 158, 186-187, 189
Pruning 164, 168-169
Purify *see* Cleansing

Quest for Jesus 92
Qumran 30, 108

Rabbi/Rabbinic 7, 14, 43-44, 66, 120
Realm 12, 22, 34-35, 46-48, 50-51, 70, 147, 151, 170, 199
Rebirth *see* Birth of the Spirit
Recall *see* Remembrance
Reconciliation 81, 129, 133-134, 143, 145, 147, 229
Recreation 216-217
Rejection 11-12, 22, 24-25, 27-28, 30, 42, 49, 52, 71, 73, 80, 82, 84, 91, 94-95, 102, 104, 111-112, 118, 119-121, 135-136, 147, 155, 170, 180, 183, 197, 200, 203, 209, 230
Relationship 14, 25, 27, 36, 54, 57, 60, 64, 74, 81, 84-86, 101-102, 106, 113, 116, 120-121, 142, 144-146, 151, 153, 155-156, 159, 165, 167, 169-170, 183, 185, 196, 212, 214, 217, 220, 222, 225, 230
Remaining (in/with Jesus) 11, 34, 59, 63, 81, 84, 102, 146, 163-169, 173, 189, 227, 230
Remarriage 119
Remembrance 17, 41, 82, 131-132, 142, 160, 172-174, 181
Reminding *see* Remembrance
Responses to Jesus 9,12, 15, 25, 28, 36, 41, 44, 49, 58-59, 63, 68-69, 82-85, 94-95, 111-112, 117-121, 124, 126-127, 134, 137, 146, 204, 221, 229-230
Restoration 29-30, 45-46, 113, 134-135, 145, 196, 210, 216, 223-226, 229
Resurrection 12-13, 15, 18, 39, 41, 70, 93, 117, 119, 122-128, 131, 141, 143, 148, 158, 160, 176, 178-180, 182, 184, 191, 206, 213-214, 217-218, 223
Revelation 4, 9, 11-13, 22, 30, 34-36, 47, 49-52, 55, 57, 78-79, 84, 87-88, 100, 112, 116, 118, 124, 152-153, 173, 182-183, 185, 192, 214, 230
Revolution(ary) 29, 120, 126, 192, 200, 204
Romans/Roman rule 7, 29, 62-63, 76, 102, 126, 131, 160, 191, 193-194, 197, 199, 201, 203-204

Royal official 12, 28, 36-37, 61-63, 67, 113, 118, 183, 229
Sabbath 41, 67-68, 70, 90, 109, 114, 140, 208, 213
Sacrament(alism) 17-18, 46, 82
Sacrifice 41, 84, 116, 127, 137, 210, 229
Salvation (*see also* Eternal life) 12, 15, 17, 23, 30-32, 36-38, 42, 44-49, 55, 61, 77, 80, 85-87, 90, 92, 100, 106, 113, 116, 119, 120, 134-135, 142, 155, 160, 169, 215, 217-219, 222
Samaria 16, 36, 54
Samaritan woman 15, 28, 36-37, 53-60, 63, 67, 78, 90, 93, 106, 109, 111, 118, 124-125, 166, 183, 229-230
Samaritans 16, 54, 58-59, 61-62, 117
Sanctify 121, 186-187, 189-190
Sanhedrin 43, 126, 193-194, 211
Satan *see* Devil
Saving knowledge/truth/wisdom 27, 31, 35-36, 48, 85, 105, 155, 199
Scripture 7, 11, 16, 45, 71-72, 74, 89-91, 93, 98, 171, 207, 209, 214
Second coming of Jesus *see* Parousia
Secret believers 136-137, 174, 210-212
Seeing (*see also* Spiritual sight) 11-12, 26, 33, 36, 44-45, 51-52, 62, 69, 71, 83, 85, 90, 103, 110-112, 131, 135-136, 153, 157, 158, 170, 178-179, 203, 215, 220, 222, 226
Seeking 67, 69-71, 77, 79, 84, 89-90, 92, 95, 105-106, 112, 168, 181, 192
Sending 48-49, 52, 73, 79, 86, 89, 117, 121, 144, 150, 154, 157-158, 162, 170, 186, 197, 215
Serpent 47
Servant(hood) 31, 54, 62, 79, 133, 135, 138, 142-143, 146-147, 149, 167, 170, 173, 192
Sheep 13, 70, 114-116, 118-120, 126-127, 138, 141, 146-147, 188, 214, 227
Sheepfold 115, 117, 194
Shepherd 13, 70, 114-119, 126-127, 130, 131, 138, 141, 147, 188, 214

Sickness *see* Illness
Sign (*see also* Miracle) 9, 11-13, 18, 28, 36, 39-40, 43-44, 49, 62-64, 71, 75-78, 84, 91, 95, 122, 125-126, 135, 139, 170, 220-221, 225
Sin(ner) 12, 17, 31-33, 35, 41, 50, 56, 60, 67-68, 74, 81, 84-85, 97, 99, 101, 103, 106-111, 113, 134, 143, 155, 170, 175-176, 194, 202, 210, 212, 219
Social action *see* Social justice
Social justice 90, 107, 113
Son of Man 35, 48, 70, 82, 97, 111, 125, 148, 201
Sorrow 160, 175, 178-180, 215
Spirit(-Paraclete) 3, 12, 14-15, 31-32, 36, 41, 44-49, 51-53, 55, 57, 83-85, 93-94, 124, 144, 156-160, 162, 171-173, 175-178, 181-182, 186-189, 208, 215-219
- as Advocate 156-158, 173, 175-178
- as 'second blessing' 31, 222
- as Teacher 160-171, 173, 177-178
- baptism in/with the Holy Spirit 31-32, 51
- the giving of the Spirit 51, 94, 142, 175, 208, 212, 215-219, 222
Spiritual birth *see* Birth of the Spirit
Spiritual sight (*see also* Seeing) 69, 108, 111-112
Spring 54, 59, 92-93
Stem-cell research 119
Stoicism 22
Study (of Scripture) 3, 11, 71-72, 74, 89-90, 98, 118
Suffering 31-32, 180, 192, 206-207
Symbolism 3, 7, 11-12, 37-42, 58, 60, 87, 92, 100, 118, 121, 143, 145, 163, 183, 207, 208, 212, 216, 218, 225
Synagogue 5-7, 13, 89, 110-111, 136, 172, 195, 211
Synoptics 10-11, 15, 24, 40, 117-118, 130, 133, 138, 161, 180, 192, 205-206, 214, 223

Tabernacle 25
Table-fellowship 79, 144

Teacher 7, 43-44, 74, 99, 118, 146, 150, 160, 171, 173, 177-178, 214
Teaching, Jesus' 15-16, 55-56, 65, 70, 75, 79, 82-85, 89-91, 93-96, 99, 101-106, 117-118, 121, 135-144, 146-148, 150, 152-153, 157-159, 163-164, 166-167, 169-170, 172-175, 177, 180-190, 195-196, 201-203, 210, 214, 221
Temple 37, 40-42, 57, 66-67, 72, 89, 92, 94, 96, 100, 105, 108, 120-121, 127, 129, 191, 195
Testament *see* Farewell discourse
Testify/Testimony 5, 8-9, 11, 14-15, 22-35, 43, 47, 50-51, 53, 58-60, 63, 70-74, 89, 97, 100-101, 106, 108-110, 112, 119, 122, 124, 136, 141, 145, 149, 157-158, 163, 169, 171-174, 176-177, 179, 186-190, 195, 199, 209, 214-215, 222, 228-229
Thinking 'from above' 76, 85, 101, 155, 181, 193
Thirst 55-56, 58, 79, 93, 133, 138, 163, 206-207
Thomas xi, 111, 123, 148, 151-153, 175, 213, 219-220, 222
Throne 185, 207, 212
Transsexual 60
Trial 14, 24, 27, 70, 73, 89, 112, 128, 156-158, 174, 189, 191, 193-198, 201, 203-205, 210
Trinitarian belief 220
Truth 8, 11-13, 22, 25-26, 57, 85, 100, 102-103, 105-106, 109, 152-153, 155, 157, 172, 176-177, 186-190, 199, 204, 228

Unbelief 49, 71, 83, 120, 135-137, 170, 176, 220-221
Understand(ing) 1, 3-4, 13, 15, 23-25, 31-32, 36, 41, 48-50, 53, 56, 58-59, 61-64, 70, 78, 80-81, 83-86, 88-91, 94, 98, 101-102, 105, 109, 111-112, 115, 118, 124-125, 131-132, 134-135, 142, 144-145, 147, 149-151, 154-155, 162, 172, 181, 183-185, 229

Unity (*see also* Oneness) 120, 136
Untouchable *see* Dalit

Vine 13, 163-166
Voice, Jesus' 70, 115-117, 119-120, 125-126, 167, 199, 214

Water 3, 11-13, 17, 25, 30, 36-39, 45-46, 53-56, 59, 61, 66, 76, 78-79, 85, 87, 92-93, 98, 100, 114, 138, 163, 209, 217, 225
Way (*see also* Path) 13, 48, 106, 118, 133, 138, 146-147, 149, 151-155, 196, 227
Wedding 15, 36-39, 42, 61, 88
Well *see* Spring
Wisdom *see* Jesus as Wisdom *and* Saving wisdom
Witness *see* Testimony

Women 15, 100, 195, 206, 214, 229
Word, Jesus' *see* Teaching, Jesus'
Work 13-14, 28, 39, 46, 48, 56, 68-73, 77, 90, 101, 104, 108, 120-121, 123, 128, 153, 158, 161-162, 168, 170, 175, 177-178, 180, 185, 189, 207-208
World 7, 12-17, 23-25, 27, 31-33, 35, 49, 58-60, 73-78, 81, 84, 86-88, 95, 100-102, 105-108, 111-112, 114, 1117, 119, 121, 123, 127-128, 132-134, 136, 138-139, 141, 144, 147-151, 157-163, 169-173, 175-180, 182-190, 192-195, 197-199, 204-205, 207, 212, 215-219
Worldview 12, 25, 28, 34, 51, 63, 112, 128, 155, 230
Worship 15, 38, 40, 56-57, 66, 72, 108, 110-111, 172

www.ingramcontent.com/pod-product-compliance
Lightning Source LLC
Chambersburg PA
CBHW072022240426
43667CB00044B/2254